The Beti Colditz

The Story of Ronald Bolton Littledale

Kees Koenen

BARNTHORN
PUBLISHING

Copyright © Kees Koenen 2025

All rights reserved.

Published by Barnthorn Publishing Limited.

www.barnthornpublishing.co.uk

ISBN: 978-1-917120-26-5

'The whole story of Colditz will, no doubt, one day be told, and it will make an enthralling story; but it must be written by one of the men who was there.'

A. J. Evans, *Escape and Liberation, 1940-1945*

'Really?'

Kees Koenen, *The Betrayal of Colditz*

CONTENTS

1	Death of an Officer	1
2	A Radio Play	7
3	Family	14
4	Education	26
5	King's Royal Rifle Corps	36
6	Calais	48
7	Laufen	55
8	Fort VIII in Posen	61
9	Escape from Posen	70
10	The Border	79
11	The Balkans	86
12	Hiding in Prague	110
13	Gris	123
14	Colditz, 14 October 1942	132
15	Switzerland	162
16	Annemasse	174
17	Via Spain to England	178
18	Confessions	186
19	The Gallows	196
20	Mike	219

21	Normandy	228
22	Airaines	237
23	The Long Way to Tipperary	253
24	A Funeral in Berlin	272
	Index	283
	Bibliography	295
	Acknowledgements	303

1

DEATH OF AN OFFICER

'If I should die, think only this of me
That there's some corner of a foreign field
That is forever England.'

The Soldier, Rupert Brooke, 1914.

Nervously, Mike Sinclair walks along the barbed wire. It is Monday 25 September 1944. High above him looms the gloomy castle of Colditz, the castle that has held him prisoner for more than two years. Around him, officers walk around the sports ground, talking to each other, reading. Guards patrol on the other side of the fencing. The small fenced-off area in the deer park is surrounded by a high wall. A few years earlier, a Frenchman managed to jump the fence, clamber over the wall in a rain of bullets, and get away. Eventually, he managed to reach Spain. But that was years ago when the war in the west was just a year old. But times have changed. The Americans are at Maastricht and Nijmegen, the Russians at the gates of Warsaw, Nazi Germany is on the losing side. On the great chessboard of the world stage, Mike Sinclair, as a lone pawn, no longer plays any significant role. But his mind is made up. He has ended up on the other side of the fence often enough, and just as often the long German arm has grabbed him by the neck and brought him back again. Faces loom in his confused mind. Kaller, Maria Jasińska, Wolf, Olga, Zbigniew: all those Poles who took him deep into Yugoslavia on his flight float before his eyes and look at him. He has abandoned them.

His fellow inmates will later say it was a suicide attempt. They think he has gone insane as he approaches the fence in broad daylight and is about to climb over it. When Mike thinks the sentries are not paying attention, he takes his chance. He wriggles his young body and tired mind over the barbed wire and pays no attention to the reactions around him. On the other side of the fence, he drops down and sets off. He's running like a madman. Puzzled eyes stare at him. Inmates start shouting for him to stop. They fear the worst and know that the whole effort is not worth it, especially not now, at this point in the war. The guards, now aware of what is happening in front of them, are also shouting at him to stop. Mike ignores them and runs on between a creek that separates the grounds of the castle from a shed standing in the field. The guards are now shooting continuously at the Englishman, who is running like the devil is after him. They can hear the noise of the gunfire back in the castle and the prisoners in their courtyard know something terrible is happening. The guards are shooting together as one now, but nothing can stop Mike in his desperate attempt to reach freedom. He almost reaches a low wooden fence, when a poorly-aimed shot ricochets off his elbow and pierces his heart. Mike falls forward and lies motionless. The silence around him is deafening. The prisoners on the sports ground start screaming, knowing the worst has happened to their comrade. Sinclair no longer hears it, The Red Fox is dead.

***

Summer 2013: We are at a campsite in Long, France, located on the Somme, not far from Abbeville. The river's name is forever linked to the First World War. The starting signal for the Battle of the Somme is given at La Boiselle, some 65 km east. On 1 July 1916, an under-mined German position got blown skywards here, and we will see the result today. Our Lord is invoked as my wife looks over the edge of a huge crater: 'Jesus Christ!' 100 m in diameter, 30 m deep, this ominous moon crater, is overgrown with grass, with chalk lines pointing into its depths. The beast has a name: Lochnagar. We walk around it on some planking, getting dizzy as we go, and meet some Englishmen who tell us they lost an ancestor in the battle. The explosion must have been heard as far away as London. Around us, the landscape is peaceful and sunny. What a contrast.

Benches with commemorative plaques in English are arranged around the well, and we pass a cross in memory of Private George Nugent of the Northumberland Fusiliers who went missing on the day of the explosion and wasn't found until 1998. He was 'lucky', a little further down the road at Thiepval is a huge memorial commemorating 72,000 missing boys who literally dissolved into the annals of history. Wreaths of poppies, on wooden stakes, at the entrance bid us farewell as we leave the site.

Summer 1916: At half past seven in the morning on 1 July, thousands of British and French troops crawl up from their trenches and march towards the German lines, rifles at the ready, bayonets raised. After all, nothing can go wrong? For days, howitzers, cannons and other field artillery with more than 3,000,000 shells have battered the enemy positions. Allied troops intend to take the initiative and attack to relieve the front at Verdun. There they were forced onto the defensive, but here on the Somme they can make a difference. The shelling is so immense, so destructive, that no resistance from the Germans is expected when the British and French Armies approach their trenches. Once these are taken, the order is to push on to Bapaume, but instead, the whole plan collapses into a massive failure. The Germans have dug deep into the limestone formations. Their quarters, set up 10 m underground, are reinforced with concrete. The bombardment has little effect. Even the barbed-wire fencing in front of their trenches appears to be still intact, despite the massive barrage. The British are unaware of all this because they don't have any forward observers to tell them. The Germans wait, prepared for what is coming. Machine gun nests have been set up in strategic locations. The shelling stops. A pause. And then the whistle blows and the British attack. The time between the end of the bombardment and the signal for the attack has given the Germans time to take position behind their guns to spread death and destruction among the often young men who believe this battle could become decisive. The first men fall, a stubborn march continues. The German machine guns are boiling hot. The British keep coming., one soldier after another drops dead. By the end of the day, more than 20,000 will not rise anymore. The ease with which the Germans kill their enemy leaves some in distress. They no longer even fire at the retreating troops, over 35,000 of whom are left wounded. When the Battle of the

Somme bleeds to death, undecided, in November, there will be more than 1,300,000 German and British casualties. Undecided, unless the few kilometres of ground gained on the Allied side could be considered a victory.

Summer 2013: We are going to Airaines, a disregarded village south of Long, but I know where it is and why we are driving there. Through a hilly landscape with beautiful colours of rapeseed, buttercups and fire-red poppies, we approach the place. It is still fairly bare here. In the distance we can see groves betraying the gully where the Somme flows. As we enter Airaines, we have to search carefully for the spot I figured out months ago. Google Street View is years behind, because when we stand in front of the cemetery on Rue d'Hangest we do not see a bare fence, but a green, overgrown wall with an entrance.

In an area inextricably linked to the First World War, it's odd to go to visit the grave of a soldier inextricably linked to the Second World War, but here, in this place, on 1 September 1944, a British officer, Major Ronnie Littledale, died. All I knew about him at the time of this visit was that he had had an eventful history behind him when he met his end here. Littledale had escaped from the infamous Prisoner of War camp at Colditz Castle with three other British officers in October 1942. He'd made his way back to England, was involved in D-Day, and eventually found his final resting place here. It shows perseverance to get this far. We walk into the cemetery and find his grave; Commonwealth War Graves, first row, second from the left. I'd already found that out, besides, there is only one row. I pause awhile to read the letters on his headstone.

We drive out of the village towards Long and are less than 10 m away from the cemetery when a haze of purple to our left stops us from further driving. We have to see this! Flax, up to the horizon, undulating in the wind like water, with a poppy here and there. What an experience! We have just visited the grave, now this! We are silent. The lines of a famous First World War poem come to mind:

> In Flanders fields the poppies blow
> Between the crosses, row on row
> That mark our place; and in the sky
> The larks, still bravely singing, fly

Scarce heard amid the guns below.
We are the dead. Short days ago
We lived, felt dawn, saw sunset glow
Loved, and were loved, and now we lie
In Flanders fields.
Take up our quarrel with the foe:
To you from failing hands we throw
The torch; be yours to hold it high.
If ye break faith with us who die
We shall not sleep, though poppies grow
In Flanders fields.

The 1915 poem by Lieutenant Colonel John McCrae (1872-1918) that made the poppy the symbol of the First World War could have been written here. The red colour of blood, the black centre as a symbol of mourning, the cross shape at the heart of the flower, the fact that poppies bloom when other plants nearby are dead: how strong can the link between war and peace be? The thoughts wander through my mind as we pick a field bouquet of the delicate flowers.

A few days later… again I am standing in front of the gate of the cemetery in Airaines. In my hand a wooden cross with a poppy and the text: 'From Colditz to Airaines… you almost made it, Ronnie– Rest in Peace'. As if I knew Ronald Littledale personally. On the back my name, email address and the somewhat haughty announcement that I am a 'Colditz Explorer', which, after all, is not entirely untrue.

It's early, and… the gate is closed. Back on the night of 14-15 October 1942 at Oflag IV-C Colditz Castle PoW camp, four British officers are lying on their bellies in a courtyard surrounded by the four high walls of the German *Kommandantur* on their way to freedom. And the door to one of the buildings on their escape route is shut. Even after an hour of tinkering, the lock will not open. Ronnie Littledale is one of the men. Like him then, I am now trying to move forward, but something or someone has decided otherwise. Sometimes, you just need someone to persevere. Ronnie and his mates discover a basement hatch and escape successfully. Luckily my wife is with me, and she understands that the big gate is only open during the day, when a procession has to pass through, but that a small gate to the side will be open. What will I do without her, with only my childlike imagination? But I have to go on alone. I place the cross next to the gravestone, right there and then, I vow to write the life story of Major Ronald B. Littledale.

On the way back, we take some poppies for the scrapbook we are making from this trip, and put them to dry between two heavy books, annuals of the magazine *L'Ilustration* bound together, a 1909 French weekly, bought at the flea market in Picquigny.

2

A RADIO PLAY

On 6 August 1972, the second part of the radio play *Daleka jest droga do Tipperary* by Anna Sudlitz, was broadcasted for Polish radio station *Teatr Polskiego Radia*. To date, Sudlitz, a journalist working in the literary editorial board of Polish Radio III, had been involved in numerous broadcasts, including a programme on the Warsaw Ghetto and a series on the Warsaw Uprising.

The play's cast of characters not only included such names as Zbigniew Klichowski, Bronisław Sobkowiak, Maria Klichowska, Bolesław and Mieczyslaw Kierczyński, Maria Jasińska, Olga Kamińska-Prokopowa, Bodenstein and Giebelhausen, but also, unusually, two British officers: Major Ronald Bolton Littledale, and a man identified only as Porucznik, which translates as lieutenant in Polish. Littledale was one of the few PoWs who managed to escape from the heavily guarded castle in Colditz in the Second World War. The other man, Porucznik, is unmistakably his regimental colleague, Lieutenant Michael Sinclair, who later gained a reputation at Colditz as the greatest ever escaper. So how did these two British officers, Littledale and Sinclair, end up in a Polish radio play? What roles did the Poles and Germans play in this story?

Answering that is what this book is about.

In 2019, more than 300 microscopic samples of Nazi victims recovered three years earlier from the estate of Professor of Anatomy, Hermann Stieve, will be buried in Berlin. Stieve carried out research during the Second World War, mainly on women. One of his victims was Olga Kamińska-Prokopowa. Apart from her role in the radio play, she also plays a prominent role in the lives of Littledale and Sinclair alongside Maria Jasińska, a pharmacy assistant from Lodz, remembered annually in Poland as a Resistance hero. Another character, Albrecht Giebelhausen, was *Kriminalpolizeisekretär* of

Abteilung IV der Stapo Litzmannstadt, now Lódz, during the war. How does he fit into the story?

And then Colditz, or *Sonderlager Oflag IV-C*, to give it its German administrative name. Colditz is central to this book. The Castle is a world unto itself, in which Littledale and Sinclair played very different roles. As a result of what happened there in the Second World War, Colditz is a much-used metaphor, for regimes and environments of harsh rules and intractability. So when UK Foreign Secretary Boris Johnson, in *The Evening Standard* of 18 January 2017, denounced French President Hollande as 'a Colditz guard' who wanted to give 'punishment beatings' to 'escapers', when Johnson likened the UK's Brexit 'escape from the EU', to an escape attempt from Colditz, he alluded to a phenomenon wide-spread in the Anglo-Saxon community.

From being a German *Schloss* and a Second World War Prisoner-of-War camp, Colditz has also become synonymous with ingenious and resourceful escape, under the most difficult of conditions. The former PoW camp is also well-known in the Netherlands, mainly through the BBC series broadcasted in the early 1970s. What has particularly stuck in the minds of viewers are the thrilling stories of spectacular escapes from a medieval castle near Leipzig, hatched by brave and clever Allied officers from Britain, France, Poland and the Netherlands.

The portrayal of Allied PoWs in general, and of Colditz in particular, contrasts sharply with reality: hundreds of thousands of men spent up to five long years trying to survive under difficult conditions. There are books about Colditz (*The Colditz Story*, *The Latter Days At Colditz*, *They Have Their Exits*), books about Stalag Luft III in Sagan, now in Poland, which was a camp for air force personnel, with a similar reputation to Colditz (*The Great Escape*, *The Wooden Horse*). Then there were movies based on these books and then TV series based around the movies. These books, and the films and TV shows that followed them almost all depict exciting stories with the plucky Allies as the eventual victors over a dark and dastardly foe. That picture rarely matches reality.

Although they were not the first books to appear about Colditz, *The Colditz Story* and Pat Reid's *The Latter Days* created a lasting picture, a portrait of life there that resembled that at an English public school, like Eton or Harrow. The final part of Reid's trilogy, *The Full Story*, published 32 years later, paints a more realistic picture of life in the camp. Meanwhile, *The Great Escape* and *The Wooden Horse* mainly concern themselves with the accounts of their respective escapes and barely discuss at all the living conditions in the camps. The book, *Castle of the Eagles–Escape from Mussolini's Colditz*, merely benefits from attaching itself to an icon: it has nothing to do with Colditz. And this is especially true of a title like *The Colditz Cock*, a booklet with an ambiguous title and a sugar-sweet cover depicting an amorous couple, which is likewise attempting to invoke some of that ol' Colditz magic for itself, and otherwise ignore reality.

Three films have been dedicated to Colditz: *The Colditz Story* (1955), *The Birdmen*, a fictional depiction of the Colditz glider project (1971), and *Colditz* (2005) with an inevitable love story. The 1963 film, *The Great Escape*, depicts the 1944 mass escape from Stalag Luft III, albeit greatly fictionalised. Like the books, these films feature adventure storylines with easily identifiable heroes and villains and escape as the main theme. This is also the case with films such as *The Wooden Horse*, *Albert R. N.*, *Escape to Victory*, *Stalag 17* and the TV series *Colditz* (BBC) and *P.O.W.* (ITV). Moreover, every genre deserves a parody: Oflag IV-C and Stalag Luft III spawned such items as *The Two Ronnies-Colditz*, the US series, *Hogan's Heroes* and an episode of the BBC's *Ripping Yarns, Escape From Stalag Luft 112B*. These paint a humorous picture of the Allies as PoWs and the Germans as inept guards. With such offerings as these, it is no wonder that the media portrayal of PoWs, or *Kriegies*, in German captivity has led to the experience of those former inmates being generally misrepresented and poorly understood.

The creation of a view is determined not only by what information is available but also and perhaps even more so by what is not. History is written by the victors, so it is inevitable that in Western Europe, the emphasis is on the story of the Allied (usually British) soldier who ends up in German captivity. The Germans, as both instigators and losers of the war, (equally inevitably) do not get the same attention or positive portrayal as their Allied counterparts. Perhaps the only exception is Franz von Werra, a 27-year-old air force captain, who was the only German PoW to manage to escape from captivity and return to Germany via Canada and the USA. The situation of PoWs in Asia seems to be the biggest blind spot in the public consciousness. Films like *Merry Christmas, Mr Lawrence* and *The Bridge on the River Kwai* do injustice to the degrading conditions prisoners had to live and work under.

Commerce and merchandising have helped to shape Colditz's image. We speak of a 'Colditz industry'. How else can we think of a board game designed by Pat Reid with a map of the castle; an LP, also devised by him, with mysterious music depicting the mood of prisoners; and Action Man dolls, with German & British uniforms, escape kits and sentry boxes, reducing the entire Colditz experience to the level of a game for children. Further examples of this commercialism can be found in the video game *Prisoner of War*, which features a PoW American officer on the cover, German soldiers and the outline of Colditz Castle in the background. In the 1980s, a construction kit of Colditz Castle was marketed in Spain. Its contents included scale models of all the buildings of the castle to recreate the complete *schloss*. Jigsaw puzzles, tea mugs, novels, mouse pads and construction kits of the glider almost make you forget that this was a Prisoner-of-War camp, where men were locked up for up to five years enduring hardship and privation. Even the BBC series was not immune: actor Robert Wagner was added to the cast as a bankable American Hollywood star in order to help the series appeal to American audiences, thus making it a viable commercial property in the States. The lengths they were prepared to go to cater to the American market can be seen in that the character he plays successfully escapes at the end of Series 1 and makes a return part way through Series 2. His character is one of the leading roles from the start of the series, even though in reality, the first American prisoners in Colditz didn't get there until August 1944.

The disparity between fact and fiction is examined in detail by military historian Simon MacKenzie in his book *The Colditz Myth* (2006). This paints us a considerably more nuanced picture of the soldiers' struggle for survival in German captivity than the movies that have hitherto formed the accepted view of the Second World War and PoWs. His position is supported to a great extent by a dissertation published that same year: *British World War Two Films 1945-65: Catharsis or National Regeneration?* In this work, philosopher Esther O'Neill discusses at length the role of film in the perception of the war and society, and the dominant role played by, among others, the film *The Colditz Story* ('setting the mythical benchmark') regarding the perception of the PoW in Europe. O'Neill asserts that film audiences are happy to be duped and accept distortions or the omission of facts, especially when it affirms the sacred shibboleths of their 'finest hour'.

A biography is ideally suited to give an objective, fundamental impression of a person's life or particular experience, like incarceration at Oflag IV-C. However, there is very little biographical material available of the officers at Colditz beyond those meagre details given to us by Reid et al. A few biographies have been published about Airey Neave, the first British officer to escape from Colditz: *The Man Who Was Saturday* by Patrick Bishop and *Public Servant, Secret Agent* by Paul Routledge, among others. In the voluminous Colditz literature, he is an exception. One of the others is Sir Douglas Bader, the RAF pilot famous even before the war. Australian author Paul Brickhill, with (partial) expertise, manages to re-package Bader's wartime history into a romanticised story entitled *Reach for the Sky*. Brickhill himself was a pilot in the Royal Australian Air Force and a POW for many years in Stalag Luft III. Here, in March 1944, he became involved in the mass escape, which he describes in and as *The Great Escape*. There have also been some thin booklets published on Vincent 'Bush' Parker, and most recently the biography of Geoffrey Stephenson. But that's about it.

According to Simon Mackenzie, serious research into the subject of Allied POWs is limited and primarily circulates in academic circles. While lengthy books have been written about Colditz, hardly a pen has been put to paper about the people who were imprisoned there. For those trying to gain insight into the lives of the men at Colditz, the lavish library is a boon, but the subject matter in Colditz literature, is limited to the art of escape, as this is perceived by publishers as being what the target readership wants and what will sell. This is in stark contrast to the harsh reality in prison camps as detailed by Mackenzie in *The Colditz Myth*, which is based on first-hand witness accounts. Mackenzie describes the specific conditions during capture after a lost battle that often leave deep marks on the soldiers: the sometimes heavy-handed interrogations by an enemy who does not always abide by the Geneva Convention; the boredom and hunger; the gangs, threats and theft between prisoners; the traitors among their own men; punitive measures by the Germans, and the playing off of different nationalities against each other by the guards. Only in a few cases did prisoners engage in escaping. Many who are captured stay where they are (*Sitting It Out* as American POW, David Westheimer, calls his memoirs) and only move when they are transferred by the Germans. Or when the British, the Americans or the Russians come to liberate them.

With his book *Colditz: The Full Story*, former British Escape Officer Pat Reid completes his trilogy about the famous PoW camp. The first two volumes, *The Colditz Story* and *The Latter Days*, are light-hearted in tone, exuding a *Boys' Own* vision boarding-school of jolly japes and plucky derring-do in the adventures of Allied officers in German captivity during their intelligent and brutal attempts to escape from the castle. His third book is more contemplative and is a more or less successful attempt to provide some solid historical authenticity. Through his books and consulting work for the 1955 film *The Colditz Story* and for the 1970s BBC TV series, Reid earned the (not entirely affectionate) nickname, Mr Colditz. Reid himself successfully escaped from the fortress on the evening of 14 October 1942 along with three others: Hank Wardle, with whom he eventually arrived in Switzerland, William Stephens and Ronald Littledale, who devised the plan for the daring escape. The latter three have remained in Reid's shadow. This is not very strange considering that Littledale did not survive the war and along with Wardle and Stephens, never recorded or published his memoirs. Reid did.

'No doubt the whole history of Colditz will one day be told, and it will be a fascinating story; but it must be written by one of the men who was imprisoned there.' So says Alfred John Evans in the preface to *The Colditz Story*. A. J. Evans knows what he is talking about. He escaped from Fort 9, Ingolstadt, as a British officer during the First World War in 1917 and wrote the book *The Escape Club* about the event, a title Pat Reid studied diligently as a boy at school according to the same foreword in *The Colditz Story*. Evans got it right: the history of Colditz is a fascinating story and the telling of it by someone who was there led to its becoming world-famous. Because of the success of Reid's books, over the years there followed the film, the TV series and the flood of associated literature written by other ex-prisoners, guards and fans of the genre. Especially in England, where Colditz was a British story, pure and simple, despite their being outnumbered by the international communities of Poles, French, Belgians, Dutch, Czechs, some Americans and a Yugoslav. The Dutch are mostly familiar with the series and perhaps Reid's books, which were promoted to Dutch audiences during the broadcast in the Netherlands.

One of the most striking aspects of the literature on Colditz and the small number of biographies of the officers who were imprisoned there is the lack of a published biography of Lieutenant Sinclair. Gavin

Worrell and Nick Jackson called him 'The Greatest Escaper of All'. Yet the book they announced in 2013 as 'a stunning tribute to one of Colditz's greatest legends' has yet to appear. Sinclair was killed by German gunfire attempting to escape the Castle grounds, the only fatal escape attempt in the history of the camp. Exceptionally, he was posthumously awarded a Distinctive Service Order (DSO). He turns up in almost every book about Colditz and he is widely lauded and revered for his many ingenious escape attempts. Sinclair and Littledale were regimental confreres and mates and they shared each other's fate. As noted, Littledale is far less well-known than Pat Reid: he did not survive the war. Reid did and wrote his histories of Colditz and thereby controlled the narrative. However, both have remained in the shadow of Colditz icon, Mike Sinclair, who died trying to get away and never returned home. At least Littledale did that.

This book, the story of the virtually forgotten Littledale, not only breaks the myth of Colditz through the telling of a personal account, but also sheds light on the mystery of why there has been no published biography of Mike Sinclair, Colditz's most highly-regarded prisoner. The solution of this puzzle also answers the question of how Littledale and Sinclair end up in a Polish radio play in 1972, why it is not their 'finest hour', but even more so, illustrates why Pat Reid's *Colditz: The Full Story* is not the whole story.

3

FAMILY

I am wondering: just how much can you find out about someone who was born some 120 years ago and has been dead for over three quarters of a century? Not just anyone, someone specific, whose name is inextricably linked to Colditz, of renown, yet fairly unknown. An email from 2001. It floats ghost-like across the ether of the internet, drifting my way as I delve into the life of that specific someone: British Major Ronald Bolton Littledale:

Subject: Littledale family, Sandiway Bank

My husband and I are writing a book on St. George Littledale and his wife Teresa, who explored Central Asia in the 1890s with a fox terrier. I am looking for papers (correspondence, diaries, photos, etc.) in the Littledale family line that comes down from John Bolton Littledale (1823-89). His son John Bolton Littledale, Jr. (born 1868) lived at Sandiway Bank. (Perhaps his father did before him as well.) I do not know when he died. He had a son Ronald Bolton Littledale of Sandiway Bank, born June 14, 1901. He is most likely gone now. Are there any Littledales still living there? How do I find out?

Regarding your biography of Mary Jowitt nee Hindley, here is the paragraph that caught my eye during an Internet search:

Samuel Hindley remarried on April 22nd 1868, again at Weaverham church, to Susannah Taylor from Wigan and Mary grew up with her father, step mother, two half brothers (George and James) and two half sisters (Jane and Sarah) on the smallholding on Littledale's Lane, between Sandiway and Hartford. Both her father and one of her uncles (David Hindley who lived nearby) were gamekeepers, Samuel to John Bollin

Littledales and David to A H Smith Barry. We would greatly appreciate any information that you might be able to provide.
Elizabeth Clinch
Palo Alto, California, USA

Elizabeth Clinch and her late husband, Nicholas, are looking for information on St George Littledale and his wife, Teresa, who set out with their fox terrier to explore Central Asia in the last years of the 19th Century. That name, Littledale, is already very familiar to me, so the sentence, 'He had a son Ronald Bolton Littledale of Sandiway Bank born June 14, 1901. He is most likely gone now' grabs my attention, and causes me to grow silent. Elizabeth Clinch, researcher for the Encyclopaedia Britannica and National Geographic in Washington DC, has found nothing about Ronald during her years of research. Instead, along with her husband, Nicholas, expedition leader and former president of the American Alpine Club, she has focused mainly on St George Littledale and his wife Teresa. In their book about the Littledales' great travels through Central Asia, they describe their prodigious search for information on this couple, who turned up at the gates of Lhasa, the capital of Tibet, in the late 19th Century.

Reading Elizabeth Clinch's post, I see before me the portrait of a young officer. A youthful Ronald Bolton Littledale looks into the camera, wearing a determined expression, along with his well-fitting uniform. Since 1 February 1923, he has been a second lieutenant in the 2nd Battalion of the King's Royal Rifle Corps. He looks like a man of action, barely restrained by the leather Sam Browne belt he wears across his chest. His cap is slightly askew, giving him a roguish air, but this takes nothing away from the combative look in his eyes. His face is slightly crooked, and he seems to be smiling like someone with a toothache. Nothing could be further from the truth: This is someone determined not only to achieve the goals he sets for himself but also those for others.

Elizabeth Clinch sadly admits that she knows nothing about Ronald Bolton Littledale, emailing me when I send her a copy of her 15-year-old message. But when I come across St George Littledale's name in the Visitation of England and Wales I know that he and Ronald are related. St George is the brother of Ronald's grandfather: his great uncle. Elizabeth wishes me 'Good luck with your own project' and says that 'it sounds like a winner of a book'. That simple email from 2001, and the Clinch couple's sleuthing leads me to their 2008 book *Through a Land of Extremes: The Littledales of Central Asia*, and a wealth of descriptions of the Littledale family. The contours surrounding Ronald Bolton Littledale are slowly revealing themselves, his black-and-white photograph as a young lieutenant is beginning to take on colour.

The small hamlet of Sandiway is about 7 km from the town of Northwich, not far from the mighty Mersey River that connects Liverpool to the rest of the world. Sandiway is on the outskirts of Northwich, where the wealthy people live. Not far east of the triangular hamlet, a narrow country road winds through the fields, surrounded by bushes and walls, occasionally flanked by a house. The winding road, called Littledales Lane, is named after John Bolton Littledale, a local businessman and landowner, who is also commemorated by the name of a small wood, Littledales Covert. John was born on 22 March 1823, the son of Thomas Littledale, who by then was already past 50.

The Littledale family hails from the Lake District area in the county of Cumbria in North-West England. Thomas Littledale Sr, John Bolton's grandfather, leaves that picturesque region and moves to Liverpool. The Littledales are merchants, transporting goods to Liverpool and the European continent. Thomas Sr. starts a brokerage in Liverpool with his cousin Isaac, under the name T and I. Littledale. The main commodity of this highly successful firm is cotton. As the firm grows, they also expand into shipping other items such as wool, silk, tea, coffee and sugar. Business is so good that Thomas Sr's family buys an estate in West Darby: Highfield House, a gigantic villa. However, in 1847, there is a financial crisis and T. and I. Littledale lose their account at their local bank. The estate agents receive a £100,000 loan from the Bank of England without any consideration, purely based on their excellent reputation.

In 1815, Thomas Sr. marries Ann Molyneux of West Derby, who is 15 years younger than himself, and whom he will outlive by 22 years. She gives birth to six children. The first child is named Thomas, after his father. The child lives only briefly: six days after his birth in 1817, the baby is buried at St Mary's, Walton-on-the-Hill, on 9 September. A year later, another son arrives, also to be named Thomas. Besides a sister, Ann Mary and two brothers Alfred and Isaac, who will live only four months, Thomas will have another brother, John Bolton, born in Liverpool in 1823. Like his father, John Bolton Sr. will marry a much younger woman, Mary Pickford, born in Manchester in 1845.

Thomas Littledale Sr. becomes bailiff of Liverpool a few years later, and from 1826 to 1827 he is mayor of the city. On 8 June 1827, he lays the foundation stone for the lighthouse at New Brighton in Wallasey, on the south-west side of the Mersey estuary. On 1 March 1830, the lighthouse is officially opened. It replaces a wooden stake to which a light was attached. This wooden stake is less than effective as a guide for shipping: it often just washes away. The *Liverpool Mercury* of 15 June reports that 'the mayor is accompanied by several members of the Common Council, and some 100 to 150 merchants and respectable inhabitants of the city.' Littledale receives a silver trowel from the architect John Foster, with which he layers a brick with mortar before putting it in place. 'May the blessing of God be upon this undertaking,' he declares, 'and may it be a means that will save the lives of the sailors of England as well as people of other countries visiting our shores.' The 27-metre-high lighthouse can be seen from 23 km away.

Not only does Thomas Sr. becomes mayor of Liverpool, but also his eldest son. Thomas Littledale Jr. owes this in part to his fearless courage and helpfulness. It is Thursday, 24 August 1848. On leaving Liverpool harbour, the ship *The Ocean Monarch* passes the New Brighton lighthouse. It is the pride of Boston's Train's Line, built by the famous local shipbuilder Donald McKay, and is en route to the United States with nearly 400 passengers on board, including 322 Irish emigrants. In the cargo hold is some 4,000 tonnes of Chinese porcelain. The ship pokes her bows out of the sea channel at around 8 am. Near the Great Orme Head, northeast of Llandudno in North Wales, disaster strikes. What happens is not exactly clear, but possibly one of the passengers, mistaking a ventilation shaft for a chimney, makes the unforgivable error choosing it to light a fire in. By the time Captain Murdoch is alerted, smoke is already pouring through the cabins, and frantic attempts to extinguish the fire have only caused the flames to blaze even higher in no time. Passengers are panicking and women jump overboard with their children in their arms. The captain unsuccessfully tries to manoeuvre the ship so that the wind does not fan the flames, so he has to lower the anchors instead. Pieces of wood are thrown into the water so the passengers who leapt overboard have something to cling to that keeps them afloat. At around this time, Thomas Littledale Jnr., the nearly 30-year-old son of the former mayor of Liverpool, and commodore of the Royal Mersey Yacht Club, is returning from the Beaumaris Regatta with a bunch of friends on his yacht, *Queen of the Ocean*. He is passing the scene of this disaster just at the right time for him to steer his yacht to where he can best help, and eventually manages to save 32 lives. He later describes this terrible disaster as 'horrific, bewildering and heartbreaking'.

After half an hour, a Brazilian steam frigate, *Afonso*, comes to assist. The crew manage to attach a rope to the burning ship, keeping it steady, so that rescue boats can sail back and forth to take off those on board the unfortunate vessel saving them from the looming inferno. Other ships have also come to the rescue: the steamer, *Prince of Wales*, and the packet boat, *New World*. Thomas' yacht, *Queen of the Ocean*, remains alongside until 3 pm in the afternoon, until the *Ocean Monarch* is finally burned to the waterline. Captain Murdoch is one of those who manages to get aboard Thomas' yacht. The *Ocean Monarch* is finally lost, sinking 25 m to the seabed, just north-east off the Great Orme.

Later, the captain disputes the finding that the fire was caused by a mistake. He maintains that it was caused by passengers' pipe smoking. He had already taken several pipes from them. No matter the cause, this has been one of the biggest and most disturbing in Liverpool's history. 178 souls were lost on the *Ocean Monarch*, which burned for 13 hours before sinking, going down with a priceless cargo of fine porcelain in its hold. Hundreds of emigrants, seeing no future for themselves in their motherland, and who lugged their few possessions up the gangway and into the deep cellars of the belly of the ill-fated ship, literally and figuratively burned their boats seeking a better life on the other side of the ocean. Meanwhile, Thomas Littledale, fortuitously returning from a regatta with friends, lent a helping hand with his sailing ship. The social class from which Ronald Littledale emerges could not have been more aptly portrayed.

Clement St. George Littledale, the protagonist of Elizabeth and Nicholas Clinch's book is one of six children of Thomas Littledale Jr. and his wife Julia Royds. He is born on 8 December 1851. When Julia gives birth to her son, his father is busy carrying out his mayoral duties, receiving the royal family at Liverpool Town Hall and then at St George's Hall, where musical festivities are held, quite a departure from its usual function as a courthouse among other things. The boy is given his grandfather's names as well as that of the building where his father is currently showing around Queen Victoria. Clement St. George Royds Littledale. He will be called St. George. When he is still a child, his father dies of a heart ailment in 1861 at the age of 42, just as he is visiting a doctor in London for a consultation. He is buried in a family plot in St John's Church near Highfield House. Young St George briefly attends Rugby School, followed by Shrewsbury School, but does not complete his studies. He is a restless soul. When he is 21 he receives his inheritance and in 1874, he sets off on a world tour.

For scions of the aristocracy and the wealthy, it is considered a rite of passage to learn how to hunt foxes and shoot game. St. George is no different and he becomes skilful at field sports at an early age, possibly learning from his Uncle John Bolton Littledale, his father's brother. Seemingly, then, a family trait: Ronald acquired his passion for hunting in-house. Travelling through the British West Indies and the USA, St. George hunts birds and mammals, specimens of which he sends to the Liverpool Museum. In October 1874, traveling in Japan, he meets a Canadian woman 12 years his senior, Mrs Teresa Scott, and her husband, subsequently spending eight months travelling with them. A year later, on the return voyage to Liverpool, Mr Scott dies. Three years on, in 1877, St. George and Teresa marry. They become renowned as the greatest travelling couple of their time. The list of places and regions they travel around is impressive: Kashmir; the Rocky Mountains in Wyoming; Alaska; the Caucasus; the Pamir Mountains; Russian Central Asia; Mongolia; India; China; Tibet; Siberia; Kamchatka and Newfoundland.

In 1887, St. George is in touch with Thomas Moore, director of the Liverpool Museum, who introduces him to Albert Gunther, Head of the Zoology Department at the Natural History Museum in London. From then onwards, during their numerous trips, the couple collect specimens of all kinds of birds, insects, reptiles and fish for the museum and plants for the Royal Botanic Gardens in Kew. St. George, in the meantime, has become known as a big game hunter, once shooting an unknown breed of sheep in the Tianshan Mountains in the border region of Kazakhstan, Kyrgyzstan and the Chinese region of Xinjiang and having it named after him in Latin: the Ovis Littledalei (today Littledale Argali, Ovis Ammon Littledalei).

Journeying through Tibet, a trip which eventually lasts 14 months, the Littledales get stranded some 80 km from the gates of Lhasa, trying to reach the forbidden city. Between 1846 and 1904, no other European will manage to get this close to the Buddhist capital. This feat will earn St George the gold Patrons medal of the Royal

Geographical Society, of which he will eventually become a Fellow.

Accompanying them on the expedition is William Alfred Littledale Fletcher, son of Edith, one of St George's sisters. He is 25 when he, St. George and Teresa come face-to-face with an armed Tibetan force, a stone's throw away from Lhasa. Born on 25 August 1869 in Wavertree and baptised on 12 October 1869 in Liverpool, William is the right person for his aunt and uncle to have along whilst traveling through inhospitable 19th Century Asia. An uncanny parallel exists between the lives of William and Ronald. By birth, they are both great grandsons of Thomas Littledale, Mayor of Liverpool. Both are old Etonians; both reach the rank of lieutenant-colonel; both are awarded DSO for their wartime exploits and both become casualties of a world war.

William is a sportsman, rowing and playing football at Eton. He coaches the rowing team while studying at Oxford and in adulthood, he is a big game hunter, explorer and soldier. In 1901, he is a long way distant from coaching his oarsmen on the River Thames: he is in South Africa, taking part in the Boer War, serving as a lieutenant in the Lancashire Hussars. He earns his DSO on 28 September 1901 when, as part of a small body of men, he defends a remote farm near Colesburg against an overwhelming force of 300 Boers until they finally withdraw. In the Great War of 1914-1918, he is a captain in the 2/6th Rifle Battalion of the King's Liverpool Regiment. His unit is subjected to a mustard gas attack at Armentieres in July 1917, which knocks out two companies. Among the casualties, 440 of them who can no longer take part in the battle, is William Fletcher. After two-months' recovery time, he returns to the fray, resuming command of his beloved unit. Nevertheless, in July 1918, even though he finds it hard leaving his men, he has to bow to the inevitable when it is apparent that the effects of the gas attack were worse for him than he had previously thought. On 14 February 1919, his weakened lungs give out, thanks to pneumonia, caught in the Spanish flu pandemic sweeping the world at that time.

***

Travel north along Littledales Lane, the low buildings of Paddock Cottage pop up on the left of the road. These are the former stables and tied cottages of John Bolton Littledale Sr's estate staff, who looked after the horses. At the time, these buildings were part of the Sandiway House estate. The house itself is on the other side of the road. It is a large sandstone manor house, built in 1860, covering 840 square metres. In the late 19th century, the area where Sandiway House stands was part of Weaverham cum Milton. The house, consisting of two floors and an attic, stands slightly elevated from its surroundings and is surrounded by farmland. From the imposing entrance, there are impressive views over the Chesire Plain. In the 21st Century, the manor is hidden from view by modern executive housing.

John Bolton Sr. is an avid follower of foxes and hounds. Resplendent in classic white riding breeches and fiery hunting pink, a black top-hat crowning his copiously side-burned head, he loves the battle with the fox in the surrounding countryside. Unusually, he has a warm regard for his prey. It is said of him that he even goes out into the cold at night after dinner to see that nothing serious has happened to the foxes on his estate that day. The Samuel Hindley mentioned in Elizabeth Clinch's email is John Bolton Sr.'s gamekeeper, employed on the estate. His working life starts at the age of 16 as an apprentice, presumably with his father who is a shoemaker. Some three years later he joins Littledale, first as an apprentice and later as a gamekeeper, which situation he will remain for the rest of his life. In 1861, he marries Ann Newton, a spinster who works as a domestic servant and, like Hindley, lives in Sandiway. Ann dies in childbirth, aged 30. Two years after her death, in 1868 Hindley married Suzannah Taylor. His sister Jane, eight years his junior, is also employed in the Littledale household, as a maid. Their fortunes are tied inexorably to the fortune of the Littledale family.

Samuel Hindley's family settles in a tied-cottage on Littledales Lane. An excellent marksman, Hindley is also a sergeant with the Hartford Company of The Cheshire Rifle Volunteers up until 1887, of which he is a member from its inception. Shooting earns him many prizes. He also breeds racing dogs and is an expert at training them. Hunting is a passion he shares with John Bolton Sr, also an excellent rider, and a member of the Cheshire Hunt, that meets regularly at The Blue Cap, a pub not far from Sandiway House. The Opening Meet is in October of every year, and The Blue Cap buzzes with activity as the hunting season commences. Horsemen and their hounds congregate, carriages with eager spectators block the road and, in the fields, horses and riders wait for the spectacle to begin.

John Bolton Sr. is appointed captain in the 23rd Company of Cheshire Rifle Volunteers at Weaverham on 28 March 1860, ending his military career as colonel of the 2nd Battalion Cheshire Rifle Volunteers. With his wife Mary, he leads the life of the landed gentry. Sandiway House has a staff of nine: a governess, a cook with a kitchen assistant, several other servants to keep things running and an elderly couple, James and Margaret Gregory, butler and housekeeper respectively, who live in a separate lodge. Mary has her own personal servant, Mary Ann Wilson.

On 5 May 1889, John Bolton Sr. dies at the age of 66. He is buried four days later in the Hartford churchyard, and his friends have a window panel placed in the church to his memory. His son, John Bolton Jr. turns 31 a month later. He was educated at Eton, studied at Christ Church College, Oxford and served in the army reaching the rank of captain, before marrying Clara Violet Stevenson, a Scot, four years younger than himself. The big event was on 12 October 1899 at St Mary's church in Burnham, and the marriage is blessed by the Reverend Canon Hunter, assisted by the Reverend Clement Leigh Coldwell. On 14 June 1902, their only child, Ronald Bolton Littledale, is born. He is baptised on 22 July at St Mary's Anglican Church in Weaverham. There is some uncertainty about the year Ronald is born.

Volume 13 of Visitation of England and Wales is published in 1905, edited by Frederick Arthur Crisp, who duplicates the book in an edition of 500 copies on his own printing press. This book and its previous and subsequent volumes acts as a kind of census for the nobility and gentry, keeping a record of coats of arms and pedigrees. They contain the family trees of numerous families from the ranks of the wealthy, aristocratic and noted. The famous Vice Admiral Horatio Nelson has a full biographical page to himself, among other lesser-known Britons. The Littledales of Highfield, West Derby, co. Lancaster are in there too: their family tree begins with the image of a coat of arms with the motto 'Fac et Spera': 'Do and Hope'. Thomas Littledale of Highfield House as the progenitor of the Littledale family, resides at the top of the tree, with subsequent generations below him. At the very bottom dangles a small entry about this tree's latest shoot:

> Ronald Bolton Littledale, born at Sandiway Bank 14 June,
> bapt. at Weaverham, co. Chester, 22 July 1901.

Anyone baptised in 1901 cannot possibly have been born in 1902. Several necrologies claim 1902 as the year of Ronald's birth. This is then repeated as fact ad infinitum elsewhere. The cemetery in Airaines, where Ronald finds his final resting place, sheds no light onto the darkness of this mystery. It records only the date of his death, 1st September 1944, carved into the white stone. Under the reference number '18289' of its War Memorials Register, the Imperial War Museum (IWM) in London reports that a memorial to Ronald Littledale and his father John Bolton Littledale has been erected at the Parish Church in Bunbury, Cheshire, some 20 km south of Sandiway House. The text of the inscription reads:

> CAPTAIN JOHN LITTLEDALE AND MAJOR RONALD LITTLEDALE. MAJOR LITTLEDALE ESCAPED FROM COLDITZ, WAS AWARDED THE DSO, RETURNED TO SERVICE AND AS A LT COL WAS KILLED BY A LANDMINE IN NORMANDY IN 1944

Accompanying the entry is the dubious warning that this text contains 'not [the] exact wording'. This cannot be questioned. Neither is it entirely accurate. That Ronald was killed in Normandy is plainly an error, since Airaines is in the Somme department, not Normandy. His being killed by a landmine is also of questionable veracity. Other sources cite an ambush in which Ronald was killed. But what does the actual text say? And in which church in Bunbury is it located? In my internet researches, I stumble upon a walled-in stone, framed with a green marble border in St. Boniface Church in Bunbury, and I do not know whether the text hints at the truth or just spreads further obscuring mist about the Littledale mystery. It reads:

> In loving memory of
> John Bolton Littledale
> Born 15th June 1869
> Died 24th Dec. 1942
> And of Lieut. Col.
> Ronald Bolton Littledale D.S.O.
> Born 14th June 1902
> Killed in Normandy Sept. 1944
> While commanding the 2nd Battalion

The Kings Royal Rifle Corps

Again, the statement that Ronald was killed in Normandy is certainly not correct, and further, the year of birth... 1902. Even more striking is the birth year of his father: Visitation of England and Wales states that John Bolton was baptised in Hartford on 30 July 1868. Baptism prior to birth is still not an option available to people, so we are left with a small mystery. Is Visitation of England and Wales wrong? Possibly. Elizabeth Clinch, too, in her email, speaks of 1868 as the birth year of John Bolton Littledale. Did she get her information from the Visitation or was it somewhere else?

In 1872, George Hindley's wife Susannah gives birth to a son, George. George begins his working life as an apprentice wheelwright and lives with his parents on Littledales Lane. He is probably like a fish out of water here, seeking a bit of adventure in his life. At 27, he becomes a soldier in the Cheshire Imperial Yeomanry where he serves for a year and a half, rising to the rank of corporal. He fights in the Boer War in South Africa and receives several decorations. Returning to England, where his father Samuel is now 67 years old and at the end of his working life, George takes up the option of following in his father's footsteps. The 1911 Census records him as a gamekeeper on the Littledales' estate in Sandiway. However, his will not be a lifelong situation there. John Bolton Jr. has financial problems, and is forced to let George Hindley go. However, he manages to find him another position as gamekeeper, most likely in Rhydtalog, Tyddyn, in North Wales.

John Bolton Jr.'s financial distress is presumably one of the reasons why he moves with his family in 1911 to a property near Bunbury, Tarporley. Financial distress in this instance is only a relative term: Bunbury House has eighteen rooms, including the kitchen, but not, for example, the bathroom. Still living on private means, the family has a nanny, a cook, a kitchen maid, a housemaid and a saloon lady, all of whom live in the property. This is truly a household representing the kind of financial distress anyone could live with.

The move to Bunbury under no circumstances means peace for little Ronald. It marks the start of a life of geographical flux. He travels in England for his education, around the world as an army officer; to France when the war in the west begins, then through Europe keeping away from the Germans and then his return to England. And then his final trip to France. In or around 1910, Ronald moves for the second time in his short life, heading for the south coast. This time he is on his own. St Aubyns Preparatory School in Rottingdean his destination.

4

EDUCATION

Young Ronald attends St Aubyns school in Rottingdean, on the south coast of England near Brighton in Sussex, some 400 km from Bunbury. It is not hard to imagine that, at such a great distance from his parents, he is already filled with the independent spirit he would later exhibit as a grown man. There is a beautiful drawing of Ronald as a child, in which, even at an early age, his dark eyes look out with confidence below his blonde, half-curly hair. This self-assurance expresses his independence right from the start of his life. It is a lifelong, characteristic trait. The nameplate attached to the frame shows 1902 as the year of his birth. And the date… 19 June instead of 14 June. Confident, independent, self-reliant, elusive.

St. Aubyns pupils don't have much contact with the Rottingdean townsfolk. It is only occasionally that the young scholars are seen playing sports on the two-and-a-half-acre field behind the school overlooking the sea, or when they stroll through the village. Just one misplaced kick can ensure their ball flies over the white cliffs straight into the sea. Across the water lie the white cliffs of France's Pas de Calais department. It is less than 180 km from St Aubyns, and young Ronald can have no idea what the land across the water will one day mean to him.

St Aubyns is a prep (preparatory) school, so called because it prepares students for their later public school education. It is a world unto itself, an institution with its own rules and regulations, separate from what lies beyond its walls. There has been an educational establishment in Rottingdean as early as the 18th Century when the colourful vicar Dr Thomas Redman Hooker taught pupils at The Grange. Notable pupils from this time include Henry Manning, later Archbishop of Westminster, and Henry Fox Talbot, one of the inventors of photography. As the school grows, rooms are built in the attic as sleeping accommodation for the pupils. The boys' beds line up tightly in this small space, separated only by a chair. Behind the chairs, there is a spot for a photo to stand, the only reminder of home. At the foot of the bed are wicker baskets for the bedding. A fireplace at the end of the room with morally uplifting prints above it completes the children's living environment. The school's evidently good reputation means it needs to expand into bigger premises. Therefore, Hooker moves the school into a building at 76 High Street. In 1894, Hooker's school was bought by two brothers, who moved their establishment elsewhere in Rottingdean. The empty buildings were bought in 1895 by Charles Stanford, who founded St Aubyn's. He was the headmaster until he sold the school on to his deputy, Vaughan Lang in 1919. In 1940, the school changed its name from St Aubyn's to St Aubyns. It provided education for boys aged 3 to 13.

For the first hundred years of its existence, the institution was virtually in a state of stasis. It changed little or not at all, always accommodating around 60 to 100 pupils. A chapel is built in 1912 and inaugurated the following year. This will eventually record the names of 102 old boys, who died in the First and Second World Wars. From brown-bordered frames, the uniformed fallen peer down on visitors in the chapel. Under stained-glass windows at the head of the chapel depicting Saint George, Saint Alban and, in the centre, The Good Shepherd, the young men who gave their lives in battle are commemorated on a dark, wooden panel, with gold lettered text:

> We remember with honour these old boys of St. Aubyns who gave their lives for King and Country.
> God proved them and found them worthy for himself.

The panel is flanked by two tall candlesticks and candles, a simple metal cross set up in front. Immediately above the candlestick on the left is the name of one of the most famous men commemorated here: John Kipling, born in Rottingdean in 1897 and son of the famous writer Rudyard Kipling, author of the *Jungle Book*. From 1907 to 1911, young John went to school here, and although five years older than Ronald, there is a chance they met. At the age of 18, lieutenant of the Irish Guards John Kipling went missing in the battle of French Loos during the Great War in 1915. A body was found and identified as John, but it was so mutilated that it was not until 1992 that it could be said with any certainty that it was indeed Kipling. His picture hangs on the west wall in the chapel, along with those of his fallen comrades from the First World War.

There are 47 boys who attended prep school here in Rottingdean and who gave their lives for their country in the First World War. Portraits of 32 of these boys have been collected by the headmasters. They are flanked by 37 of the 55 boys who fell during the Second World War. Their names also appear on the wooden panels in the chapel. Outside on the sports fields, a red-stone cross stands on three plinths, bearing the names of all 102 young men. The youthful Ronald, on taking his first steps into the school's premises, would have no idea that his name too will one day appear on these walls. In 2013, the school is closed. The locals are greatly concerned, until it is certain what will happen to the chapel, a unique memorial site is in danger of disappearing under the violent advance of time.

After leaving St Aubyns, Ronald is sent to Eton School, or King's College of Our Lady of Eton, besides Windsor, to announce its full name. Ronald again finds himself among young men, just like at St Aubyns. It is the story of his life. Women make almost no appearance in this biographical history, and where they do, it proves to be dramatic. He remains a lifelong bachelor, married only to the army. Eton is in the county of Berkshire and while it may be 100 km closer to his native soil than Rottingdean, these 300 km do not mean Ronald can count on more visits from his parents than at St Aubyns. One wonders how the distance between parents and children affects the family relationships, but that is not the point of an institution like Eton. Boarding school may be its official function, but it is mainly the elite's springboard to top positions in the Establishment, given the many military figures, athletes, statesmen and writers it has produced. Independent thinking and a questioning mind were and are encouraged by education, sport and debate.

Ronald is immediately preceded to this establishment by his father John Bolton Jr., who began his education there in 1883, but there are others too. In a portrait of him at Eton in 1887, he gazes out to his future with inquisitive eyes and a determined twitch to his lips. Neatly dressed in suit and tie and buckled tips on his collar, the 18-year-old young man is following a family tradition. In slightly shaky handwriting (his own ?), the name J. B. Littledale is written below the picture. A note has been added in blue ink, 'coll. Field + cricket. Mixed Wall

1887'.

The monochrome picture is in a College album started in 1866 by a G. Symonds, President of the College Debating Society. In addition to his scholarship, John is an enthusiastic footballer who regularly appears in the *Eton College Chronicle*. First published on 14 May 1863, this magazine records sports events and other school activities such as exhibitions and open-air concerts. The *Chronicle* also gives potted biographies of Etonians and old boys, even if they graduated years ago. The opening issue begins with an introduction explaining the aims of the magazine:

> The Editors of the ETON COLLEGE CHRONICLE feel great pleasure, not unmingled with trepidation, at bringing before the Eton Public for the first time an entirely new publication, of such a nature as has never before been attempted at Eton. Its want has long been felt; for the many and various-named Periodicals, which from time to time have appeared, in no way supplied it, giving no news of interest to Etonians, but merely wasting paper with foolish stories and crippled translations in prose and poetry, through which it was impossible to wade. The door of the Portions has forever closed; the Observer no longer exists; and the Phoenix long since has soared aloft, to return to Eton no more! But the CHRONICLE is of quite a different character to these before-mentioned periodicals, for it is to be entirely composed of facts, not fiction.

The *Chronicle* also relates the activities of the various school societies such as the Eton Society, the Literary Society, and also features many In Memoriams columns of deceased old Etonians. The stories of boys who progressed from Eton to the Royal Military College (RMC), the officers' college at Sandhurst, also populate the magazine's pages. Sports such as swimming, cricket, boxing, rowing, fencing and football are prominently featured, with individual performances given the same prominence as those of teams.

The footballing John Bolton Jr. competes against teams of Old Etonians and former Etonians now studying at Cambridge, as an Oppidan Scholar (a boy at Eton College who has distinguished himself academically and whose family is wealthy) against footballers from the colleges. Sometimes things get rough according to one description:

'Was a very tough and trustworthy, 'flying-man' but was hurt lately, and so is unable to play.' On 1 October 1887, a team from Eton plays against a team from RMC Sandhurst in poor weather conditions. When John goes up to Oxford in 1888 and plays with a team from the university town against another team from Cambridge, it is mentioned by the *Eton College Chronicle*. In 1887, still at Eton, he plays in the Mixed Wall team with his younger brother Thomas Bolton who also is in the year below him. Mixed Wall, The Collegers and The Oppidans: those are the three teams participating in that most famous of the school's curious traditions, the Eton Wall Game. The Wall is a slightly curved edifice built in 1717. On a strip of ground along the wall 5 m wide and over 100 m long that bears the name Furrow, a rough game is played in which the young men routinely get scrapes and lose skin on arms and legs. The Eton Wall Game is best described as All-in Football, a combination of rugby and football, where pushing and pulling are permitted tactics and many an elite head has been introduced to the famous wall in a distinctly disagreeable manner. Egged on by their fellow students, sitting on the wall in their striking school uniforms, the team with the ball attempts to get it to the opposing team's end. As John's parents have access to a staff of nine at home in Sandiway, and they all live off family capital, it is funny to consider him and his similarly aristocratic and wealthy confreres, preparing for their future eminent and significant roles leading the world, by charging around, up to their ears in the mud, with the sole aim of getting a ball to the other end.

    A more philosophical education is experienced by John Bolton when he joins Pop. The Eton Society of Pop is the school's most important and influential society, and being elected a member counts as the most coveted social award in Eton. Pop has its own clubroom where the president addresses his members, where new members are elected and where debates are occasionally held. Thus, the art of debating, speaking and arguing is practiced with discussions like, for example, whether 'Queen Elizabeth was justified in having the Scottish Queen Mary executed in 1587'. In 1887, the *Eton College Chronicle* reports on a discussion on 5 December involving John Bolton Jr. The issue before it then is whether 'it is justified in all circumstances to tell a lie'. One of the participants is Style, who defines a lie as a misrepresentation where the facts are concerned. According to him, telling a lie is permissible under some circumstances. As an example, he mentions a seriously ill man, who would presumably die if he knew the true facts. In response, another debater, Brocklebank, argues that a lie cannot be justified under any circumstances. Honesty, according to him, is not only the best but also the wisest choice to make. Although he can imagine situations where a lie is easier and perhaps better, he cannot imagine that a lie can ever be justified. Two other participants in the discussion agree. Then John Bolton Jr. speaks. He mentions an example of ambassadors who should be allowed to not always adhere to the truth, because they make their statements in the interest of their country and not for themselves. The debate ripples on until eventually, President Lord Ampthill sums up the evening, pointing out that whether a lie is justifiable ultimately lies between the two extreme positions advocating for or against. Finally, a large majority of the members opt for the position put forward by Brocklebank, that a lie cannot be justified under any circumstances. A few days later, the opponents are back together on the football field.

The conversation held in the clubroom of the Eton Society on 5 December 1887 and the academic position taken by John Bolton Jr. in the process casts an ominous shadow more than half a century ahead when, in 1941, John's son, Ronald, finds himself in a situation where he actually has to make the choice: truth or a lie. On his decision at that crucial moment, the nature of the rest of his life, the life of his regimental comrade, Lieutenant Mike Sinclair and the lives of several Polish Resistance fighters will be determined and sealed.

In 1915, Ronald put his signature in the Eton College entrance book in which the newly arrived boy confirms his admission to this elite establishment, at the start of its new academic year. Two more boys from St Aubyns follow him on his way to Eton, R. H. Bayford and A. M. Boase. The contact person for Ronald is not his father but his mother: Mrs L., Bunbury House, Bunbury, Cheshire. Two years later, a certain Eric Arthur Blair also signs the book. A year before[9] Ronald moves from St Aubyns to Eton, a major world fire has been lit on the European continent. The barrel of gunpowder that is called Bosnia Herzegovina is ignited with a gunshot in Sarajevo when 19-year-old Gavrilo Princip assassinates the Austrian heir to the throne, Franz Ferdinand. His wife Sophie is also hit and dies. One by one, the dominoes on the European stage fall, creating immeasurable chaos that envelopes the Russian Empire, the Dual Monarchy of Austria-Hungary, the German Empire, France, Belgium and Britain. Full of good cheer, soldiers go to war with the belief in a quick victory before Christmas that soon ends up mired in a bitter trench warfare the likes of which the world has never seen before. During the war years, the columns of the Eton College Chronicle, previously filled with enthralling accounts of football matches or the Wall Game are filled with detailed descriptions of Etonians who have fallen in battle, either from the fire of a German sniper or as a result of the crash of a double-decker. As the years go by, the In Memoriams get shorter, until under the heading *ETONA NON IMMEMOR*, only the name, rank and date of death are recorded.

Sports coverage, on the other hand, becomes more comprehensive. On 23 May 1918, for instance, an account appears of a football match played in Scheveningen on 10 April, involving two teams consisting of officers, old Etonians all. The men had arrived in neutral Holland from Germany shortly before, where they had been interned. Meanwhile, the slaughter continues unabated. In 1916, a fund is set up to allow the sons of fallen officers who studied at Eton to continue their education there. It is noted that in several cases the money should be available even before the war is over. The College puts £10,000 into the fund. There is also a desire to erect a lasting memorial to fallen Etonians in the form of a monument. By the end of 1918, £140,000 is available and dozens of scholarships have been provided. By the time the fund and a monument take shape, more than 700 Etonians have been killed and more than 5,000 are on active service on one of the many battlefields. Captain, temporary Lieutenant Colonel, William Fletcher of the King's Liverpool Regiment is one of them. He becomes a casualty during an attack by his unit at Armentieres in July 1917 when he inhales mustard gas. Ronald's 48-year-old great-nephew does not return to active service until September, but will not return to action. He returns to England on 23 July 1918, 'broken in health'.

Ronald is placed in Well's House, named after his home tutor Cyril Mowbray Wells, who acts as both student tutor and guardian. When the boys enter Eton at around 12-years-old, they join a residential community, a House, under the supervision of a Housemaster, who rewards the pupils' good behavior and corrects bad behavior where possible. The Houses are grouped around the college buildings, and the boys each have their own room, which may be small, about 15 square metres, but equipped with a folding bed, a washing facility with bath, a fireplace, a study table with chair and sometimes a bookcase and a sofa. Most of the boys' time is spent together, subject to a tight schedule of school and chapel attendance, football, cricket and participation in debating clubs until the time the front door is locked. Nothing has changed for Ronald since St Aubyns. His is a life spent in closed male communities.

For the first few years at Eton, was a keen cricketer, but when he was nearly 15, this ceded room, briefly, to boxing, competing in the Paper Weight class. Boxing is all very well, but cricket remains his favourite. In July 1918, as the Great War draws to a close, aged just 16, he plays for Well's House in the Junior House Cup final. He did well enough to gain the attention of his Housemaster. The match itself is reported to have ended disastrously for the losing team, deprived as they were of their two best players due to the Spanish Flu epidemic. At the beginning of the following year, Ronald plays for Well's House again, but this time in the final of the House Football Cup. Controversially, someone suggests they do not play the match on the hallowed but deplorable turf of The Field, but elsewhere, on a better pitch. Unthinkable! The Field it has always been and The Field it will be now. The ground, though, is so boggy that the match is played 'not on but a few inches below the pitch'. Everything and everyone is covered in mud.

It is not long after that the Spanish flu strikes again, this time closer to home. One of its victims is William Fletcher. His lungs, damaged by mustard gas, are too weak to resist the deadly virus and he dies on 14 February 1919 in Allerton. His parents survive him, but not for long. His father Alfred dies the same year: the following year, so does his mother, Edith.

A few months later, Ronald's father, John Bolton, paid a visit to his son. The occasion on 8 July is the Warre-Cornish Annual House Dinner, named after the former Vice-President of Eton, Francis Warre Warre-Cornish, who had died a few years earlier. This the first time since 1914 that the dinner will be held at the Trocadero Restaurant.

Apart from matches against teams from other Houses or old Etonians studying at Oxford, Ronald also represents his school in matches against teams from outside the school. In October 1920, he is a member of the Eton XI that beat teams from the 1st Battalion Coldstream Guards and the 60th Rifles of the King's Royal Rifle Corps. One day, Ronnie will switch sides and play for the 60th Rifles against Eton.

Like his father, Ronald is elected to Pop, but generally, he is an unremarkable presence in the columns of the *Eton College Chronicle*. The town's most important and influential society is an elite within the elite of Eton. As described earlier, Pop is a highly prestigious and exclusive society where the art of debating is practiced to perfection. At the bottom of the Chapel Steps, a formal portrait is taken of the Society members wearing their distinctive attire, consisting of a tailcoat with white trousers. Even as a member of Pop, though, Ronald remains a shadowy presence: The Eton College Chronicle reports no interesting debates to which Ronald contributed.

On Thursday 24 June 1920, a monument is unveiled in the Cloister at Eton in memory of the officers of the King's Royal Rifle Corps, all old Etonians. It is modelled from a design by Captain E. L. Warre who served with the KRRC. The top of the impressive tableau with the 75 names reads:

IN LASTING AND GLORIOUS MEMORY OF 75 OLD ETONIANS OF THE KING'S ROYAL RIFLE CORPS WHO GAVE THEIR LIVES FOR THEIR KING AND EMPIRE IN THE GREAT WAR 1914-1918

The panel of white Portland stone is flanked by two pillars and is inlaid with red marble. Three columns list the men, sorted by rank and the year they left Eton. At the bottom of the tableau, it is stated that 'this tablet is erected by Etonian Brother Officers'. The school is a conduit to the corps of some 250 men. The monument is unveiled by Field-Marshal Lord Grenfell after a service held in the chapel at 3.30 pm. Before prayers and psalms, the ceremony begins with a speech by the provost and then the names of the victims of the First World War are read out. Once Lord Grenfell unveils the monument with a short speech expressing his deep sympathy and that of the regiment to the relatives of the fallen, there follows singing by The College and Lower Chapel Choirs. Finally, the Last Post sounds from Lupton's Tower. There is little doubt that Ronald must have been here at least for some of this. These were the last of his days at Eton. Perhaps he was present at the solemn unveiling of the panel. He certainly would not have imagined at the time that several decades later, his name would appear on a new panel to the left of the 1914-1918 memorial.

Ronald leaves Eton in 1920 during Michaelmas Half term. The

following year, Eric Arthur Blair too completes his education. The *Eton College Chronicle*, in its issue of 2 February 1921, reports that Blair leaves Eton in Fifth Form. Unlike Ronald's parents, Eric Blair's parents have no money to be able to send him to university. Instead, he joins the Indian Imperial Service in Burma in 1922, where he works as a police officer. When he returns on leave to England in 1927, he resigns. Seven years later, a novel called *Burmese Days* is published. This is the first novel Eric Blair wrote under his nom de plume, George Orwell. The protagonist is John Flory, an avowed opponent of British colonialism and imperialism. The book is partly based on Orwell's experiences in Burma. He defends himself in 1946 against criticism of his book saying that, except for some inaccuracies, he has only described what he observed.

Ronald Littledale does not follow the footsteps of his father John, his uncle Thomas and his great-nephew William footsteps to Oxford or Cambridge University. His family is wealthy enough to afford for him to go to any university he wanted, but no. Instead, like Blair/Orwell, he chooses the army. This is not a great act of rebellious independence, because his family also has a military tradition: his grandfather had been a colonel, his great-uncle Thomas Littledale, who came to the aid of the sailors of the *Ocean Monarch*, a captain, and William Fletcher dies as a lieutenant colonel.

A week after reporting his departure from Eton, the *Eton College Chronicle* congratulates Ronald on passing his final Army Entrance Examination for Sandhurst. During his training at the military academy, Ronald returns to Eton several times when he plays football for the RMC in October 1921 and 1922 against a team from his alma mater. He occasionally shows some traces of his old form, but the rest of his teammates are completely outclassed. The first game is lost by the RMC 9-0, the second 6-0.

5

KING'S ROYAL RIFLE CORPS

'Dear Sir,–It may be of interest to you to record that the following Old Etonians attended the Fourth of June dinner at Cologne.' What follows is a list of 28 names including that of R. Littledale (late C. M. W.) who attend a dinner in Cologne. The message to the editor of the *Eton College Chronicle* published in the 14 June 1923 issue, Ronald's birthday, was sent by the 2nd Bn. KRRC, British Forces on the Rhine, Cologne, and is signed by 'The usual pen-weary' Le G. G. W. Horton. A message has also reached the editor from the British Embassy in Constantinople in which the 1st Guards Brigade reports a highly successful dinner at which 44 men celebrated the Fourth of June under the auspices of Colonel Commander J. Steele. The date is significant in Eton's history; it is the birthday of King George III under whose reign the school experienced an unprecedented boom. The monarch visited the school regularly and received pupils at Windsor Castle. As a tribute to him, Eton declared his birthday a public holiday, with cricket matches, recitals, a boat parade and a picnic on Agar's Plough, a large field north of Eton on the Jubilee River. 100 years later, former pupils sit at a banquet far away in Germany, a country defeated after four years of war. As a result of the 1918 Armistice Treaty of Compiegne, which ended the First World War, among other things, the western bank of the Rhine is occupied by the victorious armies. An Allied ring is also placed around Cologne, Koblenz, Mainz and Kehl, seeking to protect France from future attack by Germany, and as a guarantee that Germany will meet its reparations. The Treaty of Versailles, adopting the previously formulated demands from the Treaty of Compiegne, limits the presence of Allied troops to a period of 15 years. In 1934, the occupation will be ended. Troops from the UK, including the 2nd Bn. KRRC are stationed around Cologne, occupying a relatively small part of the zone.

On 2 February 1923, *The London Gazette* reports that Second Lieutenant Ronald Bolton Littledale has signed on to this elite corps. The KRRC is an infantry regiment founded in America in 1756 under the name 62nd (Royal American) Regiment. It recruited its men from local settlers. For over 200 years, the regiment will serve in the British Empire. The Corps' original task in America was to protect the 13 British colonies attacks by the French, who were taking advantage of the original inhabitants of America to conquer the British possession. On 4 March that year, four battalions were formed, each with 1,000 men, made up not only of British settlers but also Swiss, German and Americans. They are mostly Protestant, and are willing to fight the Catholic French. Officers are recruited from Europe: there are English, Scottish, Irish, Dutch, and again Swiss and Germans. In 1757, the corps is renumbered 60th Regiment. A regime of discipline and personal initiative and responsibility is implemented. After the Napoleonic Wars, when the British colonies in North America are long gone, the regiment is renamed. In 1815, it is called The Duke of York's Own Rifle Corps, 15 years later it becomes the King's Royal Rifle Corps. The nickname 60th Rifles resulted. In the First World War, the regiment earns its spurs on the Western Front, in Macedonia and in Italy. It also takes part in the Battle of the Somme, in which over 200 officers and 4,000 men lose their lives between 1 July and 15 November 1916. Overall, in addition to 2,000 decorations, the 60th loses nearly 13,000 men. Seven members receive the highest award, the Victoria Cross.

By 1920, the British Empire consists of a patchwork of possessions, protectorates and mandate territories around the world, connected by a strong navy. A land army is needed to maintain governance in Canada, Singapore, an immense strip of land across Africa from Egypt to South Africa, Australia, British Guiana, the Middle East including Mesopotamia (present-day Iraq and Jordan), countless islands scattered across the oceans, even pieces of the South Pole, and the jewel in the crown, India. Apart from governing this global empire, further motivation to join the army is provided by the bloody, First World War, that held Europe in particular in its iron grip between 1914 and 1918. The thought of 'never again' may have played a role for many men to join up. It is not inconceivable that Littledale may have cursed the fact that he was just too young to participate in this conflict. On the other hand, there were plenty of young British boys just his age who did fight in the trenches, and lied about their age to be able to do so. The lure of adventure will no doubt have played its part.

The 2nd KRRC has served all over the world since its founding in 1756 in North America. It has been stationed in Canada, the West Indies, Spain, Ireland, Gibraltar, the Ionian Islands in Greece, South Africa, India, China, Malta, and, in between, regular sojourns lasting several years at its base in England. From July 1922 until leaving in January 1925, it is stationed in Cologne as part of the 2nd Rhine Brigade, transferring there from Silesia.

After the Treaty of Versailles, Poland is restored as a state. As a result of a plebiscite deciding the fate of Upper Silesia, there is dispute over whether the area should become German or Polish, and a veritable Polish uprising ensues in May 1921. To put down the flare-up of violence between armed Germans and Poles, British units already in the Rhineland are sent to the conflict to assist the Italian and French troops already in attendance. The 2nd has a small role in border control and escorting train traffic in the closing stages of this conflict. On 25 July 1922, the unit leaves for the Rhineland where it will remain for several years.

Littledale, second lieutenant with Service Number 25378 is one of many old Etonians serving in the 2nd Bn 60th Rifles in the Rhineland. Around his 22nd birthday in June 1924, 25 of them send their warm greetings to the editors of the *Eton College Chronicle*, expressing their wish to be at Eton on this Fourth of June. *Floreat Etona*!

When the force is built up in early 1923, one of its tasks is to guard the railway lines over which the French occupying force transports its men and equipment to the area between the Franco-German border and the Rhine. Patrols guard various lines and sectors in the strip as part of its task of occupation. In the summer of '23 and '24, time is spent mainly on field training and gunnery exercises. As part of the training, distances between locations are covered on foot at marching pace. There is even a Rhine Army Inter-Unit Route March Competition, which is won by the 2nd.

On 3 February 1925, *The London Gazette* announces that Littledale has been promoted to lieutenant. The promotion takes place around the time his battalion returns to its home base in Aldershot where it will remain until 1932 before leaving for Northern Ireland. The 1st Battalion stays in India between 1922 and 1934. Littledale's 2nd Battalion replaces personnel from the 1st who return to England for leave, among other things. The cycle of training, sporting, temporary postings to India, and being permanently available as Home Battalion for every conceivable occasion is broken in April 1926 when the 2nd is converted to the British Army's first motorised infantry battalion. By the end of 1931, the 2nd has access to trucks, motorbikes, semi-cruisers for transporting Lewis Guns and carriers. At the training ground in Aldershot, the Carden-Loyd machine-gun carriers roll through the tall tussocks of grass like strange insects. The gun turret-less 'tankette' carries a gunner in addition to the driver, but also serves as an artillery tractor for transporting guns and howitzers.

Littledale's life during this period is described by KRRC historians as 'Soldiering while the Nation slept'; the interwar period is a period of relative calm between the atrocities of the First World War and the horrors of the Second. Not much is happening, so Littledale cannot be blamed for playing in a football match in 1928. At Eton, of course. The KRRC plays against The School 2nd XI on 6 October and loses 4-0. The visitors are very much out of form. A month later, things are slightly improved when the school plays against an Army delegation and the match ends in a draw.

As part of the regular exchange of troops, Littledale temporarily moves from the 2nd Battalion to the 1st, stationed in India. In June 1929, the traditional Fourth of June telegram was sent to the editor of *Eton College Chronicle*, this time from Lucknow, near the border with Nepal. It read: 'Five sweltering Sixtieth Riflemen send warmest greetings White Littledale Whitbread Grenfell and Wingfield'. Warm it certainly was, in June temperatures can reach 37 degrees.

The 1st has been in India for a long time. From 1922 to 1934, the battalion is stationed at several places in the Jewel in the Crown. From Ireland to India in 1922, it is billeted in Rawalpindi for the first three years. On 16 November 1926, the men march to Razmak, 420 km away in the North Waziristan district, near the border with Afghanistan. The group, dressed in tropical uniform and with the rifle at the shoulder, consists of 14 officers and more than 600 other ranks led by Lieutenant Colonel Willan. Fortunately for them, their packs are transported by train to their destination, as are 80 troops in the company of two officers. It is a 22-day march, and it includes crossing the Kuram River, wading over it ankle-deep in its water on 1 December. Game is hunted along the way, but not much is bagged. The commander is reluctant to cover the entire journey on foot. In his own words, he is afraid of getting a stiff back if he had travelled the route on horseback. Such are the privileges of command.

On arrival in Razmak on 8 December, the column is greeted by a veritable snowstorm, the last thing the men must have expected in the blisteringly hot climate. They remain in Razmak for just under a year, helping the police keep apart rival factions of Muslims and Hindus, and put down any possible uprising. In November 1927, the 1st moves on to Lucknow, the former capital of Oudh, a state in northern India that now longer exists. This is where the 'Five sweltering Sixtieth Riflemen', including Littledale, send their warm greetings to their Alma Mater in Eton. John Goddard, son of a sergeant working in the officers' mess, gives a good account in his childhood memories of the conditions under which the corps is housed and how it fills its days.

The scorching temperatures of these tropical conditions are somewhat tempered indoors by large ceiling fans. Small lizards, mosquitoes and large spiders are uninvited guests, making themselves comfortable in everyone's quarters, men and officers alike. What the ceiling fans cannot stop, however, are malaria and sandfly fever. Solid instruction and excellent advice is there to prevent any cases of venereal diseases among the men who are, in the main, single. The soldiers are excellently looked after by native servants, who cook, do their laundry, mend clothes, tend the garden or fetch water when it is time to bathe. At night, a Chowkidar walks around, a retired Gurka who keeps a watchful eye and ensures that no intruders sneak into the quarters. As long as that does not happen, and the police do not need military support, the officers have a great time in the Officers' Mess. There are leather armchairs, there are thick carpets, and paintings and trophies hang on the wall. Dinner is announced by a series of trumpet blasts. After the meal, there is music as the regimental band puts on a performance and the men listen and converse over a glass of whisky and soda.

There are other regiments stationed in Lucknow besides the 1st KRRC, like the East Yorkshire Regiment and the 3rd The King's Own Hussars. On Sundays, there is a veritable parade as the men make their way to church for the weekly service. Littledale, raised in the tradition of the Church of England, will also have attended these services. The 1st always shows up last, but with a brisk marching rhythm of 140 paces per minute, they are still on time, in full dress uniform, with troop helmet, rifle and cartridge holder. There is a reason for this, which goes back to 1857, when unarmed men were massacred at church in Meerut during a rebellion by Indians in the service of the British Army. The weapons have since been carried in the pews during word, song and prayer.

In late 1931, the 1st leave for Kolkata (Calcutta), almost 1,000 km south-east, but no less tropical for all that. And probably not on foot this time. The corps takes up residence in Fort William, in the city centre on the Hugli River. It is a matter of debate whether the thick walls and bastions of the 18th Century fort have constituted as strong a defence against the heat as they have against would-be assailants. The climate is so extreme that only ceremonial duties are still justified, such as the visit in early 1932 of the Maharajah of Nepal, Bhim Shumsher Jang Bahadur Rana, who will die not long after, along with the Viceroy and the Governor General, who is the head of the colonial government in British India. Additionally, there are regular inspections of the battalion by the Commander in Chief and Adjutant General; there is the King's Emperor's Birthday Anniversary Parade in June, and the Proclamation Day Parade which is organised on 1 January. Anything else can be put off till it cools down a bit.

Only when things get very heated between rival religious groups, like setting fire to each other's shops, does the KRRC intervene. This being the army, the men are encouraged to participate in a variety of sports. Apart from swimming in the pond at Fort William and boxing in the dry moat, there is football and athletics. The regimental hockey team plays at the highest level, in the First Division of the Bengal Hockey League. At the Christmas dinner in December 1931, when the old Etonians dutifully visit each other, they decided to organize a football match between a team of the 60th Rifles against a team called The Ditchers. Both teams will play with ten men. On 19 January 1932, the match takes place on the only available pitch next to Fort William. Refereeing is provided by Messrs. Mytton and Cunningham, both of course Etonians. The pitch is small, the match is hard, and the conditions are sweltering, mainly due to the humidity. Littledale plays an excellently and his team is constantly on the attack. In the first half, William Heathcoat-Amory scores to make it 1-0 for the 60th Rifles. In the second half, the pressure is increased, and the match ends, without any significant incidents, in a comprehensive 5-0 victory for Littledale's team. The only hazard was that the ball regularly ends up in the fort's moat. When the players are listed for the match report afterwards, they discover that the 60th Rifles fielded 11 players, not ten! This retrospective observation somewhat tempers The Ditchers' disappointment. They hope, therefore, for a revenge match before the regiment leaves Kolkata. If indeed this putative revenge match ever took place, the *Eton College Chronicle* makes no mention of it.

The relaxed and privileged atmosphere in which professional soldier Littledale enjoys his posting in India and the closed regimental world to which he belongs are in stark contrast to the wretched conditions which can exist in Calcutta. Indubitably, he will have been aware of the slums and of the large groups of homeless people living, eating and sleeping on the streets, if not directly witnessing them himself. The sharp divide between rich and poor, and the extreme poverty among the population may have been food for thought, especially given his own elite and wealthy background, but he was not moved to take a fierce stand against British colonialism, as was George Orwell in his novel *Burmese Days*. He is too absorbed and pre-occupied in his role as a professional soldier. In a photograph with fellow officers of the 1st in 1932, a relaxed Littledale, in tropical uniform with shorts and long socks, gazes at the camera. The determination in the 1923 photo is still there, but the reality of being part of a world empire where the sun never sets has removed some of the doggedness around the corners of his mouth.

Postings abroad alternate with longer periods in England. Apart from football, Littledale is keen on shooting. His marksmanship with rifle and revolver is excellent, coming out on top in several competitive shoots. In competition at Bisley, in 1934, he comes third. In 1935, he has dropped out of the top three. Despite this apparent decline, he will go on to become one of the best marksmen in the British Army. Another hobby developed during these years is dog racing, in which he was undoubtedly encouraged by his father. His parents regularly go on fishing expeditions in Scotland and Norway, and Ronnie too has his heart set on Scotland. Not surprising with a Scottish mother. Fishing is a passion shared by the whole family.

In 1936, after Littledale's stay in occupied Germany and colonial India, the British Mandate territory of Palestine is in need of his unit's ministrations. The Australian, New South Wales newspaper, *The Barrier Miner,* announces, in its columns on Thursday 10 September 1936, that King Edward VIII has arrived in Vienna by train the previous day with Mrs Wallis Simpson on their return to England after a cruise on the

Mediterranean. Here, he visits an ear specialist Professor Heinrich Neumann, who spends an hour examining the effects of an infection in the royal aural appendage, for which he will treat the king during his three-day stay. More important things are happening on the world stage. The War Ministry announces the dates of preparations for embarking reinforcements to the British Mandate Territory of Palestine, where there are ominous rumblings of discontent. Every two to three days, a ship bound for the Middle East leaves the port of Southampton. Headquarters staff and administrative units leave by the steamship, *Laurentic*, on 14 September. On the 18th, the 2nd KRRC embarks on the steamship *Neuralia*. Before this, on 3 May that year, Littledale is promoted to captain, and on 8 September, prior to the *Neuralia*'s voyage to the conflict zone in Palestine, he receives a temporary promotion to staff captain.

After the collapse of the Ottoman Empire, Palestine emerges as a mandate territory in 1920. The country is entrusted by the League of Nations to the authority of the United Kingdom. The combination of increasing Jewish immigration, especially after Hitler comes to power in Germany in 1933, and British authority leads to protests among the Arab population. There are casualties in riots in the early 1920s, followed by a period of relative calm at the end of the decade. Sheikh Izz ad-Din al-Qassam founds the Black Hand, a radical militant group, responsible for attacks on Jewish and British targets. In 1935, the British track him down and kill him in a firefight. On 19 April 1936, fighting flares up again after a general strike by followers of the Sheikh. In the uprising, British and Jewish targets are again attacked. These disturbances culminate in the assassination of the British administrator of Nazareth, Andrews, in 1937. The reaction of the British enforcers is brutal and violent. The number of troops increases to 20,000 men. The mission is to stamp out the Arab revolt. The 2nd Battalion KRRC with Captain Littledale will remain in Palestine for 14 months.

As early as 3 September, the 2nd prepares for the trip to the Middle East. Tropical uniforms need to be arranged as well as vaccinations. But on 18 September, it is time to go. Thousands of troops and reservists gather at the port of Southampton. Soldiers from the 2nd Wiltshire Regiment and the 2nd KRRC march up the gangway boarding the ship, rifles with bayonets attached. They are accompanied by the sounds of the Wiltshire's marching band. The detachment boarding the steamer consists of 600 men. The voyage lasts ten days and the time is well spent in preparation. The reservists are trained separately and educated about conditions in Palestine. On the ship's arrival in Haifa, however, a car accident knocks out the only two staff officers who know exactly the regiment's role and destination. Equally and typically unfortunately, nothing is written down on paper. No-one knows where to go, or what to do when they get there. The woollen clothing the men are wearing turns out to be far too hot, and already on the quay they change into lighter, cooler khaki uniforms. Littledale, though, is used to the heat after his stay in India. Most of the regiment is encamped in Sarafand-al-Amar, three hours south of Haifa, on the Palestinian Plain. There are dozens of barracks with pitched roofs, burning in the sun, lying in a barren expanse of land. A few weeks after arrival, units are assembled to escort convoys passing through the country, and occasionally dispatch snipers. In addition, the corps carries out night-time surveillance of railway lines and cordons off villages during searches. On 6 November, many reservists return to Britain after an appeal by the Arab Higher Committee, the central political body of Arab residents of the Mandate Territory of Palestine, to end the hostilities. The size of the corps drops to 300 men, and a period of relative calm sets in. Time is put to good use with exercises, including lengthy marches and training on motorized manoeuvres.

In October 1937, fighting flares up again. The 2nd is deployed to surround villages where searches are conducted and houses marked where weapons are found. These weapons are confiscated and the houses eventually are destroyed. Throughout the campaign, thousands of dwellings are reduced to rubble. A curfew is imposed, Arab leaders are arrested and 150 Arabs are killed. It is discovered much later that Nazi Germany helped finance the uprising.

Once again, on 12 November 1937, Littledale plays in a football match with a team of old Etonians against The Black Watch, part of the 2nd, who are in turn, also all former Eton pupils. No grass this time, as at Eton. Nor mud. And fortunately, no moat either. This match will be played on dry desert sand, on a pitch marked off on one side with an irregular row of trees, while the other side is not clearly defined. Only after being postponed three times due to political developments can the game go ahead. Things get a little rough, and the ball ends up stuck in the branches, high up one of the trees. Or on the other side of the barbed wire of the Sarafand encampment. Unfortunately, Littledale just fails to score and the match, played without a referee, ends 0-0.

On 29 November 1937, the 2nd is relieved of duty in Tel Aviv, and the journey to England via the port of Haifa begins. By 10 December, they have made it back home in Aldershot. A day earlier, Littledale relinquishes his post as temporary staff captain. For his participation in the Middle East campaign, he receives the George VI General Service Medal. The round silver medal displays the crowned portrait of King George VI, who succeeded his brother Edward in November 1936, after the latter abdicated to marry Mrs Simpson. The clasp, which is attached to a hanging bracket on the purple-green-purple ribbon, a permanent part of the award, mentions the location where the award was earned. For Littledale, PALESTINE is listed.

***

On 26 February 1918, in London's Knightsbridge district, a boy is born whose name and fate will forever be linked to Ronald Littledale. His name is Albert Michael 'Mike' Sinclair. He is the second son of Colonel Thomas Charles Sinclair of Winchester, and Lucy Iris Sinclair. He has an older brother Christopher, and a younger brother John. Mike attends Reverend P. C. Underhill's preparatory school, Wellington House, in Westgate-on-Sea, Kent, and later Winchester College, a private boys' school. It is the oldest school in England continuously located in the same building. The institute has such notable old Wykehamists, as pupils at Winchester College are known, as Alfred (Bosie) Douglas, the poet and writer but, above all, intimate friend of Oscar Wilde; the mountaineer George Mallory, who went missing on Everest in 1924 and whose body was finally discovered in 1999; and Oswald Mosley, founder of the New Party, later the British Union of Fascists.

In Winchester, Mike lives in Turners House from 1931 to 1936. His brother Christopher attends the elite boarding school from 1929 to 1934. For the last two years of Mike's stay at Winchester, his younger brother John is there too. One of Mike's classmates is Willie Whitelaw, four months younger than Mike, a future Northern Ireland Secretary, and one of the key ministers in Margaret Thatcher's cabinet from 1979 to 1988. In 1936, Mike and Willie are in the cricket team that captures the Turner Cup. That year, Wykehamist Mike leaves boarding school as Commoner Prefect.

Mike enrols to study Modern Languages and History at Trinity College in Cambridge. In surroundings as medieval as Winchester, he learns to speak excellent German, a great benefit in his future. His brother John, at Winchester a good golfer and fencer and adept at field running follows him to Cambridge a few years later to study French. In July 1939, Mike gets a Regular University Commission in the 2nd Battalion King's Royal Rifle Corps, the same battalion Ronald has been in for over 16 years. Ronald is almost 16 years older than Mike. From then on, their lives and fates will be intertwined. John Sinclair also enters the army on the completion of his training in 1940 and becomes an excellent officer. Just like Mike.

1938, Aldershot, England, home of the battalion. 24 officers of the 2nd KRRC stand in front of the camera in evening dress. It looks much like the portrait of the Eton Society on the Chapel Steps when Littledale joined it 18 years earlier. Only one of them, Lieutenant Turnor, is dressed in uniform with the insignia characteristic of the corps across the breastband. The rest wear a dinner jacket with a black bow tie. Second Lieutenant Mike Sinclair in the front row does not wear one, Captain Ronald Littledale, fourth in the row behind him does. A faithful dog with collar lies like a mascot at the feet of Lieutenant Colonel Barker, who has his decorations hanging on his chest. The dog, a Greyhound, is the symbol of the regiment, whose crest bears the motto *Celer et Audux*: Swift and Bold. Littledale wears no decorations. What did the men talk about after the picture was taken, or over dinner, or after with brandy and cigars? The situation in Czechoslovakia, perhaps? Things are rumbling there.

Hitler is keen to protect the Sudeten Germans present in the country, an ethnic minority that makes up a quarter of the population. So he says. In reality, he is just looking for an excuse to increase his position of power. Fears among France and Great Britain that a war with Nazi Germany is imminent leads to the decision in Munich in September 1938 that Czechoslovakia should cede the Sudetenland, the border region where most Sudeten Germans live. On 15 March 1939, it is the rest of the country's turn and Hitler's troops cross the border without facing any resistance. One day later in Prague, the Führer proclaims the protectorate of Bohemia and Moravia. Hitler the blackmailer expands his empire without a fight.

The mechanization of the 2nd that was halted in 1932 is resumed. In the threatening situation that has arisen on the world stage, the deployment of a mechanized corps could become decisive. With the prospect of a possible war with Germany in mind, an advertising campaign to attract new recruits is already being pursued in 1938. A recruitment poster from this year features the following recruiting text.

> Don't miss this opportunity
> The King's Royal Rifle Corps is one of the only two
> Infantry Regiments in the
> MOBILE DIVISION
> and is
> COMPLETELY MECHANISED
> You have every opportunity of becoming an
> Expert Mechanic or a Wireless Operator
> JOIN NOW AT THE NEAREST RECRUITING OFFICE

As trucks pull up in column, advanced by an armoured car, a trumpeter in dress uniform of the KRRC stands in front playing his instrument. The regimental coat of arms in the form of a Maltese cross with the motto *Celer et Audax* and the names of the numerous battlefields the corps has fought on is dominantly displayed on the poster. The drawing of the Carden-Loyd tankette shows a vehicle that does not appear to have made any progress in development since its first tentative practice sessions on the grassy field at Aldershot a decade earlier. The only difference is an antenna to facilitate communication on the battlefield.

Littledale, in his dinner jacket with bow tie, in the company of fellow officers at Aldershot, can have no idea at the time when the photographer makes the image, and things are unsettled far away in Czechoslovakia, that an assassination attempt in Prague four years later will unleash unprecedented forces that will eventually have him send to Colditz.

6

CALAIS

At lightning speed, German troops storm towards the Channel. May 1940 marks a tipping point in the months-long armed peace between Nazi Germany and the West since Poland was overrun in September 1939. Developments follow rapidly, and French troops and the British Expeditionary Force know there is no stopping them. They are retreating to northern France, to Dunkirk and nearby Calais. There, while fierce rearguard battles take place, boats and ships of all shapes and sizes cross the Channel to evacuate the main force. More than 300,000 British and French troops are taken to safety. This rescue is only successful because thousands of Allied troops stay behind and sacrifice their chances of evacuation to hold up the Germans for as long as possible. In this narrow defensive belt around Calais, Littledale takes on the difficult task of getting his countrymen to safety.

On 10 May, German troops invade the Low Countries. Holland, Belgium, Luxembourg: one by one, these barely protected countries fall like ripe apples into the Führer's lap. And France is next. The British Prime Minister, Neville Chamberlain finally resigns; his policy of appeasement in tatters: there is no negotiating with Hitler. The more war-like Winston Churchill takes over the helm from Chamberlain.

After overrunning the Low Countries, Hitler's forces proceed at breakneck speed through France, heading inexorably toward that country's northern shores and the English Channel. At the spearhead is General Heinz Guderian's XIX Panzer Corps. On 20 May, they occupy Abbeville at the mouth of the Somme River. The 10th Panzer Division are then sent north to cut off the English and French forces in and around Calais and Dunkirk from the main French army in the south. They reached Boulogne on 22 May. In Calais, the defending troops are beginning to suffer food shortages. At the same time, over in Dover, urgent discussions are being held about how to evacuate the troops from Calais and Dunkirk and get them safely back across the Channel. Plans are also being developed to try and break out and make contact with the French main force in the South. London is in the dark about the condition of the surrounded armies, but Churchill decrees that Calais must be retained at all costs. He will concede after the war:

> I personally ordered the troops in Calais to hold their ground and fight to the bitter end. I agreed to evacuate Boulogne, albeit with reluctance. And when I think back on it I think I should have given the order to continue fighting there as well. However, the order to hold out in Calais certainly meant that almost the entire garrison would be killed or captured. The decision was the only time in the war when I was unable to eat. I was almost sick at the table.

He added that the steadfastness of the troops in Calais and the strange order from Hitler for the German army command to halt on 24 May gave two vital days to evacuate the force in Dunkirk.

As a result of Churchill's decree, a brigade is formed in England to cross the Channel and augment the forces already in Calais. It consists of units from The Rifle Brigade, 60th Rifles, Queen Victoria's Rifles, and the Royal Tank Regiment. The preparations have to be done in a hurry, resulting in several serious deficiencies. The troops haven't had chance to form a solid combat unit together. They have no infantry experience, have no rifles, only small arms. There is little space on the transports taking them over the Channel, which not only ensures that not enough anti-tank artillery is carried but also that a third of the force does not even get taken.

The troops who do make it over find that the battleground poses a challenge in itself. Calais with its ports is on the northern coast of France in an area of canals, rivers and dunes. Central to the city is the Citadel, which has been regularly expanded and fortified since the 16th Century. Around the city are 12 bastions connected by ramparts, still strong enough for troops to hold off a siege for some time, however, the defensive force does not include a Corps of Engineers capable of blowing up bridges to impede the enemy's progress. Although the 2nd Battalion KRRC specialize in mobile warfare, their options are limited.

The 30th Infantry Brigade headed by Brigadier Nicholson crosses the Channel to Calais the next day with the task of advancing to

Boulogne, but they are too late. The tanks of the 3rd Battalion of the Royal Tank Regiment are struggling against Guderian's armoured corps, and the route to Boulogne has been cut off. Despite the threat of siege, Nicholson elects to stay in Calais; but even that proves impossible. German artillery bombardment and unabated attacks from the Luftwaffe ensure he is forced to further withdraw his troops.

Nicholson settles his headquarters in the Citadel, protected by a combination of French and British troops. Three bridges in southern Calais are guarded by the 2nd Battalion and units of the Queen Victoria's Rifles. Littledale, promoted to major in February 1940, acts as transport officer for the 30th Infantry Brigade after recently resigning his position as company commander of the 2nd Battalion. He had landed, along with his unit, on 23 May at around 1 pm. He finds himself in a chaotic battle, in an area getting smaller by the minute due to German pressure from land and air. Lieutenant Mike Sinclair is in charge of several Bren Gun carriers and walks around with a large map upon which he tracks the battlefield situation.

The next day, the 24th, strangely, Guderian's Panzers come to a halt. This gives the beleaguered troop force railed against them a chance for some respite from the struggle. The wounded and troops not involved in the fighting are evacuated out of Calais on board transport ships still loaded with vehicles and ammunition meant for the Rifle Brigade. Back they go to England with the evacuees, under the assumption that their cargo of materiel is no longer needed. The Germans pile on the pressure again, and finally the port of Calais, the main supply line for the Allies, is abandoned to them. The soldiers who remain behind are exhausted and battle-weary. Sinclair presents a bedraggled appearance, almost unrecognizable after not having shaved for several days. They've run out of ammunition, the last of the food is gone, and contact with Dunkirk is lost.

On 25 May, Littledale is in the Citadel and receives word at about 1 pm to deliver fuel for the tanks in the area around Bastion 9, defended by the 2nd Battalion KRRC. He is also ordered to reinforce the Rifle Brigade Company outside the rail station. The KRRC was once formed with Germans in its ranks to fight the French intent on capturing British colonies in North America. It is now fighting alongside the French against aggressive German forces intent on gaining French territory. Its task is initially 'to hold Calais at all costs' but now it's 'Every man for himself', the last order received in the hornet's nest of Calais. It is in this environment and under these circumstances that Littledale has the difficult task of getting his countrymen to safety.

He reaches Bastion 9 and finds that although he's got the fuel, there are no tanks around to receive it, so he retreats to a fort in the harbour mouth. This is almost certainly Fort Risban, located on the outer harbour and tidal dock, the Bassin des Chasses de l'Ouest. It was originally built as a defensive stronghold to protect the harbour, but now it is the last stronghold of a rearguard action to defend retreating British troops. The combination of 'fort' and 'Littledale' will become defining features of his life several more times.

The next day, on 26 May, he tries to return to his unit but only succeeds in running into the arms of a German patrol near the fort. *Für ihn ist der Krieg vorbei*: for him, the war is over. He is a Prisoner of War. Meanwhile, B Company of the Queen Victoria's Rifles and C Company of the 60th Rifles withdraw from the harbour area across the bridge to the centre. He is that close.

Huge Bruce is 21-years-old and a lieutenant, within the 85 Royal Marines commanded by Captain Darby Courtice. Shortly after midnight on 25 May, he lands in Calais with his unit to assist French Marines defend the citadel in the centre of the old town. This turns out to be a hopeless task. Despite fierce resistance, he too eventually abandons the battle. He describes how he came to encounter the XIX Panzer Corps. The battle has ceased, everything is quiet. It is a warm summer evening, the defenders are surrounded, are out of ammo. There is no ship in sight, the wharves are deserted. Bruce thinks about hiding but he realises the Germans are taking Prisoners of War. He abandons an attempt to swim off, knowing the Germans have already surrounded the citadel and will spot him in no time. He returns to his post, dismantles his machine gun and removes from his camera the film he has shot of the gruesome battle. Just then, a lone German soldier approaches him. Despite the difference in language and circumstance, the two men greet each other.

He hands over his camera and a pair of binoculars to the German, along with a scrap paper with an address hastily scribbled on it. He asks if he will get the items back after the war, he certainly hopes so. He cannot take much more than a knapsack with a toothbrush and razor, two cans of meat and a meal for the next day. Without putting up a fight, Hugh Bruce becomes a Prisoner of War. After the violence of the past few days, this is a complete anticlimax. He joins the swelling stream of defeated soldiers, a desolate company of which Littledale and the recently-captured Mike Sinclair are also part of this desolate company, on their plod to an indeterminate future. Bruce is not the only one who considered a watery escape from the Germans. Littledale is captured almost naked by the conquerors after swimming across a creek. With borrowed clothes and boots, he sets off on foot to Germany.

In a seemingly endless column, the defeated Allied armies trudge in the opposite direction to the victorious German units. The Germans are on their way to Paris, where within six weeks, they will bring France to its knees. For ten days, Littledale and the others tramp through northern France. They pass the graves of compatriots who gave their lives in the previous war fighting the same country that is now once again their enemy.

'*Aus, auf, los!*' There is no lack of clarity from the Germans. The dusty column of defeated soldiers and officers are ordered into motion, weary day after weary day. Philip Pardoe, from the same regiment as Littledale and Sinclair, remembers joining a group of mostly Frenchmen stretching for a mile and a half. Germans on bicycles buzz around them like flies. A machine gun truck accompanies the procession, a lethal reminder. Rotting corpses of horses lie stinking beside the road. The route first heads south, passing through Guînes, Marquise, and Le Wast, then Desvres, Hucqueliers, Hesding, Frévent, Doullens: unknown dots on the map, north of the Somme River. The first night's stop for Pardoe is a church in Guînes. Somewhere before, on the road, he meets Mike Sinclair.

The prisoners are thirsty and hungry. There was barely any time to grab a quick bite during the battle in Calais and now the defeated armies are entirely dependent on the Germans for sustenance. It is hot, and water is even more important than food to the men walking to Germany. Thousands of marching prisoners converge at Le Wast to spend the night in a stadium. Somewhere in this endless chain of humanity beset by hunger, thirst, dust, broken soles, heat and rain, burnt car wrecks and cadavers, Major Ronald Littledale walks on, swept along like a twig on the raging surge of an endless human river. His borrowed boots give him blisters on his feet: he must surely have regretted that unfortunate swim when trying to escape. Pardoe has developed a pain in his chest which interferes with his breathing, so he has to sleep upright at night. Mike Sinclair suffers from mild rheumatism.

Grismond Davies-Scourfield is six months younger than Mike Sinclair and, like him, attended Winchester College. On 25 August 1938, shortly after his twentieth birthday, he is promoted to second lieutenant in the 60th Rifles. On 22 May 1940, he sails on the MV *Royal Daffodil* from Southampton via Dover to Calais where he arrives the next day. The ship will later become involved in Operation Dynamo, the major evacuation at Dunkirk. In Calais, as platoon commander of the 2nd KRRC, Gris experiences the battle for the city in all its intensity, ending up far worse off than Littledale, Sinclair and Pardoe. He is badly wounded by mortar shelling and machine-gun fire. His wounds are severe enough to merit his being driven to captivity in a truck, so maybe he is better off. They pass through Boulogne, and on the way, he sees the famous white cliffs of England in the distance. It'll be five years before he will see them again. The truck takes him to Malmedy and then he gets put on train to Mainz. Meanwhile, Pardoe's column reaches Hucqueliers, where the group is too large to accommodate. The unlucky ones have to spend the night outside on wet grass. At Doullens, the column comes together with a group of prisoners from St. Valery moving north via Airaines.

Occasionally the PoWs are given food by the population, or they turn up en masse at a vegetable garden along the route. The Germans try to create discord between the French and British by giving the French preferential treatment, calling them out first when food is distributed. On 2 June, the procession arrives in Bapaume, then proceeds to Cambrai. Here a woman throws sweets into the crowd, and the men rush toward her. She is nearly crushed and bursts into tears. All chances of a possible escape are lost as the column turns north, and the lines south of the prisoners are farther away than ever. Increasing hunger, fatigue and disorientation further diminish the impulse to reach the Allied troops. On and on they plod through the monotonously flat French countryside. Wheat fields point the way to the Belgian border. Via Dinant and La Roche, the grey crowds finally arrive at Bastogne, northwest of Luxembourg. At the town's small train station, Pardoe, and elsewhere in the crowd, Littledale and Sinclair take their 'seats' on a crowded train bound for Trier, just east of Luxembourg. Last Class all the way. There's 60 of them in a cattle car. It's crowded, but way more preferable to that dreadful trudge from

Calais, even if some have diarrhoea, along with the ever-present hunger and fatigue.

The camp in Trier is just outside the city. Thousands of French and English troops are crowded into huts, which they share with thousands of insects. The men just want to sleep. At last there is a chance to write home, to let those waiting there in uncertainty know they're still alive. The Germans immediately warn everyone that the chances of mail reaching England are slim. Lists of items needed are sent along too. There is a shortage of everything: clothing, reading materials, and above all food: they're desperately hungry. When something like soup is finally served, there's an interminable wait for it in an endless line in front of the canteen. It is Littledale's second time in the Rhineland but this time under very different circumstances. Now he is not an occupier, and he will only be there for a week until a train takes the PoWs on to Mainz. The railroad runs along Mosel and Rhine, and the vines growing up against the hillsides remind the men of home.

In Mainz is yet another camp, where they stay for four days. Here they are told that virtually the entire British Expeditionary Force has been evacuated and, moreover, that the defense of Calais, experienced as chaos by the men, is considered to be one of the most successful rearguard actions ever. Churchill will later declare: 'Together with our position on the Gravelines line, which was slowly overrun, Calais gave us two vital days,' which proved to be enough to make the Dunkirk evacuation a success. The MV *Royal Daffodil*, only one year old and Gris Scourfield-Davis' erstwhile home, sailed back and forth across the Channel seven times, bringing 9,500 men home safely. Left behind is an occupied France, an abandoned Dunkirk and a smouldering mess in Calais.

After their short stay in Mainz, the prisoners are crammed back into their cattle wagon, unable to see much of the landscape. All they do know now is their destination. Deep in southern Germany, the train arrives at a station. It is mid-June 1940. They've reached the end of the line: Laufen. With jaded eyes and exhausted minds, Littledale, Sinclair and Pardoe take in the snow-covered peaks of the Austrian Alps visible in the distance. Nearby is the Berghof on Mount Obersalz near Berchtesgaden, Hitler's Alpine stronghold. Littledale certainly imagined his 38th birthday on 14 June differently.

7

LAUFEN

In southern Bavaria, on the border with Austria, lies the town of Laufen. Some 50 km away is Berchtesgaden, where Adolf Hitler has his headquarters, and even now is forging his plans for the conquest of Europe, while enjoying a terrific view of the Alps. The Salzach River, which forms the physical border between Germany and Austria, runs right through Laufen, dividing it in two. On a protruding headland that juts into the river is a huge square building that, according to one recent arrival, resembled an asylum for the insane. Pat Reid, captain in the British Army and captured near Dunkirk, was one of the first to arrive there on 5 June 1940. Walls, four storeys high, beset with numerous windows, surround a small courtyard. This is Laufen Castle: once the palace of the Archbishop of Salzburg, where Mozart and Haydn had performed during the summer months. It was now a Prisoner of War camp for mostly British officers, captured during the Battle of France.

The castle is first recorded in the year 788. Centuries later, in 1607, the Archbishop of Salzburg, Wolf Dietrich von Raitenau built a new palace on the site. This was a grander affair with four wings. From 1707, it serves as a residence for the Prince Bishops of Salzburg. In 1811, during the time of Secularisation, the castle passes from this Princely Bishopric into the hands of the Kingdom of Bavaria. Finally, in 1862 the authorities realised that this immense edifice would make an ideal prison. Space was created for 400 prisoners, to be guarded by some 70 jailers and staff. It continued thus until April 1932 when it was closed, for lack of prisoners! That would soon change. From then on, the building had a variety of uses: in 1933, the *Sturmabteilung* (SA), the notorious Brown Shirts, used it as a gym; a year later, it was the local *Reichsarbeitsdienst*, the labour exchange. Between 1935 and 1938, the complex serves as an army barracks: not the last time military personnel will be housed here.

At the beginning of the war in Western Europe, Laufen held mainly British soldiers who had participated in the French campaign. They replaced the Polish officers who were already confined in the castle. The Germans designated the place Oflag VIIC: *Offizierslager* (Officers' Prison) number VII in military zone C. The German High Command loved their bureaucracy. The bureaucratic entity Oflag VIIC only existed for a relatively short time. In early 1942, all the residents were transferred to Oflag VIIB in Eichstätt. The building was immense: according to the Germans, it could hold 1,500 men. Even after 1942, the castle served as a holding facility for anyone whom the Nazis deemed unfit for their society. Under the name Ilag VII (*Internierungslager* or Internment Camp), non-native residents of the British Channel Islands of Jersey and Guernsey were incarcerated there until liberation in May 1945 by American troops.

What were Ronnie Littledale's first impressions after he arrived there, exhausted from his long trek from Calais? Did memories come flooding back to him of his school days at Eton? Or even earlier, St. Albyns? With hundreds of people all crammed together in large buildings overlooking a courtyard, this thought is not so strange. Pat Reid describes his own arrival. The men arrive to find a place full of guards, searchlights and barbed wire. Photographs are taken for identification. Reid himself gazes sullenly into the camera, his moustache a menacing presence under his nose. The look in his eyes express the feeling shared by many of his comrades: Down, but not out. He is issued with an aluminium tag with a number on it unique to each PoW. 12 years later, Reid remembers his as 257: the photograph shows number 357.

Exactly who is number 257? Patrick Robert Reid was born in India, in 1910. His father works for the government. When he was five-years-old, he and his family leave for Ireland, where little Patrick goes to school. At 14, he goes to London where he is trained as a civil engineer. For a long time, his work determines where he will live, most recently in Liverpool. In 1935, he joins the army reserve and he serves three weeks every year in 2 Division of the RASC, the Royal Army Service Corps. The unit's responsibilities include land, sea and air transport, the army fire department, and the supply of food, water, fuel and items such as clothing, furniture and technical and military equipment. On 20 September 1939, his unit leaves for France and lands in Cherbourg, eventually being stationed on the border with Belgium. At Division Headquarters (HQ), Reid is involved in keeping combat units supplied with ammunition. On 27 May 1940, he is eventually captured during the Battle of Dunkirk.

Littledale, like all his fellow 'Kriegies' (*Kriegsgefangene*–Prisoners of War) is put through the administrative wringer at Laufen. Everything of even the slightest importance to the Germans is punctiliously entered on a '*Personalkarte*': camp number, prisoner's surname, first name, date and place of birth, religion (a not insignificant detail in Littledale's life), father's first name, mother's surname, nationality, rank, army unit, occupation in civilian life, registration number of the country of origin, place and date of capture, whether the prisoner is healthy, wounded, or ill, height and hair colour, special characteristics, and address details of relatives who are to be informed of the fate of the unfortunate new occupant of Oflag VIIC. A photograph with registration number, his right index fingerprint, and his PoW number complete the card. His photo, like everyone else's was taken with an exterior wall of the castle as a backdrop. He carries a small blackboard in his hands with a number written on it in chalk. The smudges on the board testify that many numbers preceded his. Later photos are more professionally done, with printed numbering, including the administrative designation of the camp, Oflag VIIC. Back home in England, John Bolton and his wife Clara Violet are informed that their only son has been captured by the Germans. What follows is a long period of uncertainty, as they receive no word from him. Will they ever see him again? This war could last for years, like the last one.

From this point on, Littledale was *Kriegsgefangene* No. 811. The photo on his *Personalkarte*, dated 12 June 1940, shows a man who will turn 38 in two days but who looks much older. He grimaces as he stares doggedly into the camera. The man laughing on the wrong side of his mouth in his state portrait as second lieutenant or the relaxed-looking man in tropical uniform in the 1932 photo from Calcutta has gone. His brown eyes are almost squeezed shut against the light, giving him an angry look. His head is almost bald, but not quite, some spiky hair remains. His receding hairline is only partly the cause: the Germans shaved the PoWs' heads as a matter of course. For hygienic reasons, they said.

Take out the Germans and the barbed wire and Littledale might well have considered himself back in the kind of all-male communities he knows so well from his youth. As at St. Aubyns and Eton, he now lives among men, boys even, as some of them must have seemed to him, a 38-year-old in a large common room made up of young chaps in their early to mid-twenties. His immediate environment aside, the view of the nearby Bavarian and Austrian Alps through the windows must have emphasised to him that he is a long way from home. The determination, expressed in that photograph from the 1920s, leads him and several other officers to decide to attempt an escape.

Jim Rogers, a mining engineer and officer with the 170th Tunnelling Company of the Royal Engineers, describes the situation during those first weeks as a PoW. After being captured in France during a mission to blow up a bridge, he joins the endless line of prisoners plodding their way to their camps. Upon arrival in Laufen, where more than 1,000 officers are incarcerated, Jim and his companions are crammed into overcrowded quarters, sometimes sharing space with more than a hundred others. Their quarters have three-high bunk beds with straw mattresses, called 'donkey breakfasts' by one of the prisoners. Despite the iron hand with which the camp is run, and the triumphant mood of the Germans, the prisoners are happy to have finally reached some sort of final destination, especially after the horrendous time they had getting here. That they are shaved bald upon arrival is a bit humiliating, but after the trip, some also find it refreshing. It is what it is.

The camp regime is harsh. Gazing out of the window at the snow-capped mountain peaks in the distance, or at the church spires of Salzburg is strictly forbidden. The German guards do not hesitate to shoot at unarmed men who ignore this stricture. A lieutenant who was gazing out of the window and sketching the landscape, was struck fatally by a bullet. This just provokes the others into making dolls they dangle out of the window, inviting a similar response. Inevitably, the guards fall for it and as a consequence, the bullet-ridden dolls are triumphantly hauled back insides and cherished by their creators.

The food is of decidedly questionable quality. Rotten potatoes, not even considered fit for pigs to eat, appear on the menu daily. The inmates have to cut away the most rotten parts before they tuck in. The prisoners soon start showing symptoms of starvation. Jim's heart rate drops significantly, even after walking quickly up the stairs. The doctor explains it to him: the body assumes a lower metabolic rate due to their meagre diet. What's left of the potatoes after the rotten parts are removed do not provide nearly enough nutrition.

Just a few days after arriving, Littledale and several other officers start a tunnel, in the music room, an area leading to a larger recreational space. The idea is Ronnie's and is the first of many more tunnels that will be dug at Schloss Laufen, among them one constructed by Jim Rogers, the mining engineer, whose distinctive jaw-line was the source of his nickname, The Horse. Pat Reid will tunnel his way out as well, with five others: Harry Elliott, Rupert Barry, Dick Howe, Peter Allen and Kenneth Lockwood. They got clean away from the camp only to be captured just before they reach the safety of the Swiss border. Reid and his fellow escapers are sent to a special camp after their recapture: Schloss Colditz in Saxony. These men, the Laufen Six as they will become known, are the first British group to arrive at this most famous of all camps.

Three days after work on Littledale's tunnel started, the Germans are tipped off that a tunnel is in progress. They catch two men red-handed, who are working on the tunnel at the time. Littledale, further down the tunnel at the front, manages to stay hidden. He is lucky: his mates get six weeks' worth of solitary confinement. They are Mike Sinclair, prisoner number 850, and Gris Davies-Scourfield, number 530, a lower number that he owes to the injuries that saved him from the hellish journey on foot through northern France. The photo on his *Personalkarte* shows him possessed of a full head of hair and a magnificent black moustache.

Mike and Gris's time in solitary is unpleasantly austere. They sleep on bare planks and live on bread and water, which they receive three days out of four. On every fourth day they can have a bowl of soup. They are deprived of books, writing materials and cigarettes. Any contact with the other prisoners in the camp is forbidden. At times, they are glad to be away from the crammed dormitories where 120 men or more are lodged, but they are not completely bereft of human contact. They're allowed exercise walks every alternate day in the camp grounds, sometimes between the palace and the river, or sometimes on a section of ground on the south side, fenced off with barbed wire. Occasionally, they find small gifts hidden in the snow, left there especially for them by their fellow Kriegies.

It's just bad luck that his first attempt failed, but Littledale knows that until he figures out new escape plans, he is doomed to keep wandering around the tiny courtyard or the area on the south side of the building with its barbed wire fences and German guards with dogs.

He can see the city gate on the other side of the fence, its pointed clock tower rising into the sky. It's possible that Littledale met Pat Reid here, despite the fact that the prison is crammed with so many prisoners, that no-one can expect to meet everyone. At such moments, neither of the two men can imagine that they will meet again two years later under very different circumstances, with a very different outcome to the adventures they began in Laufen.

8

FORT VIII IN POSEN

Take a map of Poznan and a compass; place the needle on the Old Market Square and the pencil tip on the centre spot of the Miejski Football Stadium, (where the European Football Championship was played in 2012), and draw a circle. 18 forts lie on this circumference, forming one of the largest protective rings around any city in Europe. The forts date from the 19th Century and when viewed from above are shaped like a trapezoid. They were ordered constructed by General Karl Von Grolman, the Prussian Army commander-in-chief between 1815 and 1819. The Prussian Army had been here since 1793 and this defensive belt was designed as their protection against the risk of uprising by rebellious Poles within the conquered city, rather than to protect the population from any threat without. There is also an inner ring of bastions surrounding the old centre of Poznan. All the forts are numbered, and one of the structures, Fort VIII, built between 1876 and 1882, is named after the general. Von Grolman died in 1843, and did not live to see the completed fortifications.

Today, most of the forts are in ruins, visible from the air only as outlines. They were originally built half sunk into the landscape, but now, trees grow where the roofs once were and the moats are empty, or filled with tall, rampantly invasive weeds, protecting no-one from anything. The northern structure, Fort VII, or Fort Colomb, has the dubious honor of being the first concentration camp situated outside Germany. The slashing, runic SS symbols once painted on the gate announced to the world what went on behind those doors. Today it is home to a memorial centre, dedicated to the victims of what happened there.

After the Germans overran Poland in September 1939, Poznan became the administrative centre of *Wehrkreis XXI, Reichsgau Wartheland*, or Military District XXI: one of the military administrative units of the German Reich and its old, German name of Posen was reinstated. Some of the forts around the city are used as prison camps, including Fort VII, which held Polish prisoners. Besides being a concentration camp, it is also a Gestapo prison and transit camp. Although the SS happily advertised their presence here, they did not want any witnesses to what they were up to. All Poles living in the area had to move.

At any one time, there were between 2,000 to 2,500 prisoners confined here, guarded by 400 SS troops. In total, from its coming onstream to its liberation, more than 18,000 people were imprisoned here, according to conservative estimates. Of these, 4,500 died under miserable conditions including 300 patients from a clinic for the mentally ill from Owinska who are murdered here: again, a conservative estimate. When the camp closed on 25 April 1944, only 750 prisoners remained. The guards are also housed in the fortress.

The gas chamber is not the only method by which the SS ensured Fort VII's residents a horrific end. They are hanged, shot, tortured or die from poor nutrition or disease. There is a steep staircase in the camp, 40 steps high, which is flooded and slippery in winter. Many poor souls meet their end when they are accidentally or deliberately pushed down the stairs. Each of the 30 cells in the fort has a floor area of 20 m by 5 m into which 200 to 300 people are crammed. Other forts, along with some satellite camps in the area, are used to house Prisoners of War, both officers and men. Together they form Stalag XXI-D and house about 3,000 people. British and French PoWs are interned in Fort VIII, Grolman's fort.

March 1941. 'Fort VIII' is written in black letters on a large white sign above the dark entrance to an immense fortress. The trees and overgrowth in the dry moat that will give the place such an ominous atmosphere more than 70 years later are absent. In addition to the moat, the red brick monolith is surrounded by a high wall inset with a gate and steel doors. Between a wooden shed and a sentry box with its characteristic and striking striped colour scheme, over four hundred officers from Laufen are waiting. A group of three men are talking to each other. Grismond Davis-Scourfield with his magnificent moustache is trying to make himself understood by two others amid the surrounding hubbub. On his right is Ronald Littledale, his face resplendent with stubbly beard growth after days without a shave. To the left is Peter Douglas. A little further away are Mike Sinclair and

Philip Pardoe, both from Littledale's regiment. Together they have made the trip from Laufen to this old 19th Century fortress in Posen. Somewhere in the crowd is Hugh Bruce, the lieutenant of the 85 Royal Marines, who destroyed his film account of the battle at Calais when he was captured. They made the trip to Posen from Laufen by train, in ordinary passenger coaches instead of cattle trucks. Gris, Mike and Ronnie stay together as much as possible during the journey. They try to make a hole in the floor of their compartment but the constant presence of the guards means their plans don't get very far: and as a consequence, neither do they. When they arrive at the station in Posen, they have got a long exhausting walk ahead of them to the fort they will be obliged to call home. They've brought with them as many belongings as they can from Oflag VIIC.

In Posen, a Lieutenant Basil Reginald Wood keeps a diary. His unit, the Princess Louise Kensington (Middlesex) Regiment, has been overrun at St. Valery in France. Captured and a PoW, he ends up in Laufen, as so many did. On 28 February 1941, he is told he will be transferred to Stalag XXI-D in Posen but later, the trip is postponed. Then, on 2 March, he discovers that he is moving out to Posen permanently in two days. In preparation for the journey, Wood spends 9 Marks on a poor-quality blanket from the canteen and sews it together to make a bag in which to carry his belongings on the train. Although he doesn't take much food with him, his blanket bag is very heavy once he has stuffed his belongings in it. On 4 March at a quarter past eight in the morning, Wood and his fellow PoWs march down to Laufen railway station where they board the train to Posen.

The journey that follows is nightmarish. The carriages are crowded, the benches are hard and it is impossible to sleep. The promise the Germans made before the train sets off, that they will be taken to a beautiful old German town is meaningless and irrelevant. It is cold on the train, and the weak soup given to the men does little to warm them. At 7 pm the next day, the train arrives at the old German-Polish border. Someone then manages to arrange some *Ersatzkaffee*, the dubious brew that is supposed to pass for coffee. It is better than nothing. At 7 am on 6 March, the tired, cold party arrives at Posen station. The SS and police are on standby to escort the men to the fort. Many of the men leave their heavy packs behind at the station because they are no longer able to carry them. On the outskirts of town, nearly 7 km from the station, their destination awaits. The fort where they end up is surrounded by a dry moat and barbed wire. Wood marches across a drawbridge into a tunnel leading into the belly of the fort.

Posen is located in an area that belonged to Germany before the First World War, but ceded to Poland after the Treaty of Versailles and was renamed Poznan. The invasion of Poland in September 1939 puts the city back in German hands and it reverts back to its German name. The reason the men are brought to this place is particularly malign. The mere capture of their enemies is not enough for the Nazis. They suspect that German PoWs in Canada are being treated badly, so in retaliation, British and French prisoners are dragged from Laufen to Posen, from Oflag VIIC to Stalag XXI-D. The former palace of the Archbishop of Salzburg is exchanged for a dank stone den with little daylight, even further away from neutral or allied borders. The men are kept in underground cells, the food is poor and, above all there is too little of it. There is an ID photo of Littledale taken here for German PoW records, that displays his PoW number. To the Germans, Littledale is Number 811. The expression in the photograph taken when he became second lieutenant in the 2nd Battalion of the King's Royal Rifle Corps more than 18 years earlier was the same as it is now, with that wry smile and determined attitude, ready for action. It is only the visage from which that expression gazes that has changed. His eyelids hang heavily over prickly eyes. The uniform jacket is tightly wrapped around him, the top button is closed. No Sam Browne leather belt crosses over his shoulder this time. His thin hair has grown back since arriving from Laufen. He looks a lot leaner than he did just under a year ago. Captivity has left its mark on the major's face.

Conditions in the camp are deplorable. The fort is covered in peat and is accessed by a bridge over a wide moat that leads to a cave-like interior. Prisoners are regularly tied to chains as reprisal for the alleged ill treatment of German PoWs at Fort Henry, Camp 31 in Canada. There are few exercise facilities, no cutlery, prisoners are locked in their rooms at night. The poor diet and lack of sunlight cause Hugh Bruce to develop a form of blistering eczema. Lieutenant Philip Pardoe, of the 60th Rifles:

> In the room where we live, eat, sleep, the beds are packed together, and many men have to sleep in the same bed. The walls are dripping with moisture, and the sheets are covered with fleas. There are lice, bedbugs, mice, beetles… The doors are locked by

the guard post… there is no storage space so the chaos is enormous, the windows are barbed wire fenced off and visibility is limited to ten meters by the presence of the wall of the moat. The moat itself stinks because of stagnant water and excess waste.

Wood continues his diary:

[When everyone has arrived at the camp] a Proclamation [was] read out by interpreter that owing to fact German Ps.O.W. in Canada were kept in Fort Henry with not a shrub or patch of shade and in bad conditions, we had been moved to this 'Fort 8' until conditions in Canada had been improved. All rooms underground, 8 and 12 tier beds, fleas, lice. Locked in rooms at night with blanket. Old and primitive aborts, some seats nailed down to give us exact number they had in Fort 8. Only exercise place about 100 yards in moat, very narrow and excreta stream running through it… No hot showers available; water supplied by pump only. All Penguin books taken in search.

Mid-March 1941. Wood writes that he had permission to go outside for two hours for exercises and fresh air. It is 'bitterly cold, ice and snow'. Hardly any food packages are coming in. There is no mail. Hunger and reading determine the rest of the day, if that's at all possible because the Germans, possibly on purpose, have limited the Prisoners to one lamp per room. Despite the cold, the camp is swarming with flies. Later, conditions slowly start to improve: parcels arrive, the men are allowed to walk around on the roof of the fort for exercise, and the number of prisoners is reduced when some of them leave for another camp in Poland. Pardoe buys a violin and continues the lessons he had already begun in Laufen. Wood's diary also mentions this changed situation. On 28 March he records that the Germans 'announced that conditions would be improved as from 1st April 1… [and the prisoners will] be allowed out on roof'. There will be more room for the officers as 120 of the men will be moved to another fort at Thorn, attached to Stalag XXA. Gradually, conditions improve: the flies disappear, the prisoners can finally do their laundry and they can get cigarettes, sweets and honey substitute from the canteen, picture frames even. But even so, the niggles persist. They still cannot get a hot shower and no-one has had any mail. The problem is this: all PoW letters, either those from them or for them, are subject to examination by German censors. No censors, no mail; and this is the situation here. The mail is stuck in the pipeline, because the Third Reich, the one that would last 1,000 years, cannot spare anyone to read its captives' post.

Morale gets a further boost when the prisoners get permission to build a stage and put on theatrical performances. John Lightfoot produces a musical called *Sir, She Said*. However, as Wood records, on 6 April, the SS searches the PoW's quarters, sending everyone outside. Do they suspect something, or is it just a routine check?

There is a reason, naturally, behind the improvements in the PoWs' lot. Strangely, a fellow countryman has pointed out to the Germans that the assumption that PoWs in Canada are being treated badly is unfounded. Franz von Werra is a pilot in the Luftwaffe, who's taken part in operations on both the Eastern and Western Fronts. On 5 September 1940, during the Battle of Britain, his plane is shot down. After several attempts to escape from England, the troublemaker is shipped to Canada. Here, he manages to evade his guards on a train he is being transported on and jumps out. He runs to the St. Lawrence River, which is frozen at the time and gets across. Once on the other side, he finds himself in the neutral United States of America. In April 1941, he returned to Berlin via the German embassy. He will be the only German to escape from captivity throughout the war. Most German prisoners believe in the certainty of the Nazi's final victory and do not bother to escape. Moreover, the conditions of their captivity are such that they have no reason to take their fate into their own hands.

It is unknown whether or not he expected anything different on his return to the Reich, but Franz von Werra is by no means greeted as a hero when he reaches Berlin. The press does not report his successful escape, and he is not allowed to recount his adventures to anyone apart from his family. For 'strategic reasons', whatever they may be, his homecoming is kept secret. It is only after several weeks have passed that Von Werra is allowed an audience with Hitler in the *Reichskanzlei*, where he receives the Knight's Cross. But this is awarded not because of his escape from Canada but because of an attack on an English air base, a different kind of flight. The Führer commends him for having 'proven that out of a situation where one is at a tactical disadvantage, he was still able to make gains'. Von Werra writes up his experiences as a training manual containing important information for aircrews should they unexpectedly find themselves in captivity.

This document opens with a game-changing statement regarding conditions in camps such as Fort VIII:

> German prisoners are being treated correctly by the British and in individual cases, mistreatment has been due to the behaviour of the German concerned.

It is *Reichsmarshall* Hermann Göring himself who orders Von Werra to visit the camps where British PoWs are confined in order to assess the situation on the ground. He will also inform the commanders of the methods used by the British to make escape impossible. He visits Stalag Luft III near Sagan, where captured air force personnel are detained. This camp will eventually become known for the spectacular mass escape in March 1944 in which 76 men participate. Only three of them reach neutral territory. 50 others, including South African pilot and organiser Roger Bushell, are executed on Hitler's orders.

A medieval Castle in Saxony, about 30 km south-east of Leipzig is also honoured with a visit by the newly-promoted Captain Franz von Werra. Used as the ultimate prison for escaped officers and those identified as Enemies of Germany, or *Deutschsfeindlich*, as the Germans call them, this castle is best known by the name of the town in which it is situated: Colditz.

Von Werra visits Fort VIII and confirms that conditions in Fort Henry in Canada were indeed poor, similar to those replicated at Posen. He then reveals that Fort Henry is a transit camp, where the men stay for 48 hours at most! The German commander apologises to the PoWs and promises to take measures to improve matters.

Just a few months after his visit, on 25 October 1941, Von Werra's Bf 109F-4 suffers engine trouble while on a training flight, and crashes near Flushing. His body is never recovered.

Despite conditions improving in the camp, some people's desire for freedom overrides any other consideration, especially when spring arrives and conditions for escape are more favourable. A group consisting of Ronnie, Mike, Gris, Philip and Peter Douglas have started a tunnel under the fort's moat. After weeks of hard and diligent work, they discover that water is seeping into the tunnel and with every shovelful of soil things are just getting worse, so they quickly abandon the scheme before there are any accidents. They start digging a fresh tunnel a bit further down the fort, but another group takes the plan to completion, and then get caught. Ronnie, Mike and Gris in the meantime are busy considering fresh ideas. Finally, they think they've hit on something.

In his diary, Wood notes that feeling he gets of the days just running into each other, so any difference between them is remarked upon. Heavy snow falls on 2 May, yet just over a week later, it's hot. Some of the more daring devils are attempting to play cricket on the leaning slopes of the fort's roof, when they see long lines of transport trains laden with tanks and other vehicles, heading east down the tracks. The men wonder if Russia will grant safe passage to the Germans so they can carry on to India, or if the two countries will clash. Parcels containing food and clothing continue to arrive slowly, but there is still no mail. Outside the camp, the war is still raging and occasionally, the prisoners get news of what's happening. On 28 May, news comes through that the Bismarck is sunk, Wood receives a parcel and reads Agatha Christie's *Cards on the Table*.

And then developments follow one another in rapid succession. Wood notes:

29th May. 1 Red Cross parcel issued. 5 officers escaped (Littledale, Davis-Seinfield (sic), Sinclair, Douglas and Corksedge).

30th May. Corksedge caught. Saw troop trains going East.

2nd Jun. Crete captured.

6th Jun. 1 Red Cross parcel issued. Read "Present Indicative" by Noel Coward. Informed we were moving to another camp, all luggage etc would be taken for us. Wonder what new camp will be like.

9th Jun. Search of all luggage in corridor. Taken down in trucks to station.

Troop trains rolling east and five British officers escaped! Wood misidentifies Grismond Davis-Scourfield as 'Davis-Seinfield'. The prisoners are told they are being transferred to another camp; their luggage is to follow them.

But not everyone is there to leave, as the following entry shows.

> 10th Jun. At parade in morning 4 officers missing, Winton, Sutherland, Silverwood-Cope...

Wood couldn't recall the name of the fourth officer at the time: he was Lieutenant John Crawford. Despite a search, the guards at Fort VIII fail to locate the foursome. At one o'clock in the afternoon, the prisoners leave for the train station for their long journey to Biberach am Riss.

Without Winton, Sutherland, Silverwood-Cope and Crawford. They are still in the fort waiting for everyone to leave.

And without Ronnie, Mike and Gris who are already on their way to Lódz.

9

ESCAPE FROM POSEN

The plan is simple. Too simple. The Germans aren't that crazy as to fall for it, are they? Two British orderlies are responsible for the daily collection of rubbish in the prisoners' quarters. They push a garbage cart around the camp, collecting the day's trash. They wheel it out of the fort and across the bridge to the large gate in the outer wall. Accompanied through the gate by a German guard, they walk about 10 m to a large pit into which they empty the cart. The party then retraces its steps back across the bridge to the brick cell complex. The plan is hatched by Ronnie, Mike and Gris is simple. One of them gets into the trash cart, hides under the rubbish and then gets wheeled over to the pit by the orderlies. Once there, the orderlies disgorge their cargo into the pit and come back for the next escaper. On a prearranged signal, the escaper in the pit leaves and heads off to wait for his comrades at an agreed meeting-place. If the cart is searched they are screwed, but that is unlikely. However, they will need a bigger cart: the current one is too small to hide a person in. Fortunately, there is plenty of wood in the camp, lying around, readily available, so they use that. The three get a lot of help from Captain Laurie, the commander of the orderlies, who also risks punishment if the attempt is discovered.

Presumably through the English Captain Hanken, initial contacts are made with the Polish Resistance. Two electricians from the firm 'Elektronie', 19-year-old Bronislaw Sobkowiak and his 15-year-old assistant, Zbigniew Klichowski, arrive at Fort VIII to carry out maintenance work on the camp's electrical circuits. From late April to 24 May 1941, they have access to the prisoners' quarters. This is when Captain Hanken asks both men for help. Potential escapees need a map of the city, paint to disguise military uniforms as civilian clothing and shelter once they are outside the barbed wire. Because of his superior language skills, most of the preparatory work falls on young Zbigniew's shoulders.

These young men, Bronislaw Sobkowiak and Zbigniew Klichowski, are just two of the brave Resistance fighters who will assist Ronald and his companions, Mike and Gris, in the coming months.

Hanken continues to roll out his plans. They'll need the help of German guards if at all possible. Otto Devant is a soldier in the Wehrmacht and is one of the camp guards. Devant and Hanken are in regular contact, as later research reveals. Hanken promises him 1,000 Marks if he helps with an escape. It is not only this enormous sum of money that motivates him to assist: there is more at play in the Wehrmacht soldier's mind. He is something of an anglophile, has visited England several times before the war and has a lot of respect for the people and the place. Consequently, he sees the captured soldiers as friends rather than enemies. A subsequent search by the Gestapo turns up a letter from Devant to Hanken, which reveals his willingness to make great sacrifices for England and to act in its interests. In the letter he expresses the hope of meeting the officers in England, and is very clear in his position on the outcome of the war.

Devant in turn contacts two other guards to help out with the escape attempt, Oswald Geerdts and Bernard Emsen, telling them of the intentions of the English, and promising them 50 Marks each for their cooperation. He also tries to schedule the guard roster in a way that ensures all three are on duty as sentries on the day of the escape. All they have to do is look the other way. Like Devant, Geerdts, who has spent 12 years in Canada and speaks perfect English, is greatly sympathetic towards the British.

Preparations for the breakout are in full swing. There's a lot that goes into making an escape a success. They need to carry their own food to keep interactions with others to minimum; they will need German money for train tickets and the like (they manage to obtain 180 Reichsmark); a map and a compass each for navigation, especially near the border crossing; a razor for shaving so they do not resemble bums during the journey, and draw unnecessary attention to themselves. They also have to do something about their clothing. They only have their military uniforms so these have to be altered to resemble civilian attire if the escapees are to pass as ordinary people. Mike will wear an old French army jacket, altered and painted black to resemble a suit jacket; black trousers and a shirt; Gris has trousers and a Dutch overcoat, painted black; and Ronnie an old raincoat and flannel trousers, also painted black. And he's acquired a civilian's cap.

28 May has arrived: breakout day. Mike is wheeled to the pit first. He is in a bag under the garbage in the cart. The sentry guarding the transport does not seem to notice anything as the cart with the garbage and Mike is emptied in the pit. Is he lazy, or is he deliberately not paying attention? When the gate is closed again, Mike receives a signal from the roof of the fort that the coast is clear. He climbs out of the pit and leaves for the town. Ronnie checks his belongings for the last time. Money, compass, map, everything is there. His civilian disguise is not very convincing but it will do. He gets the signal to go: he knows this is it. He walks through the dark corridors of Fort VIII for the last time. The dirt cart is concealed so he can climb in unseen. Without exchanging words with the two men who will roll him out, he steps over the edge, lies flat, squirms and nods. They pour the collected waste from the camp over him, lots of it, all of it until there is nothing of Major Littledale left visible. He feels the cart start to move and hears the voice of the guard escorting the transport. The cart rolls to the gate in the high wall surrounding the camp, and when the doors open, he can follow the conversation between the guard and the gatekeeper, despite the sound in his ears of his heart's rapid beating. After the cart has been pushed through the opening, the heavy gate closes and Littledale is now completely in the hands of the two orderlies. He is depending on them to do their job and empty the cart with him in it at exactly the right moment when the German sentry is not paying attention. Ronnie can't see anything from inside the cart, but he knows that it is only a short distance to the pit. Any moment now it will be time. He needs to keep silent when he drops into the pit. Then, the cart tips up and he's out, falling, taking care not to cry out. With a soft thud, he lands on the pile of rubbish at the bottom of the pit. The dirt from the cart follows him down, falling over him. He dives further into the muck, as deeply as he can and then he waits in this disgusting, malodorous place. All is quiet: there is no scream of discovery. What he fears most does not happen. The German has noticed nothing, and when the camp's gate opens and slams shut again, he knows everything is OK, the plan has worked. Cautiously, he raises his head and waits for the signal from the camp that tells him he can safely leave the pit unseen by the guards. Gris's turn is next. Again, the plan succeeds. The all-clear signal comes from the fort and Gris is out of the pit and away.

It was Peter Douglas who was on lookout duty that day and who gave the all-clear signals. In time, he will also escape from the camp and manage to reach Sweden and safety. Unlike Gris, who after his recapture and arrest, will spend the rest of the war in Colditz. He must have been enamoured with this method of escape: he tries it again later in an attempt to get free of the castle.

When he arrives at the agreed meeting point, Gris sees that Ronnie is there waiting for him, standing behind a tree and looking around nervously. He flinches and even ducks when he sees Gris. The lieutenant looks unrecognizable in his fake civilian outfit, and worse, without his trademark moustache.

The reception at the contact address of the Polish Resistance 'seemed like magic', Gris recalls in his memoirs. The young Polish electrician takes them to a safe address, where white bread, jam and cakes await them, along with Mike Sinclair, who had gone on ahead to make contact with the Polish helper there. All three escapers are together again. In the days that follow, they shelter at various addresses, often hidden in tiny rooms. They wait for the storm at Fort VIII to subside, caused by the guards' finding out that three British officers are missing. They receive better clothes from their helpers and something resembling an identity card. Their first temporary home is with a family with three children. Like all who help escaped PoWs by offering them food and shelter in their home, they take a huge risk. The fugitives have access to two rooms and a kitchen. Gris is later taken to another flat, and the constant moving of the three British officers begins, in a concerted effort to avoid being discovered or that that their presence there becomes common knowledge. During one of these moves, Gris meets Ronald again, who tells him that Mike is in contact with the Resistance. They meet a contact called the 'doctor'. After spending ten days in a room so cramped that standing upright is almost impossible, they receive news that three other officers from Fort VIII are hiding in town. Continuing their journey requires a visit to the barber, who dyes their hair. Ronald and Gris are fairly inconspicuous with their natural hair colours, but they all need to differ from their prison descriptions. Ronald's hair is dyed grey, Mike, a redhead, has his hair darkened. Gris, on the other hand, is given a striking copper colour.

The Doctor is the code name for Witold Verbno Łaszczyński. He was born in Warsaw on 27 January 1887. His father Bolesław is a painter. His mother's name is Józefa Kazimiera Moraczewska. Witold

Łaszczyński is a civil servant in Poznan and with his wife Janina Romer he has two children. His son Jędrzej dies a year after his birth in 1919. In 1922, Zuzia is born and she lives on until 2000. After attending the *Matiasgymnasium* in Wrocław, Witold attends school in Poznan, then inn Berlin and Krakow, he pursues his medical studies. He then works as a director of an insurance company and is also director of a Radiological Institute. In the years 1934-1936, he serves as Hungarian Honorary Consul in Poznan. When war breaks out in 1939, he joins a medical unit of the 7th Regional Military Hospital on the Bzura River. During the fighting, he loses an eye. When he recovers, he returns to Poznan where he returns to work at the insurance company. He also joins the *Związek Walki Zbrojnej*. The ZWZ/AK is an underground army established after the German invasion. In 1940, Witold Łaszczyński was sworn in by Major Stefan Łukowicz ('Szczepan'). In February 1942, the ZWZ is transformed into the Internal Army, *Armia Krajowa*. As second reserve lieutenant, Witold Łaszczyński becomes head of a cell charged with a special mission. By order of Poznan District Commander Rudolf Ostrihanski, the Resistance unit is involved in helping Allied prisoners who have escaped from German PoW camps. Under the name '*Dorsze*' ('Cod'), activities are organised. Escaped prisoners desperately need this help. After their escape, they end up in a strange, unknown country, a place entirely alien to them. They don't know who to trust. They don't speak the language, they have little or no money at their disposal, they have no shelter and they soon find themselves running low on essentials such as food and suitable clothing. They need travel documents, which are absolutely indispensable for the long journey to freedom. A journey that must be carefully planned and led by couriers. The organization requires the close co-operation of dozens of courageous people, who risk their lives for the freedom of just a few. The cell led by The Doctor consists of brave Poles: Michalina Gorczyca (*Kapitanowa*, Captain), who provides shelter, Bolesław Kierczyński, Klara Dolniak and Irena Markiewicz. The group also works closely with other Resistance members such as Bernard Drozd (*Marynarz*, The Sailor), Nikodem Kaliszan, brothers Zbigniew (Zbinio) and Zygmunt Klichowski and their mother Maria Klichowska-Gliszczyńska. Michalina Gorczyca befriends the Klichowska family and establishes contact with Doctor's group when, in March 1941, three British officers escape from Fort VIII. Maria's husband, Bolesław Klichowska, is a Polish officer who is in German captivity. Maria is therefore only too willing to play her role in the Resistance against the German occupiers, as is her son Zbigniew, the 15-year-old assistant to the Polish electrician who does odd jobs at Fort VIII. Her code name in the underground is Czerska. Born in Swornigacie in 1897, she is raised in the patriotic spirit of her father, a nationalist activist. At an early age, the fierce Polish identity within her asserts itself when, between 1906 and 1907, she participates in protest demonstrations against the removal of the Polish language in schools, something for which the authorities decline to thank her.

The Klichowska family lives at Ulica Słowackiego 10/15, an address used as a contact hub for the organization and which is also Gris, Mike and Ronnie's hiding place. Additionally, The Doctor's cell succeeds in winning some of the Fort VIII guards over to their cause. Three Germans are known to have been bribed: Otto Devant, Oswald Geerdts and Bernard Emsen and they played parts integral to the successful escape of prisoners 811, 850 and 520. How much of this was known to Littledale, Sinclair and Davies-Scourfield is open to debate. But those who do know, the three German sentries, are under no illusions as to what the consequences will be for their treachery, should it ever come to light.

Once at their hiding place with Maria Klichowska, Gris, Mike and Ronnie are happy to place themselves under her excellent care. It is not hard to visualize Maria working away in the kitchen making bowls of soup for the three men, to fill the officers' stomachs and satisfy their hunger. Maria was 21-years-older than Mike and Gris: she could have been their mother. For nearly a year since their capture in Calais, the three have been behind bars, barbed wire, guard posts, moats and in the company of hundreds of other men, defeated and captured like they were. These first contacts with a world reminiscent of home must have left the three men with warm feelings and the hope that maybe, they were not defeated after all. Simultaneously, they also know they must be alert and keep their wits about them. On the other side of the house there is the store entrance where Maria's husband has his tailoring shop. The local Wehrmacht, NSDAP and SS are regular customers for repairs.

The escapers are given better outfits than the sorry specimens they manufactured in the camp from old uniforms and bad paint. Gris will admit that if anyone had seen him on the streets of Poznan thus attired, it would have been immediately obvious that he was an escaped PoW.

The man responsible for procuring these new clothes is Bolesław Kierczyński, otherwise known as 'The Editor'. Kierczynski owes his nickname to his position as head of the sports department of the *Dziennik Poznański* newspaper.

Meanwhile, The Doctor's cell is busy preparing false documents and passports for Littledale, Sinclair and Scourfield-Davis. The photos for the passports are taken by Bernard Drozd. Bernard was born in 1915 in Essen, Germany, the son of an immigrant Polish family of miners. From 1919 onward, his family has been living in Połajewo. Drozd owes his nickname, The Sailor, to his naval appointment in Gdynia in 1938. A year later he returned to Połajewo and then left for Poznan where he worked as a locksmith. Nikodem Kaliszan swears him in to the SWZ in 1940, and it is Michalina Gorczyca who involves him in the *Dorsze* campaign. In addition to taking the photos, Drozd also buys authentic passports with money made available to him by The Doctor. These are essential in the area controlled by army and police. The first border they must cross is between the Reichsgau Wartheland in which Poznan lies, and the General Government. Their intended destination is neutral Russia. Although this way, they avoid the problems presented by more obvious destinations like Sweden and Switzerland–they'd need to cover a huge distance to reach both and in the case of Sweden, would need to cross the sea–there is a more pressing reason why the choice of Russia is not as strange as it seems. A 1941 atlas reveals all.

To the north of where they are now, in Posen, are German-occupied Norway and Denmark; the Netherlands, Belgium, Luxembourg, northern and western France, Vichy-France, the Czech Republic, Austria and East Prussia are in the west and south-west. The Axis powers and satellite states of Italy and Albania, Yugoslavia and Greece, and collaborating countries such as Slovakia, Hungary, Romania and Bulgaria are to the south and south east. Finally, where they stand now, Posen, is in German territory. The name of Poland no longer applies and the nation as a sovereign entity does not exist. The Nazi leadership has taken the entire concept of Poland and transformed it into the General Government.

Therefore the best possibility of escaping German, German-occupied or German-minded territory is the Russian zone running from the Baltic States, just behind Warsaw through Brest-Litovsk in the direction of Lvov to Bessarabia. Stalin had made a deal with Hitler, the Molotov-Ribbentrop Pact, and is as much an aggressor in Europe as the Germans, as the conquered populations of Estonia, Latvia, Lithuania and the eastern part of Poland could readily testify. But the arch enemy of the Nazis has presented Ronnie, Mike and Gris with an opportunity. Or so they hope. Few British soldiers as well as refugees from other nationalities who take the road to Russia are ever seen again.

This choice is not without chance of success. With the invasion of Poland, it is almost 'obvious' that the Jews are likely to bear the brunt of suffering right from the outset of the occupation. Many Jews in the German-occupied part of the country even manage to cross the porous border with the Russian-occupied part. Despite being deported afterwards, mainly to Siberia, these Jews have a considerably better chance of survival than the ones who remain behind in the ghettos of the Nazi empire.

One of the largest ghettos is in the city of Lódz just south of the Posen - Warsaw line. Immediately after Nazi occupation, the town was renamed Litzmannstadt by the Germans. This was a bitter reminder for its residents of the German General Litzmann, who led his troops to this spot in 1914, when Germany was an empire equally as aggressively acquisitive as Hitler's dictatorship. On large white signs in the city, the occupiers make it crystal clear. In thick black letters they read, *Auf Befehl des Führers heißt diese Stadt Litzmannstadt*. By order of the Führer, this city is called Litzmannstadt.

In the vicinity of the old city centre and the Bałuty district, is a part of the city isolated from the outside world by wooden walls and barbed wire fences. In this small area, some four square kilometres, Jewish people are crowded together in several dozen streets. Wooden bridges five or six meters high lead across streets where streetcars pass through the neighbourhood, alongside German troops in trucks and on motorcycles. Films from this dark time show the Jewish residents of this open-air prison, yellow stars on their clothing, passing in dense groups over the bridges. A single traffic controller keeps watch and a lone motorcycle with a sidecar carrying helmeted Germans passes among them. More than 30% of the 672,000 inhabitants are Jewish. About a quarter of these manage to flee. The rest are cooped up here and have to work for the occupying forces. Over 164,000 people are crammed together here and have no chance to leave. More and more inhabitants of other liquidated ghettos in Poland, as well as Jews from other countries, along with a group of Roma, are transported to Lódz. Some 70,000 *Volksdeutsche*, people of German descent, live in the surrounding city, an ethnic minority whose allegiance to the Nazis is not immediately apparent to anyone else. This makes it all the more difficult for well-wishers among them to offer any kind of help to the Jewish population without being noticed. The ghetto's inhabitants are completely dependent on the German occupiers, using anything or everything as a bargaining chip just to get food. Malnutrition and disease become a part of life in the ghetto, leading to strikes in the factories where the Jews work for the Germans. It is distressing to consider that these very factories provide a form of protection for the population: as long as they are productive, which they continue to be until the middle of 1944, the Jews working in them cannot be transported to the camps where certain death awaits them. However, the situation in the ghetto is increasingly dire. It is estimated that during a famine in 1942, some 18,000 people die. In late 1941, deportations to the death camps begin. To avoid their tragic fate, some families commit suicide. This, then, is the town through which runs the border that Ronnie, Mike and Gris have to cross first. Lódz is an important transfer point on the first leg of their journey to Warsaw.

Klara Dolniak is a member of The Doctor's group and has an uncle living in Lódz. This Czesław Wolf lives with his cousin in an apartment in the city and he is the contact the British trio will meet. In his memoirs, Gris describes his journey to the city that is rapidly becoming hell for its residents. In a red car, the three head to Lódz, accompanied by a Pole. Behind the wheel is a Volksdeutscher, who does not know who he is driving. Mike tells the driver that the two in the back, Ronald and Gris, are Germans suffering from nervous illness after a bombing raid in Hamburg, so they don't talk. The real reason is that their lack of knowledge of the German language is something that Mike Sinclair, educated in Cambridge and himself an excellent speaker of German, does not choose to share.

10

THE BORDER

Maria Eugenia Jasińska was born on 29 November 1906 in Lódz into a working-class family. Her father was called Ignacy and her mother was named Anna Szczygielska. She attends the Romana Konopczyńska girls' grammar school, where she is a good student and very popular with her teachers and peers. Her sister Helena will later write of Maria's generosity of spirit towards those around her, how she was supportive both materially and spiritually. She is sociable and a good organiser and is involved in founding a society for self-education. She is also very ambitious: she wants to be a doctor and found a sanatorium for children in Łagiewniki. All in all, she was caring, helpful, uncomplicated, always cheerful and unpretentious: with solid working-class virtues that made her an easy person to get on with and who could relate positively to others. She was defined as a person by her deep Christian faith. These are just some of the character traits that her biographer A. Olszewski will attribute to her.

Sadly, Maria does not achieve her ambition to make it to medical school. Instead, she pursues pharmaceutical training in Warsaw and completes her training as a pharmacy assistant in 1932. Until war broke out in 1939, she worked at the Ubezpieczalnia Społeczna pharmacy in Lódz. From then on, she helps out by collecting money for wounded soldiers, arranging for the supply of cigarettes and bandages. Very early in the war, she establishes contacts with the underground Resistance movement in the city. Her help is extended to prisoners in Durchgangslager I at ul. Łąkowa 4, to whom she gives medicine, clothing and food. She also finds shelter for people fleeing from the Nazis including Jews.

Maria changes pharmacies and ends up in the Apteka Pod Łabędziem (Under the Swan). It is the elegant nickname of Apteka Calendula, which is among the oldest pharmacies in Poland, and named after the swan depicted on the shop's signboard. The institution was founded in 1894 by Roman Mossakowski, an active member of the Pharmacists' Association in Lódz. He is a member of a committee that organises the first congress of pharmacists in Poland in 1912. Right from the start, the pharmacy promotes natural treatments with homeopathic medicines developed on the basis of homemade prescriptions. Since its inception, the pharmacy has also attracted social activists, people involved in charity and scientific activities. Alongside company directors, Stanisław Pisarski and Piotr Ilnicki, Józef Cymer is one of the most eminent representatives of the pharmacy profession. He conducts extensive research and publishes papers on antibiotics and the use of bacteriostatic agents in medicines. The workaholic Cymer combines practice with science. Maria Jasińska becomes one of the pharmacy's key employees, ensuring her work there forms an intrinsic part of helping people deal with the awful reality that surrounds them all.

She works hard and well as a pharmacy assistant, gaining the trust of her manager. Apart from being able to get medicine for the prisoners, she can also use the pharmacy's basement at night after her work shift has finished. It is an ideal location from which to work, forging papers for the underground movement in Lódz. She rents a flat in Fuldaerstrasse, as she does not want to implicate or endanger her parents with her clandestine activities. When her sister Helena notices that she looks very tired, she simply replies that there are people who need her help, people who are ill or hungry. 'We are not dying of hunger yet' she says, a simple and effective explanation. Maria Jasińska's final meeting with Littledale, Sinclair and Davies-Scourfield will end very dramatically.

From their hiding place in Posen, Littledale, Sinclair and Davies-Scourfield are taken to Lódz, where they stay in a flat owned by Czesław Wolf at 9 m. 49 Böhmische Linie. Here they are looked after by Krystyna Kallerowa and provided with cigarettes, playing cards and magazines. Jerzy Szczepkowski, who rents a room in Wolf's house, puts the group in contact with Maria Jasińska, who is already up to her ears in illegalities. The men are completely dependent on Polish Resistance fighters. They do not know the region, have no papers, and rely on a large group of people for food and care, all risking their lives for the fleeing PoWs, something about which they would feel much concern: their presence brought much danger to a lot of people.

Maria gets the necessary documents to them by way of a certain Zofia Kolińska-Grabarczykowa. But she does much more to help them. Their route to neutral territory involves going through Warsaw. To get there, the three have to cross the border between the Reichsgau Wartheland and the General Government. Maria Jasińska is ultimately responsible for helping the three escapees make what Littledale's Polish helpers had told him was an extremely dangerous crossing.

There are many women and girls who risk their lives as Resistance fighters in the Second World War. Because their activities are highly illegal under the Nazi regime, they are forced to work underground. They rescue Jewish children from the ghettos in Warsaw, Vilnius and Bialystok, work as nurses in children's homes and provide bandages, food and drink. They participate in setting up relief hospitals and shelters for refugees in school buildings, cinemas, offices and shelters for children. They also distribute illegal reading materials. And more: they help organise escapes from camps and hospitals and provide hiding places at safe houses. As couriers, they accompany escaped prisoners of war on their flight across Europe.

In June 1941, Jerzy Szczepkowski visits Maria Jasińska's pharmacy to meet an acquaintance, Tadeusz Kotynia, who also works there. He tells Maria he will soon be visiting the town of Gałkówek near the General Government border in order to see if there are any suitable properties there to use as temporary shelter for escapees. He says he then intends to travel on to Warsaw. Presumably, he asks Jasińska for assistance crossing the border. They agree to meet at the end of tram line 10 in Widzew, on the east side of Lódz, the following evening to discuss matters further. It's a huge surprise for Maria, therefore, when Szczepkowski shows up the next evening with two of the three British officers, Ronald and Gris, who are staying with him in Wolf's flat. Also present at this meeting is Resistance fighter, Bernard Drozd, who has come to Lódz by train from Poznan, and another Pole, Nikodem Kaliszan, who was sworn in by Bernard to the ZWZ in 1940. Although Jasińska is surprised and alarmed when Szczepkowski arrives at their meeting with so many people with him, she is mollified when everyone gets introduced to her properly and proves to be friendly and polite. Returning the gesture, Jasińska does not reveal she has realised that Szczepkowski's two housemates are British. In his memoirs, *In Presence of my Foes*, Gris recalls that he and Nikodem, referred to as Nicholas, left Lódz together for Widzew.

The original plan was for all of them to continue in a car, but the driver demurs. He is worried that such a large group will be too conspicuous, attracting unwanted attention from the Nazis. Maria, however, insists they carry on, finding another way to get the thing done. Szczepkowski suggests she take the two Englishmen to Gałkówek and shelter them with friends there. However, the group splits off into two. Drozd, Kaliszan and Littledale will remain in Widzew, while Jasińska and Davies-Scourfield leave by car for Gałkówek.

Near Ustynowa, the driver suddenly stops and again refuses to continue. This time, Maria and Gris are forced to continue on foot. So there they are, stuck on the edge of a forest full of thorny bushes, and it is midnight. There is nothing else to it but to spend the night under the trees. In the morning, they set off again. When they finally reach Gałkówek, Gris is handed over to the Zrobek family at their farm. Maria had met Mrs Zrobek through a mutual friend, Karoline Ostrowska, with whom she had worked at a hospital pharmacy before the war. Shortly after their arrival, Bernard Drozd turns up with Ronnie Littledale, and Jasińska accompanies both officers to the farm.

Once the two escaped PoWs have settled in with the Zrobek family at their farm, Jasińska goes off in search of the Nowak family, who live near the border with the General Government. She wants to see if she can rent a summer house there in which she can spend her holidays. She can't find either Henryka Nowak or her mother, so she returns to Lódz the same afternoon, and goes back to the pharmacy to finish her shift as if nothing had happened. Shortly afterwards, Jerzy Szczepkowski calls on her again. He wants to know if she would also take the third British officer, to Gałkówek. It is Mike Sinclair, still staying in Wolf's flat. Reluctant at first, she finally agrees to take the refugee to the Zrobek's farm by the same route.

Meanwhile, Mrs Zrobek is taking Gris and Ronnie along with Bernard Drozd to the border region, where she hands over the responsibility for their journey to Henryka Nowak, who knows the border area better than she does. Henryka is rather young to be doing this kind of thing, she will turn 16 in July, but she readily takes on this hazardous assignment. So the three of them, Ronnie, Gris and Henryka, make their way to the border where, after waiting to ensure there are no patrols about, they all make the crossing. Once over the demarcation line, they go to Żakowice, where Henryka arranges accommodation for them at an inn.

Back at Gałkówek, when Maria and Mike finally arrives at the Zrobek family farm she discovers that Gris and Ronnie have already moved on to Żakowice. So she, Mike and Nikodem Kaliszan, also present, set off for the inn. Unfortunately, it is late and they get lost in the dark, and have to spend the night hiding out in a field. The next day they finally reach the inn, 24 hours or so after Ronnie and Gris. The three officers of the 2nd KRRC are reunited. It is 22 June 1941. The three have finally left Germany.

When Fort VIII is closed in June 1941, partly due to the exculpatory statements of Luftwaffe pilot Franz von Werra, four British officers– Winton, Sutherland, Silverwood-Cope and Crawford–stay behind, hidden away in a secret room in the camp. They have been able to contact Witold 'The Doctor' Łaszczyński's Resistance group. After getting clear of the fort, they spend ten long weeks in Czesław Wolf's flat in Lódz, passing the time reading, smoking, eating, sleeping, playing cards and waiting for Wolf to come home from work so that they can have some news from the outside world. All around them conditions for the Jews in the ghetto are deteriorating. The main reason for the delay in setting off is that it is now taking much longer to make the arrangements to get the men out and on their way to Warsaw. One of the members from Doctor's Resistance group, Bolesław Kierczyński, has a brother in Lódz. Bolesław inundates his brother Miecsysław, a 35-year-old merchant, with letters asking him to help arrange the transport of the four to Warsaw. At first, Miecsysław wants nothing to do with this and refuses to respond. Eventually, Bolesław turns up in Lódz to confront his brother in person. Face to face with Miecsysław, his repeatedly asking him to help almost turns his request into an order. Affronted by his brother's intransigence, he threatens to tell their mother what is going on. Miecsysław, for his part, slowly changes his mind. Unsurprisingly, he would prefer their mother not to get involved in all this and eventually, he writes to agree to help out with getting the four refugees from Fort VIII across the Reichsgau Wartheland, General Government border.

When Miecsysław tries to contact Wolf at the apartment, he finds that Wolf is not in; there is only the group of British PoWs, wearing civilian clothes. After chatting with them for a while, Miecsysław realises that they are indeed who they claim to be. One of the officers speaks German and, at his request, Miecsysław twice buys them a pound of bread. Meanwhile, he starts looking for someone suitable to accompany the four over the border. He gets in touch with Józef Połczyński, a business contact, and asks him if he can suggest anyone. But Józef says no, he cannot help. A few days later, Józef loading a supply of jam at a shipping company called Warrant, and he meets Bronisław Wieczorok, one of the employees there, to whom he confides his difficulty. Bronisław tells him that he can help: he has done this before, in a tax case, crossing without a permit. Then, he was bailed out by a Polish man named 'Józef' for ten Reichsmark. When Połczyński mentions that he wants to get someone over the border, Wieczorok says he will contact this 'Józef' to see if they can sort something out.

Probably wisely, Połczyński has not been entirely candid. He has neglected to tell Wieczorok that there is not one person who needs to cross the border, but four, and that the four are not just anybody, but escaped British PoWs from Posen. The possibilities of being discovered are huge, and the consequences are positively hair-raising. Behind the subterfuge is the fear that if Wieczorok knew the truth, there is every possibility he would back out, meaning no help from him and in turn there would be no contact made with 'Józef', who sounded a very useful character to know.

A few days later, Bronisław Wieczorok meets 'Józef' at the central railway station and they agree to meet again at six o'clock that evening at the corner of Kiliński and Przejazd. 'Józef' is already there waiting when Wieczorok turns up with Połczyński in tow. The men introduce themselves to each other and they leave for Miecsysław Kierczyński's flat. Finally the introductions are made between Miecsysław, the man who was pushed by his brother into getting four British PoWs across the border, and 'Józef', the man tasked with the job of actually making that happen. Wieczorek and Połczyński leave after five minutes, while Miecsysław and 'Józef' prepare to visit Wolf's flat, where a detailed discussion takes place about where the British can be taken once they have crossed the border.

Of such tenuous connections with much backwards and forwards are escape networks made. The next act of Operation '*Dorsze*', previously successful for Littledale, Sinclair and Davies-Scourfield, can finally proceed.

For two of the British officers, Miecsysław already has a solution. His brother gives him the address in Warsaw of Lech Dolniak, Klara's brother. There, they can find shelter. Miecsysław sends a letter to his brother in Poznan asking what he should do with the other two. His brother sends back a telegram saying that they too are welcome to stay with Lech Dolniak. Almost certainly extremely relieved with this outcome, Miecsysław passes this information on to Wolf, who can take over as far as he is concerned. By mid-August, via an unknown route, 'Józef' has delivered Silverwood-Cope and his companions to Lech Dolniak's address in Warsaw. According to Davies-Scourfield's memoirs, they travel all the way by train: the adventurous hike through the forest he and his two companions took was unnecessary. Bolesław Kierczyński, in the meantime, sends another message to his brother Miecsysław in Lódz telling him that the four escapers have arrived safely in the capital. Miecsysław can breathe a sigh of relief. At least for the time being.

On the day that Mike, Ronnie and Gris crossed the heavily guarded demarcation line and are reunited at the inn, their hopes of travelling on further to Russia are dashed: it has been invaded by Germany. *Unternehmen* (Operation) Barbarossa has placed an insurmountable barrier in their way. Not even the help of the brave Polish Resistance can get them over this one. They get the sad news over the radio during a discussion at the inn.

It does not take long, just a few weeks, for the German sword to cut deep into Russian flesh, and for the Red Army to be on the brink of defeat. In the end, the Molotov-Ribbentrop Pact was worth nothing. General Franz Halder, the German chief of general staff, writes in his war diary, 'After only two weeks, the war has been won.' Two weeks later, he adds the wry qualifier: 'But the enemy does not seem to know that he has lost…'

It is impossible for Ronnie, Gris and Mike to continue on the same path now. Their Polish accomplices want to help them find a safe address in Warsaw, but they will have to get there themselves.

11

THE BALKANS

The eastward journey to Tomaszow is about 40 km on foot, through open countryside. Littledale, Sinclair and Davies-Scourfield have been told by The Sailor, Bernard Drozd, that he has connections there and can give them somewhere to stay. The three men pass through a village where they come across some dogs who, ever alert to unfamiliar faces, start barking when they spot them. Ronnie is not happy. The ominous sound reminds him of the book *The Escaping Club* by British officer A. J. Evans, about his escape from Germany during the First World War. But no-one they meet, Poles or Germans, pay them any attention, as they make their way to Warsaw. They make sure that every so often, they have a shave. That way, they avoid looking like tramps and consequently, the gaze of suspicious Germans, always on the lookout for the out-of-the-ordinary.

Once in Tomaszow, they meet up with Drozd and Nikodem Kaliszan, who show them some worrying headlines in the newspapers. The Germans have indeed invaded Russia and are rapidly progressing east towards the Red Army ahead of them. Moreover, the police have already started to make enquiries about the escaped PoWs. This really is a matter of concern. Drozd is at a loss and does not know what to do, but Nikodem gives them an address in Warsaw where they can go, and says he has contacts there who can help them. He promises to pick them up in town when they arrive. Drozd meanwhile returns alone to Poznan.

They are still more than 100 km away from Warsaw and covering that distance is a real ordeal for the three escapers. At one point, they stop at a farm to ask for some water and an alert dog bites Mike on the leg. For sure, dogs are not these men's best friends on this trip. The men are tired, tense, doubtlessly scared and the atmosphere is getting strained. Ronnie starts arguing with Gris, over whether they eat first or drink first. Ronnie prefers to drink first because otherwise he cannot swallow, while Gris wants to do it the other way round. Mike is not bothered: he is not going to get water again. Sleeping in the open field under clouds of mosquitoes does not make things any better.

On 25 June, after two days of walking, the three arrive wearily in the capital, and then make their way immediately to the safehouse on Chmielna Street. They are not there for long: they move several times and along the way see the ruins of the city caused by the 1939 bombings. Now that Russia has been invaded by the Germans, and Hungary and the Balkan states now hostile territory, hiding in Warsaw is safer.

From that point on, their sojourn is characterised by walls and curtains. From behind them, they witness people being hunted down and rounded up by the Nazis. Jews for detention, workers for mobilisation, the Nazis are after both. Arrests are a daily phenomenon. The boredom of spending so much time indoors is mind-numbing. No matter how many different houses they shelter in, there is the same nothing to do. Nevertheless, this forced ennui is far preferable to a walk on the streets. They are added to a party of three Poles, who are travelling to Budapest and Littledale is given another set of identity papers. This time he will be travelling as a farmer. Unlike Mike's papers, his has a photograph on it. Then someone decides that three PoWs are too many, so Gris has to stay behind.

Ronnie, Mike and Gris will not be together again until they are all in Colditz Castle.

***

When war begins on 1 September 1939, and the German armies pour into Poland, many inhabitants flee. They spread out across the Balkans ending up in Yugoslavia, Greece, Albania. Even after the cessation of fighting, there is a sizeable number of Poles who want to continue. They migrate across the Balkans to Hungary and Romania, and then on to join army units in the Middle East, or France, where they can continue the fight against the Nazis. A small number remain in the Balkans. These are mainly steel workers and miners from Silesia, who find work in their professions in Yugoslavia. Alliances emerge to take in refugees, and lead them on to the Middle East. Shelters are set up for single mothers with their children.

One such home is Hommes Suisse pour l'Enfantes Polonais, founded by Maria Kujawska in Crikvenica in Yugoslavia. She was previously involved in uprisings in Silesia, and was a prominent member of the women's movement there. The home is maintained by the Swiss charity Pro Polonia. A veritable refugee colony emerges around the home in which Maria plays an active role. In April 1941, Yugoslavia is attacked by the Axis powers in Europe (Germany, Romania, Hungary, Italy and Bulgaria), and eventually Maria and her two daughters end up in Ravensbrück concentration camp. Unruffled, she continues her humanitarian work there in the infirmary where she takes in new prisoners and fights for better care. When Polish women from the capital arrive after the 1944 Warsaw uprising, she overcomes reluctance on the part of the SS and gains for them access to medical care. Moreover, in February 1945, she convinces the SS that the women in her block are not seriously ill and therefore do not merit selection for the gas chamber. That would simply be a waste. This courageous woman will survive Ravensbrück.

Russia is no longer neutral territory. Therefore, Littledale and Sinclair must radically rethink their plans. The network of Polish emigrants in the Balkans offers them the best chances of reaching freedom. It could be possible for them to be helped on to independent Turkey and from there, back to Britain. It is 26 August. While Gris is left alone in Warsaw, the result of the trio's being deemed too large and conspicuous a group to accompany, Ronnie and Mike go by train with their Polish scouts to Kraków. The next day, they continue to Zakopane in the far south of Poland on the Slovakian border. Could the Tatra mountains they are heading towards have at some point evoked memories of seeing the alpine peaks when they arrived at Oflag VIIC in Laufen?

In the evening hours of 29 August, 1941 they are smuggled past German border guards and then taken by car to Roznave, today in Hungary. On 31 August, they board the train to Budapest. Thanks to the Poles, tickets are bought and cars are paid for. Mike and Ronnie do all they can to look respectable and presentable. This means shaving and shoe polishing. The Poles supply clean underwear. At four o'clock in the afternoon, the party arrives in Budapest. They stay at what was intended to be a permanent address for the whole month of September, but when the Hungarian police start asking questions about their papers, they move and get new papers. Mike and Ronnie are also separated for some time.

Meanwhile, back at home, Ronnie's Alma Mater, Eton, has taken a keen interest in their Old Boys' various war exploits, although the school has no idea where Littledale is at the time. In a story dated 30 October 1941, *The Eton College Chronicle* posts the following bulletin:

ETONIAN PRISONERS OF WAR
The following is the first instalment of the list of Prisoners of War supplied by the O.E.A. [Office of Educational Affairs], who would be grateful for any further information. Since this list has been compiled the War Office has announced that the British Prisoners of War at Oflag VIIC and Oflag VIID have been transferred to Oflag VIB at Warburg, on the border of Westphalia and Hesse. Those previously printed in the E.C.C. do not appear in this list.

Then follows the report on Littledale

1920 Littledale, R.B. (C.M.W.), Maj. KRRC P. of W. No. 81, Oflag VB, Germany

That Littledale is erroneously recorded as being imprisoned at Oflag VB in Biberach in Baden-Württemberg may possibly have arisen because former fellow-inmates, like Hugh Ironside and Philip Pardoe, were known to have been transported there via Laufen and Poznan. The assumption could have been made that the same applied to Ronnie. The diary kept by Reginald Wood in Poznan also mentions the removal of prisoners from the fort to Biberach. Needless to say, Eton has no knowledge of the escape from Fort VIII.

A contingent of British officers were transferred from Oflag VB to Oflag VIB (Warburg) in October 1941. This included numerous future Colditz residents like Douglas Bader, Josef Bryks, Jock Hamilton-Baillie, Pete Tunstall and Dominic Bruce. Meanwhile, Littledale No. 81, or actually No. 811, and his regimental-mate Sinclair, are somewhere on the road between Budapest and the border with Serbia.

With six others, Littledale and Sinclair set off for Yugoslavia on 9 November. Mike and Ronnie's papers indicate that they are *Volksdeutscher* (Ethnic Germans). Unwilling or unable to traverse the border directly by train, they first travel to Szeged and then on foot, they make their crossing. Once in Yugoslavia, they catch a train to Pancevo near Belgrade, where they arrive around noon on 10 November. The route into Belgrade itself is blocked by the River Danube and the only means of getting there is the ferry, heavily guarded by German troops. They are lucky. That there are so many people onboard means that not everybody has their papers checked. Ronnie misses out on this dubious privilege, but Mike does not, so his papers are examined along with his bags. One of their traveling companions is a Serb speaker, which would be a help if difficulties arise. After 45 minutes of sailing, they reach the other bank and a less stringent check follows.

The journey continues by train. On 11 November, they have an awkward moment at Jagodina when their noon arrival coincides with that of two armed companies of German soldiers, allegedly from Russia. On 16 November, Sinclair and Littledale are accompanied by two Polish women as they leave by train for Sofia. They arrive in Bela Palanka after hours of travelling, where one of the women leaves them. The other woman, Olga Kamińska-Prokopowa, is 22-years-old and in an advanced stage of pregnancy. She speaks Serbian and is trying to join her husband in Turkey.

Olga was born in 1922 into a patriotic family, the first of her parents' numerous offspring, her father is a lawyer. On his death, Olga, as the eldest, becomes responsible for raising her siblings. When war breaks out in 1939, she experiences violence first-hand when her best friend Romek Wilczyński, whom she has known since school, is killed defending the *Wieża spadochronowa* (parachute tower) in Katowice. This tower, used for training paratroopers, is an excellent observation post for the 73rd infantry regiment in the early stages of the war. They also use it as a platform from which to shell attacking German troops. During the fighting, Romek is killed. Like many compatriots, Olga flees the country. Together with a group of young people from Katowice, she ends up in Hungary, where she finds shelter with the family of Romek's mother. Here she decides to rejoin the Scouting movement.

She was first involved in Scouting in 1933, when she was in a group which was centred around Wanda Gorecka-Wierzbowska. Wanda is two-years-older than Olga and they know each other from school. She was born on 16 May 1920 in Brzeszczy near Oświęcim, better known as Auschwitz. She comes from a miner's family, attends the girls' grammar school in Katowice and joins the scouts. In early 1940, she receives addresses of Polish PoWs through the Polish Red Cross from Krakow, which she distributes to friends, relatives and her fellow scouts. The idea is to put together parcels containing much needed items for the men in the camps. When the Auschwitz concentration camp is built, it becomes her main area of work. Apart from clothes for the prisoners, she organises the delivery of medicines. She establishes contact with the prisoners inside the camp through some of those who are put to work outside. Various pick-up points are set up for the collection of medication at various places like peasant barns or railway buildings. Some of the medicines come from two pharmacies in Katowice. Generous donations from friends ensure that the resources can be purchased. Later, food and medicines are brought in from anonymous sources from Cieszyn and Kraków.

Apart from delivering goods, Wanda's group pass on secret messages to and from relatives outside the camp to those inside and vice versa. When her mother is arrested on charges of having contact with camp residents, Wanda, tipped off in advance, decides to leave the area. At first, she goes to Katowice, but once the travel documents are arranged, she is escorted across the General Government border by a certain Korczyńska, along with Littledale, Sinclair and Davies-Scourfield. Her uncle in Warsaw supports her financially and she continues her work sending parcels to Auschwitz and the PoW camps. She is in Zakopane when the war finishes.

In Hungary, Olga meets Scoutmaster Jan Stanisław Prokop, who is eight years older than her, and whom she will marry sometime later. Jan Prokop is from Kraków. His father, also Jan, was an Austrian army officer and later a priest in Kraków. In 1932, young Jan finishes high school and becomes an active member of VIII Krakowskiej Drużyny Harcerzy, a Kraków Scout group. He is involved in organising a camp near Vilnius. He studies at a school of commerce and economics in Kraków and works as a clerk at the district administration of the State Railways. He completes his military reservist training and is appointed a second lieutenant, after which he serves in the army from 1935 to 1936. Three years later, he defends his country from the Germans, until it is finally overrun. Managing to find his way out, by 17 September, 1940, he is in Hungary.

In Budapest, he joins a Scout group and works with the Polish consulate. When he meets and marries Olga, she becomes his second wife and they travel together to Yugoslavia. As a fiercely patriotic Pole determined to continue the fight against his country's occupiers, he intends to join the Free Polish Army. Sadly for Olga, her pride in this is tempered by the fact she has to stay behind in Yugoslavia. Space is limited on the ship and is needed for the men who are going to fight. So instead of accompanying her new husband, this new bride has to say goodbye when he leaves Yugoslavia by ship. As a captain, he serves his country in the Middle East and after the 1943 invasion, he does so in Italy.

Olga also serves her country Yugoslavia, by working in the underground Resistance movement in the now occupied country. She finds employment in a restaurant in Jagodina, in what is now Serbia. The restaurant is financially supported from military funds. Here, she helps in the task of facilitating contact between people who wish to travel to neutral Turkey via the Balkans, and couriers who can help them do so. The restaurant is acts as a secret interchange point on the long route from Poland to Turkey. One of Olga's colleagues is another Polish woman named Wiesława Jezierska. After several months, Olga has reached the late stages of her pregnancy and wants to get to her husband as soon as possible. It is ironic that to do so, she acts as a courier for others who are also on the run.

Thus it comes to pass that Olga Kamińska-Prokopowa gets in touch with the anonymous helpers of Ronnie Littledale and Mike Sinclair and sets off for the southeastern Balkans with the British officers.

By horse and cart, the party, including Olga and the two Englishmen, arrives at the border between Yugoslavia and Bulgaria. As Littledale reports later, this was on 17 November 1941. The border they cross runs through the Moravabanate, a province of the Kingdom of Yugoslavia. The western region is occupied by the Germans, while the eastern part has been annexed by Bulgaria. Their backs covered in sweat, they pass Yugoslav border guards, who are possibly collaborating with the Germans. They arrive at a farmhouse. Mike and Ronnie are still wearing the clothes they were given in Warsaw and carry a small suitcase.

Someone had made an arrangement to pick up the two men from Fort VIII and take them by cart and horse to Pirot, but this falls through. The owner of the farm tries to arrange another cart for them. They are all walking together along a country road, on their way to sort this out, when they run straight into the arms of a Bulgarian customs officer. Suspicious, he searches everyone's luggage and demands to see their papers. They are only carrying Yugoslav documents with them. The officer takes them away. Olga quietly says it is wise to go with him, but they should be able to bluff their way out of the situation. However, this will end differently.

Once in Pirot, the customs commander subjects the party to questioning. Mike and Olga, speaking in German, try to convince him that they are Germans. He responds politely, informing them that he will contact the German garrison down the road. Perhaps they will be able to help them further. At this point, the company admits they are Poles. All but one of the officers are sympathetic, but that cannot prevent their handing the party over to the Bulgarian police. They are taken to off to headquarters for questioning.

Mike and Olga are questioned in German, Littledale questioned not at all, probably due to lack of time. They spend two days in different cells. On 19 November, they are taken under police escort to Sofia, where their fingerprints are taken, and they are asked to make written statements. In French! A Bulgarian woman who is a fluent French speaker is brought in to serve as an interpreter.

They are moved from one prison in Sofia to another. Mike and Ronnie are locked in a small cell with six Bulgarians. The place is filthy and crawling with vermin. In the females' section of the prison, the Polish women endure similar conditions. There is nothing to sustain them except bread and water. On 20 November, conditions improve when they are moved again, this time to a cell at police headquarters. Littledale learns from a fellow detainee, a Bulgarian truck driver, that he is accused of being a communist by the Germans. According to him, it is practically impossible to cross the border between Bulgaria and Turkey on foot. An interrogation with the Bulgarian police follows on 24 November with the help of a female interpreter who speaks French. Littledale is last in line. He and Sinclair have agreed to try and pass as Poles. Mike speaks the language somewhat and says he is a student wanting to leave Poland. Ronnie, with his limited knowledge of the Polish language, claims to be a Pole living in America, visiting relatives in Poland just before the war, before going to Hungary.

Littledale continues his story to the officials at MI9 in 1943. What he tells them must have been like a bombshell going off at their offices.

Our interrogator told us that our stories were false, and that if we did not tell him the truth, he would hand all three of us over to the Germans. Sinclair later told me that he had declared he was a British officer and had escaped from the Germans as a prisoner of war. His interrogator told him that if he gave a full description of his route, with the names of all those who had helped him, they would all be sent to Turkey, perhaps within days. When it was my turn for interrogation, my interrogator already knew that I was a British officer and an escaped POW. He told me he would send me to Turkey if I gave a detailed account of my route and helpers. I found this attitude very suspicious, and I started drafting a statement in English with invented routes and helpers. This plan Sinclair and I had agreed on beforehand in case we fell into German hands. While I was writing the report, Sinclair was brought in. He told me in French <u>'we must tell the truth'</u>, then was taken away again. Therefore, I thought he had gone through some experience during his interrogation that I did not have. As a result, I wrote a statement <u>truthfully</u> about our routes and helpers. When I visited the prison barber shop on 27 November, I met Sinclair, who hinted to me that some things had gone wrong. Later, we were taken to collect our luggage. While we were doing this, Sinclair told me that the police chief had seen him again and had told him he was sorry but that he was unable to send us to Turkey, and that he would hand us over to the Germans. He gave as his reason that Bulgaria had just signed the Anti-Comintern Pact, and that the Germans already knew of our whereabouts. Sinclair also said that at the time the police chief saw him, a German non-commissioned officer was present in the room. Sinclair added that he refused to say anything as long as this German was present, and demanded to speak to the police representative who had initially received us. Eventually, this request was granted. Sinclair protested vehemently to this man that we gave our statements only because we had been solemnly promised that none of us would be handed over to the Germans. Eventually, the statements Sinclair and I had given were handed over to the police representative and he was given permission to burn them. He asked if there were copies and was assured that there were not. Later, we found an opportunity to have a brief conversation with Olga and she told us that following the burning of the original statements, she noticed that there was a typed copy on our first interrogator's desk.

The concussed effects of Littledale's explosive statement is only noticeable by the underlining in the MI9 report of Sinclair's statement '<u>we must tell the truth</u>' and Littledale's confirmation: '<u>truthfully</u>'. The minuscule blinking of eyes at the British Secret Intelligence Service will ultimately be in very stark contrast to the fate of the aides identified in Littledale's and Sinclair's 'truthful' statements.

Ronald Littledale's choice between truth and falsehood when making statements, not in his personal interest but in the interest of others, does not stand comparison to that of his father more than half a century earlier during the Eton Society's discussion evening in 1887. The difference between a wartime interrogation room with Bulgarian police in which the escaped prisoner of war finds himself, and the comfortable, peacetime room at Eton with booze and friends, in which the youthful member of Pop makes his speech, does not explain why Ronald decided to come clean. He does not need to give any information to anyone other than his name, his rank and military number. It even says this in the Geneva Convention; he is therefore protected. Is his desire for freedom and the promise of being allowed free passage to Turkey the paramount factor in his decision? Or is Sinclair's experience during his interrogation and his subsequent insistence in French to Littledale that he tell the truth ultimately persuasive? The moment marks a turning point in both men's lives.

After lengthy interrogations, Sinclair and Littledale are handed over to a German non-commissioned officer on 27 November 1941. He transfers them by car to Sofia's city prison. On their way, Littledale tries to persuade a Bulgarian police officer to inform the US Consulate of the two men's fate, but the officer doubts he will succeed. Under German escort, the two men disappear into a special wing of the prison. Three days later, Littledale is visited by two Bulgarian policemen in plain clothes. One of them, a good English speaker, tells him he is allowed to write a letter to his father, as long as he keeps it short and does not give his current location.

73-year-old John Bolton has no idea what has happened to his son. *The Eton College Chronicle*, for all its contacts in high places, is equally in the dark regarding which corner of Europe he is in. Bolton and his wife Clara, now 68, are making their contributions to the war effort in Bunbury, close to home and in their own way. John is Divisional Chief Warden ARP (Air Raid Precautions) during the Blitz from 1940 to 1941. The Wardens observe the skies checking for the approach of German aircraft, and carry out their nightly rounds enforcing the blackout. Clara is a member of the Mobile Unit of the ARP. Even for this small village, snuck away in a remote corner of England, danger is ever-present. This is amply demonstrated in 1941, when the village church suffers damage after some stray German ordnance hits the building. A German bomber is on its way home after an unsuccessful raid on nearby Liverpool. As it flies over Bunbury, it drops its deadly load of 13 bombs to lose weight and ease the return flight. 12 bombs land harmlessly in the fields surrounding the village, but one projectile explodes between St. Boniface church on the edge of the village and Bunbury House, Ronald's childhood home, 150 m away. There are no casualties, the occupants having gotten out in time, but the damage to the church is enormous. Most of the windows of the house of worship and the entire roof have been destroyed. Restoration will be expensive. As a consequence, it will be 1950 before the church, built in 1320, is fully restored.

It is not known whether Littledale wrote his permitted letter to his father. Will he ever see his father John Bolton and his mother Clara again?

Littledale protests vehemently about the treatment he receives from the Bulgarians. He wants to speak to the police commander, worried that Olga will fall into German hands. Asked if she is perhaps a secret agent acting against the Germans, Littledale replies that she has only been helpful to him and Sinclair with her knowledge of the various languages spoken in the Balkans. On 2 December, Ronnie, Mike and Olga are taken under escort to Belgrade, where Olga is handed over to a German soldier. Sinclair and Littledale travel on to the military prison in Vienna, Austria, where they remain until 17 January 1942. Here the treatment is good, and in addition to Austrian military prisoners, there are Austrian guards. The Austrians in both cohorts express negative views of the Germans.

At 9 am on 17 January, Sinclair and Littledale leave Vienna's Franz Josef Bahnhof escorted by an Austrian sergeant and a German soldier. When the soldier leaves the compartment, the sergeant tells them that he hates the Germans, who treat Russian PoWs appallingly. He adds that they are going to a place near Dresden. Meanwhile, the two Englishmen agree that as soon as an opportunity arises, they will try to escape. In the toilet compartment, they manage to sabotage the window's opening and closing mechanism. All they have are the civilian clothes they are standing up in, their shaving gear and caps. They have no money, and only a little food left over from lunch.

Between Prague and Roudnice, the train begins to reduce speed. Mike requests to go to the toilet. Littledale asks shortly afterwards if he can stand in the aisle for a bit of fresh air. Mike and Ronnie have agreed on a signal: just before exiting through the toilet window, he leaves the door in a particular position. When Ronnie sees the door in this position, he enters the toilet. Feet first through the open window, he makes his exit from the moving train, like Sinclair, climbing out on to the running board. As the train regains speed, Littledale edges along the carriage and joins Sinclair. They position themselves on the balcony between the carriage they are on and the one next to them. The moment they approach Roudnice and the train slows down, Sinclair jumps. Just then, the sergeant opens the window and sees what is happening. Littledale manages to hide in time. The train stops and the sergeant runs after Sinclair, who has banged his head somehow, becoming slightly dizzy. He is soon caught. Meanwhile, Littledale avoids two searching cones of light as a pair of railway police officers in black uniforms shine torches around, desperately looking for him. He can hear their conversation about Sinclair's arrest. Fortune smiles broadly on him: a cloud of steam obscures him from their view. Sinclair is on his way to Colditz, and his fellow traveller, Littledale, does not know.

In Belgrade, Olga gave birth to a son on 25 February 1942. Jan and Olga's child is named Marek. She is transported to Vienna for further interrogation. Marek is placed in a *Kinderheim*, a Nazi state orphanage where lone children are raised as Aryans under the Germanisation policy. After many attempts, Marek is eventually placed with relatives: the story being that friends of her husband Jan manage to take the child to Kraków and hand him over to his grandmother. Olga is sent from Vienna to Berlin and ends up in the hands of the *Reichssicherheitshauptamt* (Reich Security Main Office). For more than a year, she is kept in a solitary cell in *Moabit Untersuchungsgefängnis* (Remand Centre) alongside numerous other political opponents and Resistance fighters.

Somewhere in one of the five wings of the large prison block, behind a small barred window in a sea of steep walls and barbed windows, is another Polish woman. It is Wiesława Jezierska, who ran the secret Balkan interchange with Olga at the restaurant in Jagodina. Was she, perhaps, the woman who travelled by train with Olga, Ronnie and Mike and got off in Bela Palanka? For her activities on the escape line to Turkey, she is arrested and sent to Berlin, and like Olga, an uncertain fate awaits her. Olga writes to her parents, a letter presumably smuggled out through one of the prison guards. In her letter, she makes an urgent plea regarding her child's religious upbringing. Will she ever see Marek or her husband Jan again?

Drawing of Ronald Littledale in St Boniface's Church, Bunbury (Author's Collection).

Lieutenant Ronald Littledale (National Archives, UK).

Major Ronald Littledale in Oflag VIIC Laufen, June 1940 (National Archives, UK).

Lieutenant Mike Sinclair in Oflag VIIC Laufen, June 1940 (National Archives, UK).

Zbigniew Klichowski (Public Domain).

Zygmunt Klichowski (Public Domain).

Witold Verbno-Łaszczyński 'Doctor' (Public Domain).

Bolesław Kierczyński (Public Domain).

Miecsysław Kierczyński (Public Domain).

Maria Klichowska (Public Domain).

Fort VIII in Poznan, 2015 (Author's Collection).

Fort VIII in Poznan, 2019 (Author's Collection).

Flat of Czesław Wolf in Lodz (Author's Collection).

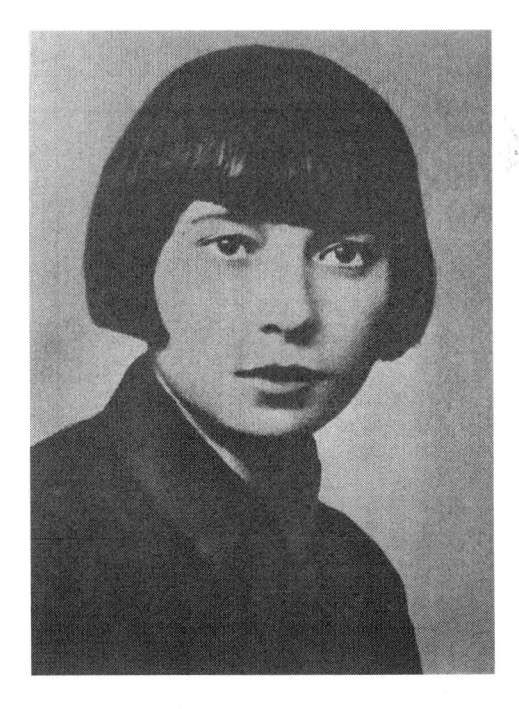

Maria Eugenia Jasińska (Public Domain).

Maria Jasińska in prison, 1943 (Public Domain).

Maria Jasińska in the pharmacy in Lódz (Public Domain).

The pharmacy in Lódz, 2025 (Author's Collection).

The pharmacy in Lódz, commemorative plaque for Maria Jasińska (Author's Collection).

Zdenka Pakova (Fotoarchief Jaroslav Čvančara).

Vladimir Bergauer (Národní Archiv Praha).

Markéta Bergauer (Národní Archiv Praha).

Hiding place of Littledale in Prague, Bergauer address (Author's Collection).

12

HIDING IN PRAGUE

After his jump from the train, Littledale walks hurriedly south along the railway track. It is bitterly cold and he has not got an overcoat. His only hope is to find help as soon as possible. He wanders around Roudnice, before hitting on a plan: he will approach someone and ask them the time in German. If they answer in Czech or in bad German he will ask for their help: if they answer in German, he will move on to someone else. The first person to whom Littledale makes himself known as an escaped Englishman says he is obliged to find a policeman and turn Littledale in. Ronnie is lucky that the person does not take things further. He finally seems to make some progress with the third encounter he has. It is a boy about 17-years-old, whom Littledale meets walking home. Here he introduces a relative who has lived in America and speaks English. Ronnie can stay here for two nights, and is given a coat, boots and some money. They tell Littledale that they do not have an underground contact in Prague, but they give him an address in Krabcice belonging to a preacher called F. Dobias. On 19 January, that is where Ronnie goes. From this man, Dobias, he gets an address in the capital, and pretty soon he is on his way, walking to Zdiby with some extra money in his pocket, courtesy of Dobias. En route, he calls in at a farm. An awkward meeting ensues: one of the two farmers present wants to know more about Littledale's identity. Despite his misgivings, Littledale feels safe enough to tell the truth. Promptly, the farmer replies that he is a German: Littledale should leave as soon as possible, he adds. The Englishman is immediately back on the road, walking towards Prague.

He catches a tram that takes him to the city centre, where he alights. It is seven o'clock in the evening. Ronnie is tired, he is having trouble walking, it is very cold, and his contact is not there. He tries to find shelter elsewhere but fails to do so. Time and temperature against him, he resorts to sitting in a railway station until about 1 am, when he notices that the police are going around checking papers. Back on the streets again, knowing he is rapidly running out of options, he is in a desperate state. Finally, he approaches a man and tells him who he is. He is in luck: this good Samaritan takes him to a restaurant.

The next day, on 20 January, he revisits his contact address, this time with better results. Littledale tells his contact that his plan is to travel to Switzerland, but no, that will not be possible until the snow melts in the mountains, in a month or two. In the meantime, he is to stay at various addresses in Prague until mid-May. It will take not much more than a week or so for external events to take a hand in deciding his fate.

***

A small ceremony takes place at Mexické ulici číslo 4 in central Prague. It is 10 April 2017, and two soldiers in British Army uniform and two in costumes that most closely resemble soldiers from Franz Josef's Austro-Hungarian Empire are lined up in front of the facade of a tall six-storey residential house. Behind them, between a shutter and a wooden door with octagonal windows, a simple white cloth hangs over a plaque. The 'Britons' stand ready with rifles, fixed-bayonets, presented; the representatives of the Dual Monarchy carry multi-coloured flags on long poles ending in what looks like a silver eagle. The 'Britons' with their field hats sloping on their heads are highly reminiscent of Jan Kubiš and Josef Gabčík, and that can hardly be a coincidence in this city during this ceremony.

On the facade, the Czech flag hangs limply high above the gathering in a street where there is hardly any wind. A few speeches are made, and when the white cloth is removed, the text on the black stone on the facade becomes visible.

V tomto dome zila obetava clenka odboje
Zdenka Pakova
Se spolupracovniky vysadky ANTHROPOID
Byla popravena nacisty 24. 10. 1942 v Mauthausenu

The memorial declares that in this house lived Zdenka Pakova, a member of the Resistance who was murdered with fellow fighters by the Nazis in Mauthausen on 24 October 1942. The codeword ANTHROPOID is written in thick letters.

Between two actors, representing Jan Kubiš and Josef Gabčík, is a yellow-coloured sign on the ground leaning against the wall. In front of it is a handful of roses. The board shows a few pictures, with the one in the upper-left corner standing out the most. It is a girl with full, thick hair with two giant braids, and a black tie. It is Zdenka Pakova as a child, who lived at this spot. Also distinguishable are a man and a woman. And a British soldier. His cap is slightly askew, set at what used to be called a rakish angle: it looks mischievous. His uniform fits like a glove, the Sam Browne across his chest restrains a man ready for action: a second lieutenant in the 2nd Battalion of the King's Royal Rifle Corps. It is a young Ronald Bolton Littledale who looks in into the camera, wearing a determined expression, here at Mexické ulici číslo 4 in central Prague. Even more remarkable is the image from the *Deutsches Kriminalpolizeiblatt* (German Criminal Police Journal) 4,409 of 16 October 1942, which reports the escape of four British officers from Colditz Castle in Saxony, Germany. On the left in the image gallery on this pamphlet is Littledale.

The other two photos on the yellow board are of the Bergauer couple. Vladimir Bergauer was born in Pisku on 18 September 1898, the son of Julius and Marii Bergauer. In 1945, two notebooks containing diary entries are found in furniture once belonging to Vladimir Bergauer and later confiscated by the Gestapo in 1942 to be sold cheaply to Nazi Party members. They describe Bergauer's student years during the period between 1914 and 1922. Student infatuations and broken relationships alternate with village politics and wider world events. These were turbulent times for the Czech Republic after its emergence in 1918. Theatre, army training, the threat of conscription and war, dance, books, art and the first steps on the path of science are described on the pages in tight, powerful strokes. On 2 July 1917, Bergauer completes his education at the grammar school in Pisek in South Bohemia, and in October that year he begins his studies in medicine at the medical faculty of the University of Prague. It does not take long for him to become a collaborator and a close assistant to the head of the Department of General Biology and Experimental Developmental Physiology, one of Czechoslovakia's leading biologists and eugenicists Professor Vladislav Ruzicka. Bergauer's field of research becomes the ageing processes of living organisms, later complemented by sexual biology.

He returns to Pisek regularly, to his family and friends, as well as to his beloved theatre, music and art. A skilled pianist, he also sings, takes photographs and performs in plays. In autumn 1918, for instance, he plays a leading role in Ladislav Novak's comedy *Duelanti*. When Spanish flu breaks out in early October, teaching at the university is interrupted. Together with his father Julius and three former classmates, Bergauer returns to Pisek. When the Czech Republic is proclaimed in October 1918, Bergauer celebrates this fantastic event with his friend Tomáš Soukup and his brother Jiri.

After graduating from the medical faculty of Karlovy University in Prague, he starts working as a lecturer in general biology. After a short while, Bergauer becomes an active participant in the Czech Eugenics movement, joining the Eugenics Committee of the Masarykova Akademie Práce. In the 1920s and 1930s, he mainly studies sexual selection and so-called differential birth rates. After Ruzicka's death in 1934, Bergauer became director of the Czech Institute of National Eugenics. From the mid-1930s, he is involved in research on voluntary sterilisation as a eugenicist. He continues this even when Bohemia and Moravia are occupied in March 1939. When the universities are closed in November 1939, Bergauer leaves for the newly formed Institute of National Biology and Eugenics, where he is head of the Department of National Demography.

He marries Markétu Knourkova, daughter of Josef and Ida Knourka. She was born on 6 February 1904 in Olomouc. Both are Catholic. She is an engineer and also works as a clerk at the building company of the Czechoslovak Revival Movement. Members are adherents of Martinism, a spiritual movement concerned with research into hidden spiritual abilities of humans and animals. He will later lead the Eugenics Society in Prague. Together with Professor Jan Belehradek of Karlovy University, he publishes the book *Obecna Biologie*, on general biology, in 1936.

Once contacts are established, things move rapidly. Littledale, through Pastor F. Dobias from Krabcice and Jan Mirejovsky, pastor of the Association of Evangelical Youth, manages to get in touch with Yaroslav Valenta in January 1942. Together with Dr Rudolf Mares, Valenta is secretary of the Academic YMCA. At that time, Valenta is involved in resistance against the Nazi occupier and a member of the ÚVOD (*Ústřední Vedení Odboje Domácího*: The Central Leadership of the

Home Resistance), a general organisation of non-communist Resistance groups in the Protectorate of Bohemia and Moravia. Valenta and Mares work on securing radio communications between the domestic Resistance and London for the purpose of sending over intelligence gathered by themselves. Together with, among others, Dr Jaroslav Šimsa, he is the founder of the Resistance organisation PVVZ (*Petiční Výbor 'Věrni Zůstaneme'*: Petition Committee: We Will Remain Faithful), mainly non-communist, left-wing intellectuals, freemasons, the National Women's Council, trade unions of postal and railway workers. Through Valenta, Littledale gets in touch with Zdenka Pakova.

In 1942, the girl with the full, thick hair with two giant braids, and a black tie in the photo in Mexické ulici číslo 4 is a 35-year-old woman. She was born on 8 November 1906 in Prague, the youngest of four children of Jiřímu Pakovi and Arnoštce Pakové-Mayerhoffer. Her father is editor of the magazine *Nový Havlíček*. Zdenka learns sewing at an industrial girls' school. Until September 1926, she works as secretary of the Building Cooperative of the Student Revival Movement and as bookkeeper of the Budeč dormitory. Designed for students of Karlovy University, the dormitory is operated by the Revival Movement of Czechoslovak Students. As there are no separate dormitories for girls in Prague and the available accommodation is inadequate, a complex is built which can eventually accommodate some two hundred female students. A businessman, Václav M. Havel, father of the renowned Czech writer and politician Václav Havel, is responsible for this. When completed in 1925, it is a very modern building with central heating, a doctor's surgery and a canteen. A fifth floor is added in 1937. Zdenka Pakova gets to know Markétu Knourkova Bergauer as director of the Budeč dormitory.

When war breaks out and her country is overrun by the Germans, Zdenka joins the Resistance. Her fellow fighters will tell you she is truthful, selfless, helpful and has an invaluable ability to restore everyone's hope and morale at especially difficult times. Yaroslav Šimsa said she always knew what was needed and helped whenever possible. Apart from Šimsa, she works with Valenta and Mareš. She arranges fake papers, food and clothes and provides shelter to those people involved in illicit activities, such as Mareš, Valenta and František Peltán. Her flat serves as a refuge and this is where Littledale will eventually find shelter. Zdenka is initially reluctant to take in

Littledale. Her branch of the Resistance is mainly concerned with information and intelligence and this is a distraction. However, her colleagues in the movement are keen to assist the British officer, so she relents. Her sister Jiřina also helps out. They are joined by Anna Kavinová-Schustlerová, Maria and Emil Brunclík, and Gertruda Šašková. Through Zdenka, Littledale meets Dr Vladimír Bergauer and his wife Markéta and it is with this brave couple that Littledale spends the longest time in hiding, until mid-May 1942. They install him in a flat at Italské ulici 615/7 in Vinohradech, Prague, some two kilometres from Zdenka's flat on Mexické ulici číslo 4. It is also next door to the Bergauers' residential address.

It goes without saying that Littledale must have been happy and grateful to find accommodation with the Bergauer couple. But would that have been the case he had he known about what Vladimír Bergauer was involved in before the German annexation of Czechoslovakia? While matters must be seen in the context of pre-war Czechoslovakia, at the time Littledale was hiding with Bergauer, it was precisely the kind of thing he was fighting against in Calais, a discipline his opposition to which motivated him to escape from Laufen through a tunnel, flee from Posen in a rubbish van, jump out of a train and skulk around Europe like hunted game for over a year. Developments that, as a deeply religious man, he must have been vehemently opposed to.

On 2 May 1915, the Czech Eugenic Society was founded in what was then Austria-Hungary. Discussions about eugenics in a scientific and social sense should lead to:

> A specialised study of biology, the dissemination of knowledge about physical and mental health in all classes of the population, a fight against hereditary diseases and infant mortality, support for the care of mothers and their newborns, and, ultimately, a fight against alcoholism and tuberculosis, as well as against venereal diseases.

The First World War hampered further development of these ideas to ennoble the human race that were in vogue at the time.

Following the formation of the state of Czechoslovakia after the collapse of Franz Josef's empire, a meeting with American eugenicists in New York in 1923 results in the establishment of the Czech Institute of National Eugenics.

From the end of the First World War until the 1930s, Eugenics was a serious field of study for scientists and jurists, not only in Czechoslovakia, but in many other Central European countries. The German '*Gesetz zur Verhütung erbkranken Nachwuchses*' (Law for the Prevention of Hereditarily Sick Offspring), passed and implemented in 1933, is the harbinger of an ominous future.

Although there were some critical voices, the idea of using sterilisation on a voluntary basis, or at the intercession of a guardian, in order to curb hereditary diseases by preventing the reproduction of carriers of these hereditary diseases gradually gained a foothold in Czechoslovakia. A three-member committee of specialists was set up in 1936 to critically examine legislation in neighbouring countries and to prepare a draft law formulating measures to this end. The three members were a legal advisor and two medical specialists in the field of eugenics. The legal advisor is Dr Jarmila Veselá. His task is to test the plans against current criminal law in order to safeguard activities from being deemed illegal. The two medical specialists are Dr Bohumil Sekla and Dr Vladimír Bergauer of Karlovy University.

Sekla has been aware since the early 1930s that genetic disorders are passed on by carriers to their descendants. This, he believes, is enough justification alone for the sterilization of carriers. He recognises that it is a huge matter for the individuals involved, but increasing state involvement in social and medical affairs is the prevailing political zeitgeist now and will be in the future. Sekla is a supporter of a programme such as the one followed in Germany because of the ideal vision of the 'perfect formal form' in which it is cast. Even so, he regularly and firmly stresses that eugenics must be separated from racial theories, of which he is a complete opponent. Dr Vladimír Bergauer, the third member of the committee has published a book on general biology, *Obecna Biologie*. This is only a faint reflection of the work he is involved in.

A memorandum laying down the basis of the draft law follows in March 1937, and is presented to the Ministry of Health and Physical Education in June that year. However, the relevant legislation is ultimately not passed or implemented in Czechoslovakia, initiatives even being taken to protect 'weaklings'. But the moment Hitler's troops roll into Prague in March 1938, everything changes and Czech Law no longer applies. The areas annexed by Germany are now subject to the laws of the Third Reich, including *Gesetz zur Verhütung erbkranken Nachwuchses* (Law for the prevention of hereditarily sick offspring). This law has already been succeeded in the Third Reich by a euthanasia programme of unprecedented scale with all its consequences.

Among Jaroslav Valenta's many contacts in the Resistance movement is 45-year-old Gertruda Šašková, professor of geography and history, and choir member of the Jednota bratrská in Žižkov, a Protestant movement founded in 1457. In addition to her other Resistance work, she is involved in helping Littledale. After months of waiting in Bergauer's flat, a plan is formulated by him for Littledale to travel to Switzerland with the help of the Resistance in Austria. Šašková is to escort the major to Vimperk in southern Czechoslovakia, some 60 km west of Budweis, and close to the tri-border point between Czechoslovakia, Germany and Austria. She accompanies the British major to Husinec to visit preacher Zelink of the Czech Brotherhood Union, with whom they spend the night. The next day, Littledale is sent on by train from the border station, eventually leaving the country. According to Littledale himself, he is helped on his way to Husinec on 18 May, and two days later by another helper from the Resistance to Linz.

Littledale travels alone to Innsbruck, on third-class tickets bought in stages, always on local trains. These are subject to fewer or no inspections by the police and are therefore safer. His contact in Innsbruck is ill and is unable to do anything for him at the moment. The journey continues by train to Bludenz, where he talks to an old man who is gardening at the time. This man tells him that heavy surveillance and snow make border crossings impossible at the moment. At Hotel Der Löwen, Littledale has a drink, but he cannot stay there, so he is forced to spend the night in a barn. On the morning of 23 May, he takes the train to Schruns, where he meets an English-speaking old priest who has been to India and later another man. He asks both men about crossing the border and gets the same answer from both: crossing is a nigh-on impossibility.

Littledale believes that Liechtenstein, where he is very close to now, is occupied by the Germans at the time. He is forced to return to Husinec, and he decides not to make another attempt to cross the border until June when the snow has disappeared. However, Liechtenstein is never occupied during the war, and Littledale has missed a golden opportunity. After travelling back via Linz and

Prachatice, he arrives in Husinec, where he spends two days in bed with a fever. On the evening of 27 May, he is told by his Resistance friends that there has been an attack on Reinhard Heydrich in Prague.

With his cold, arrogant face, Reinhard Heydrich looks exactly like the Hollywood Nazi stereotype, as defined by decades of television and movie portrayal. The long face with the sharp nose is punctuated by two small piercing eyes of which even Himmler is afraid. The Reichsprotektor of Bohemia and Moravia enjoys a lofty position in the hierarchy of Nazi leadership, and he ensures that opponents to Hitler are ruthlessly eliminated. As chairman of the Wannsee Conference on 20 January 1942, he has the dubious honour of heading up an extermination machine that industrialises the slaughter of millions of Jews. From Prague Castle, that towers high above the Czech capital, he destroys the Czech Resistance. From Britain in particular, there are strong calls for action to end his terrible reign. It will give a huge boost to national morale in Czechoslovakia if the man who bears the epithets 'The Butcher of Prague' and 'The Blonde Beast' is eliminated.

Training sessions follow and as early as late 1941, seven soldiers from the Czechoslovak army in exile are dropped in the Czech Republic. Contact is made with local Resistance groups, and after discussing and trying out various scenarios, they decide to take Heydrich down in the lion's den. The very picture of arrogant confidence, Heydrich sets off on 27 May from his home in Panenské Břežany to the Castle with his chauffeur. His open top Mercedes-Benz is unescorted on the drive from the north-east side of the city towards the Moldau. Smetana's symphony has not been heard here for a long time. Two of the assassins, Jozef Gabčík and Jan Kubiš, are ready at their posts when the car takes a sharp right turn and has to brake, losing speed. This is the moment they have been waiting for. Gabčík shoots immediately, but his Sten gun jams. Heydrich's driver, Klein, fires back but misses. Kubiš throws a grenade that detonates with a loud bang. Shrapnel tears through the car's bodywork and into Heydrich's body. The assassins manage to get away, but from this moment on, they know they are marked men.

Heydrich is wounded and hovers between life and death for several days until he dies of blood poisoning on 4 June. Hitler is furious and wants to see nothing but blood. The country is searched for the perpetrators. The towns of Lidice and Ležáky are wiped off the face of the earth as a measure of reprisal. Their populations are exterminated or put on transport and taken away. A traitor leads the SS bloodhounds to the Church of St Cyriel and Methodius in Prague, where the perpetrators of the attack are hiding. A firefight ensues, lasting several hours, with hundreds of SS men. They try to flood the crypt under the church, flush out the assassins, but that does not work. However, the attackers have to give up, preferring suicide to arrest. In the witch's cauldron that the country has become, one in which the Germans proceed ruthlessly to track down Heydrich's killers and anyone associated with them, it becomes very difficult for both Littledale and his helpers to move about freely.

At Vimperk station, Gertruda Šašková waits on a platform for her train home. An express train arrives and, to her amazement, Major Littledale gets off. To avoid attracting too much attention when she addresses him, she pretends to be tying her shoelaces. Why has he not crossed the border? She doesn't hear much more than his remark that he could not. They have to keep the conversation short so as not to be too conspicuous. Littledale moves away from her and at that moment he is approached by a Czech policeman, who asks to see his papers.

As Šašková tries to make her way out of the station, Littledale is telling the policeman in German that he has lost his papers. At that point, the policeman arrests him. Littledale makes one last attempt: realising that the man is not a Sudeten German, he tells him who he really is and asks him to help. Alas, the cop dashes all Littledale's hopes, and refuses. He ensures that at no point can Littledale escape his notice. Littledale is extremely lucky not to get caught up in the Wild Hunt the SS have invoked in their search for the killers of the Butcher of Prague. According to a later statement by Littledale (presumably at MI9), the 'SS have gone crackers when they shoot at anyone they consider suspicious'.

After Littledale's arrest at Vimperk station, someone remembers he had a companion, someone with whom he was in conversation. Who? Why? Shortly afterwards, Gertruda Šašková is arrested in her flat. Then Emil Brunclik, 53, an employee of Keramika, a ceramics manufacturing company in Prague, and his wife Maria, 44, are arrested for the possession of weapons, the distribution of illegal pamphlets and magazines, possession of an illegal radio and the hiding of Major Littledale in their flat. A total of 35 out of 65 people from the Resistance group around Šašková will be executed.

Zdenka Pakova is arrested on 26 June. She is taken to the German police prison in Pankrác and deported to the Terezín fortress around 15 October 1942. From this small fortress, she commences her journey to Mauthausen concentration camp. She is murdered there 'at 10:24 a.m.' on 24 October. Jaroslav Valenta is arrested in a police raid the night after Heydrich's murder. Rudolf Mareš is arrested after falling into a Prague Gestapo ambush in July 1942, where František Peltán is wounded and shot. Mareš is murdered in Prague's Pankrác prison in October 1944.

A plaque is unveiled at the Bergauers' house, also referring to ANTHROPOID, and the ominous date and place of 24 October 1942 in Mauthausen. A yellow plaque with pictures of the Bergauers this time, and Zdenka, but without Littledale. ANTHROPOID is Heydrich, the 'man-monkey', or ape-man, whose death the Nazis in Czechoslovakia must avenge. The wave of arrests, deportations and executions that follows Heydrich's death engulfs not only Zdenka Pakova but also the Bergauer couple. On 30 June 1942, Markéta Bergauer is arrested at three in the afternoon on the orders of the Gestapo Protectorate Police. The typewriter is working overtime at the *Kanzlei des Polizeigefängnisses Barthelemeusgasse* (Office of the Barthelemeusgasse Police Prison) as Markéta hands over her details to her guards.

The arrest warrant for Prisoner 5536, who identifies herself with her Arbeitsbuch (a personal card with a large eagle holding the ubiquitous swastika on the front cover) reveals that her father, Josef, former first lieutenant, is now no longer alive, that she has a brother also named Josef, that her mother Ida lives in Wenzigstrasse, and that after her arrest, she hands over 22 Czech Crowns, a wristwatch, two lighters, a fountain pen, a tobacco pouch, a handbag, a comb, gloves, a notebook, clothing vouchers, various papers, and a white lady's ring with a white stone. After her arrest, she is immediately handed over to the German security police. She eventually ends up in cell 18 of the *Sicherheits-Abteilung* (Security Department).

Vladimir Bergauer is arrested on the same day and suffers the same fate as his wife, from whom the Germans have separated him. He is initially deported to the prison in the small fortress of Theresienstadt (Terezin), just like Markéta. Remarkably, the Bergauers are not especially in favour of Operation ANTHROPOID, the assassination of Heydrich. But the Germans do not care about that. Anyone who helps in hiding the paratroopers who carried out the attack, or was involved in the action in any way, or who the Germans have even the slightest suspicion that they had anything to do with it is a candidate for arrest.

The Bergauers know their fate, that even the time of their death is recorded to the minute on their *Sterbeurkunde* (Death Certificate). They know how the Nazis do things, but do not accept that as a reason not to do what they did. Of a total of 294 detainees, the majority, including Pakova and the Bergauers, will be executed on 24 October 1942 at Mauthausen concentration camp, 20 km east of Linz in Austria. One by one, the victims are pushed into a bunker. Every two minutes they are led inside a room, first the women, then the men. Told that their height is being measured by 'doctors', they enter the room where they are shot, an unceremonious bullet to the back of the neck. Vladimir dies at 14.02, Markéta preceding him in death at 10.26. On 26 January the following year, the last 30 victims are murdered in cold blood. Sokol Sport Club president Frank Pechacek is torn to pieces by guard dogs.

Radim Pák, Zdenka Pakova's brother, receives a letter on 19 January 1943 from law firm Magerstein & Schmid in Prague informing him of the results of an investigation into the whereabouts of his sister Zdenka. To the author's regret, Radim has to be informed that his sister has died in a concentration camp on 24 June 1942. After the war, Radim wants to find out more about the circumstances under which his sister was arrested. He therefore writes to the Ministry of the Interior in autumn 1945. In a letter dated 27 November that year, the reply follows that:

> His sister Zdenka, the Bergauers, the Bruncliks and Gertruda Šašková were all executed at Mauthausen concentration camp on 24 October 1942 for their involvement in hiding British Major Littledale. His contacts with preacher Dobias from Krabcice and preacher Jan Mirejovsky are mentioned and how through them Zdenka and later the Bergauers provided a hiding place. Bergauer gives Littledale glasses as a disguise. Littledale is not the only one in hiding with the Bergauers. A marconist (Radio Operator) known by the pseudonym Golem, in possession of a false identity card in the name of Jiri Zeman, is also hiding. As there are doubts about the credibility of Littledale, who he claims to be, he is transferred to Mr and Mrs

Brunclik's flat. Mr and Mrs Bergauer enlist her contacts with the Resistance in Austria to bring Littledale to St Antönien in Switzerland with false papers. On the way to Austria, Littledale finds shelter, presumably for one night, with an evangelical priest named Zelinka. Eventually Littledale does not reach Switzerland as he is afraid of being buried by an avalanche. As agreed, he returns to the station in Vimperk. Just before his arrest, he speaks to Dr Sasková who is waiting for him to accompany him back. After Littledale's arrest, investigations are carried out at Vimperk station and Dr Sasková is discovered to be possibly involved. In early June 1942, she is arrested in Prague, followed by the others involved.

The possibility that the man posing as an escaped British PoW could be a secret agent of the Gestapo, infiltrating the Resistance group with the aim of plotting and eventually destroying it, is not ruled out in the final sentence of this letter. In a later communication from the ministry to Radim Pak on 21 September 1946, the fate of the British major is conclusive:

> According to the report of the British military authorities, Lieutenant Colonel Ronald Bolton Littledale, Kings Royal Rifle Corps, who was a fugitive prisoner of war, fell in battle on 1 September 1944, while commanding his regiment.

13

GRIS

When Littledale and Sinclair leave Warsaw behind in late August 1941, they also leave Gris behind, all alone. It sounds like tough luck, but it is a part of the military culture in which they were all were steeped. Despite the informalities between them, there was a two-step gap that separated Ronnie from Mike and Gris in the military hierarchy and it was a factor. He was a major, Gris and Mike both lieutenants, subalterns. It was a fact of life. As military men, it would go without saying. That they were in an escape situation actually made it all the more relevant. The escape is seen a mission. Littledale was the commanding officer, the senior British officer, to use PoW parlance. Deciding who goes and who stays, as senior officer, was Ronnie's decision to make. The only choice he had was the choice to decide on and express his philosophy of leadership in this case. He could lead from behind the lines, so to speak, or he could lead from the front. He chose the latter. So he went.

He calculates that his best chance of success is to have a companion. Of the two officers on hand, the multilingual Sinclair was the more useful to him, so Sinclair went with Littledale. The mission comes first: he chose who he saw as the best man for that mission to go with him. Their journey takes them across the Balkans to Turkey: Mike's language skills would be essential. So he went.

Before they set off, Mike wants to know every detail of the trip that awaits him and Ronnie. The Poles are less enthusiastic about this. If Mike is unexpectedly arrested and he is forced to talk it could have serious consequences for the Polish Resistance. Gris's initial concern at the time is that he feels lonely, but this changes when new officers from Fort VIII arrive at his hideout. These men were simply left behind at the fort in Poznan at the time of its closure. Taking the same route as Gris, Mike and Ronnie, they arrive in Warsaw via Wolf's flat in Lódz, and an unknown Polish hero known only as 'Józef'. Two years after Britain declared war on Germany, on 3 September, British officers Kit Silverwood-Cope, Kenneth Sutherland and Peter Winton, all three escapees from Fort VIII, sit down to dinner with Gris. Also present are Puffy and Mrs M., the woman with whom Gris is in hiding. Mrs M. is British and was a governess at the Austrian court with the imperial family. She then married a Polish official. After the First World War, the couple moved to Warsaw after which she taught English to influential families. Despite the German invasion of Poland, she continued to live in the country and set up an organization to help escaped British prisoners of war. Officers and men who have escaped or taken refuge while working outside the camp come and go in her house. Puffy is the nickname of a man who introduces himself as Mr Olszewski. He is good friends with Ms M. and helps her with the refugee line. His nickname refers to his puffy cheeks.

The days Gris spends in his room become weeks and the weeks become months. Gris waits until he too can move on, waiting for news from Ronnie and Mike, who will by now have progressed a long way in the Balkans. Although far from the front line, the violence of war is nearby. The occasional rattle of a machine gun can be heard from the ghetto near to where Gris is staying. Not that he constantly stays in the same place. He moves around the city with some regularity, sometimes as a result of unexpected police visits. But despite the help he is given, food, clothing and company, in his mind there is the fear of being arrested, and confess when questioned. Winter approaches, and Christmas is celebrated at Puffy's. Then comes a devastating message confirmed by Puffy. Two British officers have been arrested in Bulgaria, one is a major and one is called Sinclair. Gris' blood runs cold. What if they confess during interrogation? What if, under pressure, they spill the beans about where they have been all these months after their successful escape from Poznan, and who was able to hide and accompany them over this great distance for so long?

Gris is also in danger of being discovered, although as a lieutenant he is at much less risk than his Polish aides. For soldiers in wartime, the Geneva Convention and other formal, protective protocols exist to ensure that once captured, enemy soldiers and airmen are treated properly. For the Polish citizens, risking their lives to smuggle these escaped men safely to a neutral country, these rules do not apply. Gris has two options. He can continue to wait, as he has been waiting for months for an invasion to come, which is absolutely unrealistic; or he can move on with help from the Poles who have helped him so far. At the end of January 1942, he too realises that staying longer with his helpers will only increase the risk of discovery, arrest and worse for them.

For Gris, he will forever remain Mr X, and he never found out who this X really is. Through an acquaintance of Mrs M, he comes into contact with this mysterious figure. X has been running around asking where in Warsaw there are British people in hiding. He himself lives in Kraków and he claims that it is possible to take people to neutral Switzerland. Is it a serious proposal, or is he an agent provocateur, a German infiltrator? The circumstances are such that Gris has already more or less decided that it really is time to travel on, and he sees a degree of merit in this proposition, despite the ominous feelings of suspicion he harbours. Ms M., meanwhile, also has her doubts about this X.

After several long discussions, Gris decides it should go ahead. Puffy contacts X and he agrees that two men can come to him in Kraków where further transport will be arranged. The Poles tell Gris to team up with Corporal Weekes, who has been in Warsaw for some time and speaks Polish reasonably well. After making the necessary preparations and arranging travel documents, Gris and Weekes leave in the second week of February, 1942 alongside two Polish escorts, including Puffy. When they arrive in Kraków, they encounter large groups of Italians who have returned from the Eastern Front. The Russian PoWs they also see make a miserable impression. In a suburb of the city, they eventually meet the mysterious Mr X. Gris remembers that he has one blue and one brown eye. Thanks to the food he shares with everyone and his reassurances that he has dealt with this situation before, both English soldiers calm down. X tells them which route they will take, and that new papers need to be prepared. That evening, Puffy gets a call. Under no circumstances should he return home. Through his Polish contacts, he and Gris know that the underground organisation is under the microscope of the Gestapo. Puffy ignores the warning, is eventually arrested and disappears into the dark world of Auschwitz.

The Vienna Express to the capital, Innsbruck and beyond awaits the two men at Kraków station. A slight sense of euphoria takes hold of Gris as the train starts moving. At last, on the road! Closer to freedom! In Teschen, disaster strikes. At the station in this town, lying on the border of Poland and Czechoslovakia, two policemen board the train, quickly go through and check everyone. When Gris shows his documents, they are accepted, but Weekes cannot answer when he is asked a question in German. Gris tries to mediate but the police prefer to take the two men away for further investigation. Mr X watches it all happen from a distance. Examination of the men's luggage reveals all sorts of things that ordinary citizens cannot afford in these unusual times; things like chocolate and voucher cards that can only be obtained in Das Reich. Gris' story is that he is travelling to Vienna for work. Although he speaks reasonably good German, he pretends to be Belarusian. While his papers were being inspected, Gris produces a work permit. Since Weekes can only express himself in Polish, Gris takes his papers and speaks to the policemen for the both of them. When they ask them to get out of the train, Gris is relieved that he ignored advice to carry a weapon during the journey. During the interrogation, the Englishmen's story becomes more implausible by the minute, and the language barrier is only making things worse. Gris tries again to convince his interrogators that his travelling companion only speaks Polish and Belarusian, and he himself only German, despite pretending to be Belarusian. His story is that he was three years old when the Bolshevik revolution broke out. His father was murdered, and together with his mother he escapes to Germany, where he has lived ever since, and which he considers his motherland. An interpreter is eventually brought in, who detects an accent in Weekes' voice, English or American, he is not sure which. Gris and Weekes get deeper and deeper into trouble and eventually they get summoned to Kraków for in-depth questioning. Although Gris is fearful of interrogation and of the terrifying techniques that might be employed to extract the truth from him, he stalls for as long as possible before finally admitting that Weekes and he are escaped British PoWs. He hopes he was able to buy enough time to allow their Polish couriers to get away far enough not to be arrested.

Gris admits to having escaped from Fort VIII in Poznan, which make his interrogators prick up their ears. That camp was closed months ago! Where has this man been all this time? Who helped him, gave him documents, clothes, food, shelter? How did he get all the way to Teschen from Poznan? Gris remains silent. Years later, he will remember the investigation. How lives depend on his words.

But the Germans already know everything and do not need answers, they produce a list and show it to Gris. Names pass by, names of people already arrested, addresses in Poznan, Mrs M, Puffy, Mr Wolf in Lódz. Gris doesn't recognise them all, but this he does. And he remains silent. Dark thoughts fill his head, but he has to remain steadfast in the interrogation room. In his cell he is later able to have a surreptitious conversation with Weekes, who tells him that apart from Mrs M. and Puffy, none of his helpers are on the list.

Via a transit camp at Lamsdorf, today Łambinowice in Poland, Gris makes his way to Saxony. According to Pat Reid, Edward Grismond Beaumont 'Gris' Davies-Scourfield arrives at Colditz on 12 March 1942. The immense castle that towers over the town will be home for the unfortunate lieutenant for the next three years. Three years in which he thinks a lot about all the Poles who were arrested and the list presented to him at his interrogation in Kraków.

One of the first people he meets in Colditz is Mike Sinclair. 'Thank God, you're still alive,' he shouts, sincerely. He asks if Ronnie is also there in the castle. He isn't. Mike will tell him more later. Gris tells him about his interrogator's claims to have arrested the cohort Polish Resistance fighters who helped them and also about the warning Puffy received over the phone in Kraków. Mike is greatly concerned about this and believes that the claim was probably correct. Some Polish officers in Colditz will later receive confirmation of the claim via coded messages. It is suspected that Mr X, who initially seemed to be the lifeline for Gris, was in reality a Gestapo agent who infiltrated the Resistance organisation, and waited as long as possible to strike in order to cause as much damage as possible. The circumstances under which Gris was eventually arrested put him at a loss for words. Why were the two officers waiting for him and Weekes at the station? That was too convenient. Why weren't they arrested earlier? Why were they allowed to make acquaintance with X? They could just as easily have been arrested back in Kraków. Years later, Gris stumbles across a report sent from the underground to the Polish government in London, expounding the theory that there must have been a Gestapo infiltrator in the escape organisation that eventually led to the arrest of many Polish Resistance fighters.

Mike has been in Colditz since 15 January 1942. A few months later, he sees a chance to escape when he is taken to a hospital in Leipzig for treatment of chronic nasal sinusitis. Once out of the castle, there are far fewer guards around him, it should be much easier to escape. After the dramas of 1941 and since his arrival at Colditz, Mike has only one goal: to return to England, to fight against Germany. On 2 June, he climbs out of a window in the hospital and heads off. According to Gris, Mike had gone to the hospital before for treatment, and doubtless, took every opportunity to do some reconnaissance, the only advantage a chronic condition provides. Apart from scoping out the situation on the ground, he seems to have prepared well for his journey. Within days, he reaches Cologne, almost certainly by train, some 500 km away.

The route he follows suggests that his goal is Belgium and then France, where the south is not occupied by the Germans at that time, but governed by the collaborationist Vichy regime. Through these countries runs an escape line along which many Allied soldiers will reach neutral Spain with the help of the Resistance. Sinclair must have gained knowledge of this route in Colditz, among other places. However, he will not reach Spain. On 6 June, Mike is arrested. Luck, never his strong point, is not on Mike's side. Just as he arrives in Cologne, a massive search is under way for parachuted crews of shot-down aircraft, after a heavy bombing raid of the city. On the night of 30 to 31 May, 868 aircraft bomb Cologne in the first 1,000 bomber raid (involving 1,047 planes). The machines are laden with more than 3,000,000 kg of explosives. On the 31st, five de Havilland Mosquitoes from the RAF's 105 Squadron, conduct a photo reconnaissance over the city to record the results of the night's bombardment. Operation Millennium resulted in 2,500 fires, a city in ruins, and an enraged population. Any crew member of a shot down Allied aircraft is a target for police, soldiers and civilians on the ground, prey for merciless hunters. Mike, too, has gained many enemies. The poor disguise he is wearing gives him away. On 8 June, he manages to escape again, this time possibly from a cell in a neighbouring Stalag in which he is temporarily held, according to Pat Reid. Once again, though, he does not get any further than Cologne, and his arrest means a single ticket back to Colditz.

One month later, on 15 July 1942, a ghost enters the castle. Ronnie Littledale has arrived, and the three officers from Fort VIII are reunited. No doubt they have a lot to discuss. Or do they?

Over and over again, Gris must have racked his brain about that list presented to him at his interrogation. Questions like: who knew what about whom, when did they know it, and who was willing to tell what was so and what was not, and to whom was it told? The protagonists of these events are: Gris himself, his German interrogator, his escape buddy, Corporal Weekes, Michael Sinclair and Ronald Littledale. Now that Sinclair, Littledale and Gris are reunited, they have time on their hands, in their bunks and in the small courtyard to study the situation from all sides.

Gris, Mike and Ronald all know Mrs M, Puffy, and Mr Wolf from Lódz, and they all know the addresses in Poznan where they stayed after their escape from Fort VIII. Weekes, on the other hand, who is not in Colditz as he is an NCO and therefore not eligible, does not recognise anyone on the list at his interrogation except Mrs M and Puffy. This makes sense, because he arrives in Warsaw through a different route than Gris, Mike and Ronald. Littledale has revealed a list of actual names of helpers and routes that he and Sinclair followed after their arrest in Pirot, so it is logical that the list shown to Gris at his interrogation is at least based on this, and may indeed be the same one. The interrogator says that several arrests were made. However not everyone on the list was arrested at the time. According to a secret document dated 7 July 1942, from the Chief Prosecutor in the case against Maria Jasińska addressed to the General Prosecutor, it is not clear to the police at that time where Czesław Wolf has gone. They think he is staying with Lech Dolniak in Warsaw.

If Littledale's list and Gris's interrogator's list match, Mike and Ronald know which names and addresses Gris must have seen. They could have discussed this at length during Ronald's short time in Colditz. Perhaps they did, but Gris does not mention it in his later recollections. Mike and Ronald never wrote their memoirs. Only Littledale leaves an explosive document at the offices of MI9.

Now Gris possibly had his reasons for keeping quiet about this. It was never discussed between them, which is simply not plausible, or he wants to protect Mike and Ronnie. They are British officers serving in the same regiment. They are friends, and brothers in arms. He is not the first to say this. As an explanation, as detailed in his memoirs, is centred around a report from the Resistance in Poland addressed to the Polish government in exile in London. This theorises that there must have been a Gestapo infiltrator in the escape organisation who fed information back to his handlers, which led to the arrest of the Polish Resistance fighters. It is quite possible that the infiltrator was the mysterious Mr X. His asking around where there are British people hiding in Warsaw with the aim of helping them is strikingly suspicious, and that it triggers Ms M's antennae is entirely plausible. The disquiet among the escaped Englishmen about putting themselves entirely in his hands is a further red flag. In order to infiltrate the underground Polish organisation, the Gestapo needs an in. The list of names that Gris claims to have been shown during his interrogation, and Weekes' later comment that he only recognises Mrs M. and Puffy on the same list, but not the addresses in Poznan and Mr Wolf from Lódz, points firmly in the direction of an opening having been found in the escape line Gris, Mike and Ronnie followed after their escape from Fort VIII. The most logical explanation is that this was provided by Mike and Ronnie's confessions.

Placing a mole within an organisation is a means by which the Germans can not only investigate those already in the picture, but also identify any others involved. Once inside, they simply bide their time, gathering information. Indeed, as early as November 1941, they have a list of names and routes of Poles involved in '*Akcja Dorsze*'. It is only on 28 April 1942 that Maria Jasińska is arrested, shortly before Gris gets caught. Presenting Gris with a list of names and addresses during his interrogation is therefore a way of finding out if there are any others involved. However, the Germans' expectation that Gris will also make an accusatory confession is dashed by his being made of sterner stuff than they hoped. The statement he writes merely tells of where he escaped, where he was arrested and that the vow he took as an officer prevented him from betraying those who helped him. Nothing else.

He imagines himself under a lucky star with the thought that the Germans have already rolled up the escape line. If they had not, and he himself had been harshly interrogated, he doubts he would have resisted long. Gris notes that there are rumours that Mrs M. and Puffy have been under surveillance for some time, and that he does not understand why he himself was not arrested earlier, but that the Germans sat on it until he was on the train with Weekes to the border with Czechoslovakia. If true, using X as an infiltrator would then have been unnecessary. It would follow, therefore, that X, if he existed at all, did not expose the Polish escape line that helped the KRRC officers escape from Poznań and get as far as they did. That was down to Littledale and Sinclair. Under arrest and interrogation at Pirot, they talked. It was thus an easy thing for the Germans to follow their route backwards, seeing where it would lead and, of course, to whom. That they were able to arrest Gris into the bargain was just a bonus.

The three men that escaped from Fort VIII on 28 May 1941 are back together in July 1942 after more than a year of wandering through Eastern Europe. This time in Oflag IVC, Colditz. However, this reunion will not last long.

14

COLDITZ, 14 OCTOBER 1942

Gegen Mittag trat ich mit meinem Begleitern durch das alte düstere Thor der unheimlichen Irrenanstalt–'Adieu Welt!'–rief's in meinem Innern–'hier zwischen diesen dunklen Mauern, unter Wahnsinnigen und Tobsüchtigen muss ich von nun an leben!'–Ein Arzt nahm mich auf; meine Transporteure verließen mich, und ich war nun ein Irrenhäusler geworden.

(Around noon, I stepped with my companions through the old gloomy gate of the eerie lunatic asylum–'Farewell world!'–I shouted inside–'here among these dark walls, among madmen and maniacs, I must live from now on!'–A doctor took me in; my companions left me, and I had now become a lunatic.)

In the opening pages of his book, *The Colditz Story*, Pat Reid described his first PoW camp in Laufen as an insane asylum. As the saying goes, he should have waited! Colditz Castle was used as a mental institution between 1829 and 1924. The paragraph above is from a booklet entitled *Ein Fall Forbes in Sachsen, oder wie jemand nach und nach wahnsinnig werden kann* (*A Forbes Case in Saxony, or How Someone Can Gradually Go Mad*) which describes the experiences of J. A. Rodig circa 1896. It costs about 50 pfennigs a copy and the net proceeds are earmarked for the family. One of the castle's most famous residents during its time as a psychiatric facility is Ludwig Schumann, son of composer Robert Schumann. He was admitted in 1871, a severely disturbed young man, and was kept there against his will until his death in 1899, among '*diesen dunklen Maueren, unter Wahnsinnigen und Tobsüchtigen*' (these dark walls, among madmen and raving madmen).

Another notable resident of the institution is Ernst Georg August Baumgarten, a forester and inventor from Johanngeorgenstadt. His hobby was building dirigible balloons and spring-driven models. In

Grüna in 1879, he made a successful manned flight which reached a height of 25 m. He joined forces with Leipzig-born bookseller, Friedrich Hermann Wölfert, to build an airship in Dresden with three gondolas and a hand-operated propeller drive. However, two years later, the authorities ban him from any further aeronautical engineering. Baumgarten, though, does not care and quietly carries on in secret. In 1882, his secret is out and he loses his job and with it his official residence. Things go downhill from there and after he was involved in a dispute concerning his airships and even intended to fire a gun, he is deemed to be mentally incapacitated and is sent instead to the *Landesirrenanstalt* Colditz (Colditz State Mental Hospital) in January 1883. A year later, he dies of tuberculosis.

Baumgarten may have felt a certain pride and vindication if he had known that 111 years after his death, British PoWs in the same building in Colditz would (unknowingly) follow his example and build a flying machine as part of an insane plan to escape from the roof of the castle. For months, they secretly work on the project under the collective noses of a superpower of German guards. The glider is completed in early 1945, but it will never be flown. American troops liberate the castle on 16 April 1945, and so eliminate the need to risk anyone's life. That the plan could have succeeded is confirmed in 2012 when a British team builds an exact copy of the Colditz Glider at precisely the same spot in the castle and successfully launches her from the highest point. Watched by the town's population, from the bridge leading to the castle, and piloted by remote control, she dives gracefully over the Zwickau Mulde river, banks right, turns left then 'lands' exactly at the spot in a meadow next to the river that the PoWs had in mind at the time. Not much is left of Alex, though, the intrepid mannequin travelling onboard. The poor doll is decapitated in the crash.

Colditz is a small town in Saxony, about 40 km south-east of Leipzig, in the Leipzig-Chemnitz-Dresden triangle. High above the town, on a promontory, a colossal castle towers over the houses and the river Zwickau Mulde, a tributary of the Elbe. The castle, with its massive walls, seems to float on air. It is immense. It has some 700 rooms, two courtyards, its own chapel, and was built to keep the enemy out. On three sides, a would-be assailant is faced with scaling a high cliff. On its southern aspect, the castle is protected by a dry moat. On the eastern side, there is a short passage through an archway under the buildings which nowadays house a youth hostel. Over time, the castle has had many functions. It was originally built as a military fortress, and then successively served as a hunting lodge for the Elector of Saxony, an almshouse, and then between 1829 and 1924 it was an institution for psychiatric patients. Shortly after the Nazis come to power in 1933, political opponents of the regime are imprisoned in concentration camps. Colditz Castle is one of around twenty locations in Saxony used for this purpose along with other castles such as Burg Hohnstein and Burg Osterstein in Zwickau. The internees are mostly communists or liberals, who are severely tortured and forced to live in appalling conditions. From Burg Hohnstein, which is also built on a high cliff, several internees are thrown over to their deaths.

On 21 March 1933, the first prisoners arrive in KZ Colditz, at that time a *Schutzhaftlager* (Protective Custody Camp), for various groups or people deemed 'dangerous to the State'. Surveillance is alternately in the hands of police, SA and SS. Eventually, over 2,000 political opponents are locked up here. But its days as a concentration camp are numbered, as on 31 May 1934, the camp becomes part of KZ Sachsenburg and on 18 August 1934 it is closed, when the prisoners leave for Sachsenburg and other camps. Between 1936 and 1937, it is used by various local institutions. For instance, it houses part of the city museum as well as some sections of the NSDAP. It also houses the *Reichsarbeitsdienst*, the job centre. From 1938, the castle is a *Landes-Heil und Pflegeanstalt* (State Hospital and Nursing Home) for long-term and severely needy patients.

The relatively short period from November 1939, when Polish lieutenant Jedrzej Giertych arrives as the first PoW officer, until 16 April 1945, when US soldiers of 9th US Armoured Division, led by Colonel Leo W. H. Shaughnessy, take over the castle and liberate the PoWs, has put Colditz firmly and permanently on the map. During this period in the Second World War, the castle is a *Sonderlager*, a Special Camp for escaped Allied officers and *Deutschfeindliche* (Enemy of Germans or Germany) alongside a number of Hitler's personal hostages, or Prominente, whom he could use as human change as and when it suits him.

If any person could be credited for popularising this period of Colditz's history, that person is Major Patrick Robert Reid. Then captain, Reid is captured on 27 May 1940 during the Battle of Dunkirk, and detained as a PoW number 357 in Oflag VIIC, at Laufen. After a failed escape attempt, he is sent to Colditz, one of The Laufen Six.

When he sees the monolithic edifice on his walk up from the railway station, terror strikes him. The thought strikes him, escaping from here has got to be impossible. On the night of 14-15 October 1942, however, he and three companions escape and later safely reach Switzerland, thus proving himself very wrong.

It was ten years after, in 1952, that Reid publishes the first of several books about Colditz, *The Colditz Story*. A year later, it is followed by *The Latter Days*. The first book describes the author's experiences from his arrival at Laufen to the moment he shakes hands with his co-escaper Howard (Hank) Wardle under a lamppost in the Swiss town of Ramsen. The sequel takes up the story of the camp from after he left, chronicling the adventures of the camp's international PoW community, which slowly but surely becomes British only as the other nationalities are transferred out. The tone in these two books is very light-hearted, jolly and what might be called Boys' Own. The environment and the people resemble an English Public School: the German staff being the masters and the prisoners being the irrepressible schoolboys. However inaccurate a portrayal this is in actuality, it is one which jibed with the times.

While Pat and Hank's journey through Nazi Germany after their breakout from the castle is covered in detail in *The Colditz Story*, Reid tells us nothing of Ronald Littledale and William Stephens' story, other than confirming that they arrived in Switzerland 24 hours after he and Wardle.

In 1955, the film *The Colditz Story* is released by director Guy Hamilton, starring John Mills as escape officer Pat Reid. It was based on events portrayed in both of Reid's books, and he acted as Technical Consultant. In the 1970s, Reid is again Technical Consultant for the 28-part television series, a co-production by the BBC and Universal Studios. This time, Edward Hardwicke plays the role of escape officer Pat Grant, unmistakably recognisable as Reid.

Story telling in books and films occupy two very different artistic spaces. A book tells its story as it is, a film can only present a version of that story that works within its medium. Books are as long or as short as they need to be, where film is more constrained. It goes without saying that some events are presented differently onscreen to how they have been described as having taken place in reality. Characters are compressed and combined, events are concertinaed, changed in detail or omitted. This is generally accepted to be the nature of the beast. However, one person feels aggrieved by this, Lieutenant Airey Neave, the first British officer who made it to Switzerland from Colditz, together with Dutchman Tony Luteijn, in January 1942 via the camp's theatre.

The Colditz Story, book and film, portrays in reasonable detail how Neave and Luteijn crawl under the stage and then drop down through a hole in the floor underneath. The two men then emerge into a corridor that runs over the entrance gate to the courtyard and leads into the German guardhouse. They only get so far by their own efforts, now fake uniforms and darkness must do the rest. Neave and Luteijn work their way through the guardhouse and then casually walk out of the gate of the heavily guarded castle and away into the night, eventually reaching Switzerland. So far, so good. But put the book down and let's rewind the film a little. Hold on, that's Pat Reid walking out of the Guardhouse, not Airey Neave. And who's that with him? Not Tony Luteijn, that's for sure, or any other Dutchman for that matter. And who are those other two? Neave is not amused to see his thunder stolen by Reid and demands that the film's credits very clearly state that he is the first Englishman to escape. To drive the point home, he publishes his own memoirs under the title *They Have Their Exits*, an altogether more sombre account.

The TV series from the 1970s, called simply Colditz, also makes the truth subservient to a good story, whilst at the same time depicting plenty of storylines that correspond to reality. Again, Reid's escape, for example. His own actual escape is filmed pretty much exactly as it took place. The two-part episode, *Gone Away*, centres on the 14 October escape, beginning with a wild escape plan being put to Pat Grant, that he dismisses as unfeasible, but to which he finally agrees. One of the arguments, to justify going ahead with this scheme, is that to date, only two Englishmen have managed to get away from the camp and to keep up morale, they need to make another attempt. Pointedly, the name of the first man is not mentioned. But those who familiar with the history of Oflag IV-C know who and what this refers to. Airey Neave's name is not only conspicuous by its absence, so is his escape. Nothing is said. A lot is said.

As in Reid's first book, *Gone Away* follows Pat's journey through Germany, until, exhausted, he and his escape buddy fall into the Swiss snow, watched impassively by a border guard, who, with a strong German accent, tells them they are safe. No mention at all is made of the other two men involved who, after all came up with the idea of the escape in the first place.

On the evening of 17 July 1942, Major Ronald Bolton Littledale, 40, arrives at Oflag IVC Colditz. For two years he has been at large in Europe, alone or with others, trying to escape the German conquerors of the continent and return safely to England. Two years: enough time for the Germans to mark him down as 'troublesome', a reputation sufficient to warrant locking him away in a *Sonderlager* somewhere and throwing away the key. Hence, his darkening the doorstep at Schloss Colditz.

Littledale is different from his imprisoned fellow officers at Colditz. At 40, he is almost considered an old man; he is a professional soldier with a lot of experience abroad; as a major, he is a senior officer amid a cohort of mostly subalterns and captains. He is, therefore, an outsider, falling somewhere out of the pecking order. He is also an old Etonian. Although most of his companions in Colditz attended boarding school, not all of them went to Eton, the school considered, not least by itself, the cream of the crop. The old boys of Eton are a group in their own right, a breed apart. The pecking order is irrelevant to them. In the words of Padre Ellison Platt, the Colditz diarist, the Old Etonians eat together, walk their laps together in groups of two, three or four; they attend the same courses and lectures held within the castle walls. And go to the toilet together. They may not consciously isolate themselves from those around them but they stand apart from the rest.

Littledale settles in to one of the rooms in the senior officers' quarters in the Saalhaus. No dormitory for him. The room he occupies is shared with Billie Stephens, Major William Faithfull 'Andy' Anderson, Colonel Young and a colonel from the NZMC. This small party of senior officers not only sleep there, they eat there and spend most of their time there. Mornings begin with breakfast, usually before the first *appell*, their bread and *Ersatz* coffee provided by the Germans. The menu for the day is chalked up on large blackboards outside the kitchen, but the fare's limitations in quality is matched only by its lack of variety. Lunch usually consists of soup, often the dreaded kohlrabi. A bell rings to summon the duty orderly to collect it and he carries it over to the living quarters in a bucket and doles it out to his charges. The menu for the evening consists of bread with a notoriously inedible jam substitute made from the roughest of root vegetables, supplemented by cooked beef or pork from the Red Cross parcels. It is not a diet designed to please a palate cultivated at the Ritz or the Café Royale or even by nanny. Neither is it one that provides more than minimum nutrition, perhaps deliberately so: the last thing the Germans want at Colditz is a castle full of well-nourished prisoners.

What does Littledale think upon entering the courtyard under the *Flüsterbogen* (Whispering Arch)? '*Hier zwischen diesen dunklen Maueren, unter Wahnsinnigen und Tobsüchtigen muss ich von nun an leben!*' ('Here among these dark walls, among madmen and raving maniacs, I must live from now on!') or '*Adieu Welt!*' (Farewell World!)? Probably he silently voiced his determination not to stay too long among these madmen. This is not contradicted by the extensive collection of photographs taken at Colditz during its existence as Offizierslager IVC as shall be seen. This photographic record is a unique window into a particular period of the camp's history. The photographer was Herr Johannes Lange, who took over a photography business in the town of Colditz from his father Moritz. He was given a permit and the assignment to photograph inside and around the camp. He took the ID photographs for the prison records and was there to record the scenes of escape attempts, both successful and unsuccessful. These photographs were collected, reproduced and used as study material for Colditz staff and those of other camps.

The gallery of Lange's photographs is fascinating: English and Dutch officers parade in fake German uniforms; British and French officers show off their civilian outfits; a French officer is resplendent in women's clothes, complete with wig; strings of bed sheets hang guiltily from windows; the sculpted busts, Max and Moritz, used by Dutch prisoners to disguise absences at *appell*. Lange is right there with his camera and tripod, taking his pictures. Regularly, Oflag IV-C's security officer, Reinhold Eggers, has selections included in the weekly magazine *Das Abwehrblatt*, a publication specifically for the German staff in PoW camps, to illustrate the many and varied materials used in escape attempts. These include fake weapons; secret hiding places; false papers; counterfeit *Ausweise* complete with photos taken clandestinely or cut out from group portraits; stamps for officialdom cut from linoleum flooring. There are examples of ingenious hides like walnuts that contain tiny compasses, hollow badminton rackets hiding maps, gramophone records containing money.

In addition, Lange takes group portraits, copies of which are bought by the men to send to family and loved ones at home, if only to show that they are still alive and well. For some officers and orderlies, this is absolutely necessary: they are Jewish, and they know they could have no better place under the circumstances than among their fellow prisoners and friendly compatriots in a Wehrmacht-guarded castle in Germany. Camp life is captured and preserved in a host of black-and-white images depicting daily activities such as sports and drama, *appells* and those endless walks in the courtyard. One can see the religious exercises, processions, inspections of Red Cross parcels by the Germans, inspection of living conditions by Swiss authorities, a visit to the hairdresser, German surveillance and the arrival and departure of prisoners, all caught on film by Johannes Lange and his trusty camera in Colditz.

Remarkably, there is also contemporary colour cine film. The images are tinted grey-green now and the colours have faded, but nonetheless, these are unique images taken by German officer, Walter Lenger, during his brief sojourn in Colditz. This logistics supply officer shot his fascinating footage in late October, early November 1939, in the Castle's early days as a PoW camp when the first Polish officers were interned there. Memorabilia collector Karl Hoeffkes bought the film in 2012, and when he realised what he had, he alerted the authorities. Although the history of the camp is well documented in words and photographs, moving images of it from that time are extremely rare.

The shot-list is beguiling. Polish officers are on *appell* in the inner courtyard, the German guards impassively counting the rows; and then prisoners on their endless circumnavigation. This sequence is shot from a vantage point above the German kitchens, beginning at the spot where the delousing shed later stood, and where Littledale's escape started. Briefly, the Kommandantur flickers into view, the courtyard scene of tension and excitement for Littledale and his mates. Soldiers amble through the market place, the castle looming above them: German officers stroll nonchalantly out of the main gate (or are they Allies in fake uniforms?); others are fooling around on the bridge in front of the castle. One of them draws a pistol and pretends to threaten his colleagues, of whom one regards him haughtily, another draws a sabre and the rest look on in amusement. These are captivating glimpses of a time, a world, 80 years past.

There are no photographs of Littledale in Colditz. He is not even in the background of someone else's photo, an unintentional photo-bomb. It is the story of his life. Either by accident or design, he is a master at not standing out, the man who leaves no trace. He was definitely there: there is a portrait of him drawn by Lieutenant John Watton, one of the roguish community of Colditz artists who drew portraits of their comrades. It shows the profile of a man with a generous smile between a sharply protruding nose and chin. The print is included in *Escape from Colditz*, an omnibus edition of Pat Reid's first two books. Curiously, it also crops up in the 1970s BBC series as one of several similar portraits dotted around the British quarters. It is first seen attached to the side of a cupboard in one of the British rooms, but it takes a keen eye to spot it, as it is gone in a flash. From the French Leave episode onwards, the drawing pops up regularly. It would be nice to think that Pat Reid, as the series' consultant, paid quiet tribute to his escape buddy, personally seeing to it that he was so prominently featured.

The Posen Three are back together, albeit only for a brief time: Littledale, Mike Sinclair and Gris Davies-Scourfield. Mike has been in the 'escape proof' castle (a claim made by the Germans) since January 1942. Littledale is tired, exhausted and has had a tough time following his arrest. Gris remembers that Littledale rarely broached the subject. According to him, Littledale and Sinclair were held under extreme conditions by the Gestapo in Sofia after their arrest prior to their final transport to Colditz. Ronnie, as his friends call him, is devoutly religious, even to the point of carrying an army edition of the New Testament with him during escapes. This infuriates Mike. Imagine being caught with an English book somewhere in occupied Europe! His faith must have given Ronnie support in enduring the hardships in Sofia.

Whose idea was it, this crazy scheme? Who thought it was a good idea to cross the Kommandantur courtyard, quite literally behind the sentry's back, barely metres away? Who saw that its very madness and audacity would be the key to its phenomenal success? A wild idea, for sure, but just how wild?

In September 1942, Littledale is introduced to Lieutenant Commander William Stephens, like him, a new arrival at Colditz, and with whom he is to share a room. Stephens is captured during a commando raid on the port of St Nazaire, Operation Chariot, on 28 March 1942. This French coastal town is where the German war fleet hides when not out making the Atlantic an extremely dangerous ocean to cross. The Germans have a new battleship, the *Tirpitz*, sister ship of the infamous *Bismarck* and according to British intelligence, it could be heading for St Nazaire, the only place on the Atlantic coast with a dry dock large enough to accommodate her. Operation Chariot's mission is to destroy the dry dock's doors by packing an old destroyer, HMS *Campbeltown*, with explosives on delayed-action fuses and then ramming it into them. The fuses will detonate the explosives, set in concrete in the ship's bow, timed to go off the raiding party has made their getaway.

16 motor launches (MLs) accompany this floating battering ram on its way to knock on the dry dock doors early on the morning of 28 March. On one of these launches, ML192, Lieutenant Commander Stephens tries to add to the destruction, but the crew fails to complete its task. ML192 is hit by enemy fire amidships and Stephens gives orders to abandon ship. Everyone manages to swim to shore, but shortly afterwards they run into a German patrol and they are taken captive. Ten hours later, HMS *Campbeltown* explodes, destroying the doors. Operation Chariot is deemed a success, even though out of the 612 men who comprised the raiding party, only 228 made it back to England. Of the others, 169 were killed and 215 were taken as PoWs, one of them being Lieutenant Commander William 'Billie' Stephens.

Pat Reid describes Belfast-born Stephens thus:

[He had a] handsome blond appearance, with piercing blue eyes and a 'Nelsonian' nose. He constantly walked as if he were on the deck of a ship. He was a real daredevil, someone whose main aim seemed to be to penetrate the German part of the camp (Colditz) and then fight his way out with a metaphorical cutlass.

Stephens is the son of a shipping agent and timber importer in Northern Ireland. After attending boarding school in Shrewsbury, he joins his father's business. In 1930, he joins the Royal Naval Volunteer Reserve, and at the outbreak of war he is assigned to the Coastal Forces, part of the Royal Navy. Regarded by others as jovial, he is charismatic, impeccable, fit and alert. The photo of the man in navy uniform shows 'a perfect gentleman'.

The charismatic Stephens is initially confined in Stalag 133 near Rennes, along with some of his fellow St Nazaire raiders. Conditions are poor. Then he is taken to Wilhelmshaven to the Milag Nord PoW camp for Merchant Navy personnel, where he undergoes interrogation. From there, he visits several camps (first Marlag, a PoW camp for naval personnel in Westertimke near Bremen, then a camp still under construction in Bremervorde on 25 June 1942) before reaching Stalag VIIIB, a barracks camp in Lamsdorf in south-eastern Silesia on 24 July. Here, Billie has an encounter with a certain Sergeant David Ronald 'Ron' Steele, No. 2 Commando and fellow St Nazaire Raider. Sergeant Steele has an interesting story to tell.

A group of officers were on their way to Colditz. Breaking up the journey, they spend several days in isolation in Stalag VIIIB, Lamsdorf. One of these visitors is Lieutenant Commander Billie Stephens; another is the commander of a submarine disabled in the North Sea in 1940, Lieutenant Mike Harvey. Both of them plan to swap identities with two of the NCOs in the camp, who are quartered separately from the officers. This ruse has its origins in a clause in the Geneva Convention that allows detaining powers to employ captured other ranks in manual labour towards their war effort. This same clause protects captured officers from similar treatment. Although free from the obligation to work, officers are not able to join the work parties that regularly leave their camps in reluctant service of the 'Bohemian Corporal', and from which are much easier to escape than the camp. That is unless they can arrange an identity swap. Which is what Stephens is proposing to Steele now, as they converse discreetly at the fence dividing the officers from the other ranks. Fortunately for Billie, Steele agrees: he will take the place of Harvey, to whom he bears a resemblance. He agrees to look for someone similar to Stephens who is willing to go along.

Memory fails Steele, but he remembers that he ends up in the officers' section of the camp, and Harvey in his own section. A photograph is taken of Steele for Harvey's ID card, and for 24 hours they exchange details about each other's life stories, so they can pass for the other when questioned. Meanwhile, Lance Sergeant A. H. Dockerill (Dock) of No. 1 Commando agrees to take on the role of Billie Stephens. Steele cannot remember why, but Dock did not make the switch with the officer with the piercing blue eyes. While Harvey has the chance to get out and away, Stephens has to stay behind.

But Lamsdorf turned out to be just a temporary stop. They are soon en route again. Travelling with the officers on their way to Colditz as

Harvey, Steele ensures his own admission to the infamous castle. Meanwhile, Stephens, clad in a plain-buttoned RAF jacket and a cap without insignia, gets away from the train as soon as it arrives at Colditz Station, thanks to a diversionary manoeuvre, when night has fallen. Steele has to be content with walking up the steep hill to the castle looming above. Here, he is initiated into its strange and esoteric ways. A German doctor examines the newly arrived batch of prisoners, and decides they need an application of strong disinfectant to kill off the infestations of lice or other unwelcome visitors he is sure the new-arrivals have brought with them. His assistant produces a brush and a bucket containing a purple liquid with which the doctor promptly daubs their testicles! A good, liberally applied dose. The other prisoners roar with laughter: the doctor is revealed to be none other than Howard Gee, a civilian prisoner in the castle, speaker excellent German and a dab hand with a brush and a bucket of purple dye. Harvey was lucky to be spared this misery when he too ends up in Colditz.

On 3 September 1942, the day after he got away from Colditz station, Stephens is caught and is confined to solitary for a week back at the Castle. He is not the only Operation Charioteer who finds his way here. Men like Michael 'Micky' Burn and Corran Purdon also make the journey from St Nazaire to Colditz. Only dozens of metres away from Stephens, separated by thick walls, sleeps a British gentleman, under a sack of donkey food, as a mattress made of straw is called. A British gentleman with whom, not long afterwards, he embarks on an attempt to permanently leave the depressing fortress they have both ended up in.

In a private account, Stephens characterises the roommate he quickly befriends:

> Like me, Ronnie Littledale had only recently arrived in Colditz, after a remarkable escape career, during which he had travelled through almost every country in Europe without having that little bit of luck that could have got him across the border to a neutral country. He was an exceptional personality in every respect. He had gone through a very difficult time, both during the time he was on the run and when he was recaptured by the Germans. When I met him, he was very thin, looking tired and jaded. Despite all he had had to endure, he never lost the courage

to escape. Escape was his only thought and it dominated his entire life. He thought about it all day and I'm sure he dreamt about it at night.

That little bit of luck, Stephens calls it. He elaborates further: '100% Luck isn't good enough. You have to have the Devil's luck as well.' Imagine that, a devout Christian like Littledale with the Devil's luck!

Pat Reid also remembers Littledale:

Ronnie was of a strange sort on this planet. There was no flaw or gap in his character. Silent and even shy in his dealings but firm in his opinions. He was very thin, too thin. He had had a hard time, and looked a bit older than his real age. His hair was thinning on the forehead, and a sharp nose pointed to a narrow, sharply drawn chin. This complemented the image of an ascetic personality, which in fact he was. He would never have admitted it. His gentle side and watchful sense of humour belied his tight self-discipline and stubborn determination.

Under guard, Littledale and Sinclair were en route to Prague from Sofia when they tried to escape by jumping off the train. Sinclair was caught and was eventually taken on to Colditz, but Littledale got away. Months later, he was re-arrested. According to Reid, it was after this second arrest in Czechoslovakia that Littledale was 'put through the mill and tortured'. However, there seems to be little or no corroborating evidence to support this, certainly not from Littledale himself. The Gestapo, not known for the sensitivity in the way they interacted their detainees, nonetheless are said to have treated him correctly.

As his fellow officers experience him, Sinclair belies Donne's assertion that no man is an island. His secrets are clutched tightly, his friendships conducted from a distance, his counsel and company generally reserved for himself. He is driven by a desire to cause the Germans as much personal harm as possible. This he regards as his sworn duty: his own safety is second to this. This singularity of mind leaves him with few friends and his company not easy to keep. Universally admired and respected for his determination and abilities, no-one thinks about talking the small stuff with Mike Sinclair. A fellow inmate, Mike Edwards says of him: 'For Mike, there was God, then the

60th, and that was it. His only goal in life was to return to his regiment.' Pat Ferguson, a young lieutenant in the Royal Tank Regiment, notes:

> The few times I spoke to him in the courtyard of Colditz, his only desire was to get out of the castle and kill as many Germans as possible. He seemed to be on a personal crusade against the entire Hitler occupied continent.

According to Ferguson, Sinclair's determination stemmed mainly from the experiences he had with the Gestapo in Poland. The family with whom he had been in hiding in Warsaw was sent to Auschwitz, and did not survive the war.

'God, the regiment and nothing else': that also describes Littledale. Like peas in a pod, those two.

Only the men who spent time there can truly confirm or deny what conditions were like at Colditz. The picture that emerges from literature, film and television is that of a boarding school, where bullying the Germans (goon baiting) is the main activity, alongside trying to get out. The narrative rarely deviates from this party-line, to dwell upon the negative aspects of spending unwilling years in a medieval castle with more guards than prisoners. About how cold the winters are; how inadequate the food supply; the experience of being deprived of news from home or from the war outside the castle; what it is like being cooped up with the same people, day after day, year after year, people one would not necessarily choose to spend ten minutes with, let alone five years. Prisoners walking the tightrope between sanity and madness, endlessly waiting to be repatriated.

Jack Champ, one of the 20 Australian officers in Colditz, witnesses one of the men on *appell*, completely out of control, screaming desperately to be shot. The prisoners are tormented by the sheer boredom of the place so any and every form of activity is seized upon to stay healthy in mind, body and spirit. Sports, drama, reading, painting fill the day, all pursuits of the middle and upper-middle classes, a background most of the officers share. There is always someone happy to lecture about unusual experiences or specialized subjects. Then there are the courses. With Polish, Dutch, English and French officers in residence, the Colditz School of Languages offers plenty of opportunities to broaden one's linguistic horizons. Other subjects are on offer too. There are even men like Micky Burn, who does a correspondence course in Social Sciences from Oxford University. Some choose to use their abundance of time to write. Burn's book, entitled *Yes, Farewell*, is about a castle where PoWs are locked up, and will be published after the war. There are several card schools in the camp, some of them playing for serious stakes. Losses incurred in the castle and settled after the war ensure most of the practitioners of this thinking sport will not touch cards in combat again in peacetime.

One activity, however, occupies many, while dreaming in their beds or while beating the bounds around the courtyard: Escape. Many dream, but only a few take action. Everyone in Colditz is there for a reason: some because they have already escaped from another camp, or some because they are considered *Deutschfeindlich* (Enemies of Germany or Germans). Everyone has something to bring to the escape table, everyone can play a role if they choose: keeping lookout or taking observations (stooging), forging documents, making civilian outfits or fake German uniforms, or even participating in escapes. One of the biggest mistakes the Germans made concerning their PoW containment policy was the bringing together of all this expertise in one place. Littledale could not have found a better place if he'd tried.

One day, during a walk to the exercise park, at the foot of the castle, Stephens and Littledale are struck by an idea. There are two courtyards in the castle: one for the use of the prisoners, where they can get some fresh air, play volleyball or simply stroll around; the other is where the German Kommandantur is located. Between them is The Seam, running down the south side of the prisoners' area and the north side of the German area. It is enclosed on the ground floor on the PoW side by the *Evidenz Zimmer* (Interview Room) and the PoW Kitchen, where German cooks and British orderlies prepared and cooked for the officers and it is this building from whence came the muse that inspired Littledale and Stephens. On the German side, which was lower than the PoW courtyard, there were a number of similarly makeshift and badly constructed buildings.

Every escape starts with a question or a theory: What if, or, we should be able to. In this case, the theory is that it should be possible to get from one courtyard to the other through these kitchens. Stephens thinks it is crazy, sheer lunacy, and the more he considers it, the madder it seems. Ronnie, though, sees this as a strength: he is convinced that the guards would never think anyone would dare try anything so obviously insane.

Although The Posen Three are reunited, know they are a great team and are desperate to escape, they decide not to work together this time. They are too well known to the authorities and too familiar together. Maybe they will have better luck apart. So Ronnie will make the attempt with Billie. According to Pat Reid, Littledale and Stephens' plan has 'grown a beard': Ronnie and Billie were not the first to have thought of this scheme or something similar. He himself had always considered it to be the very last resort of last resorts: not to be tried until absolutely all other possibilities have been exhausted.

By April 1942, Reid has been Escape Officer for two years. He wanted to get out as much as anyone, and as Escape Officer, he played a part in every British escape attempted so far. But it was a position of trust: his role as arbiter and advisor to the escapes of others meant he was unable to escape himself. If he wanted to get out, he had to resign his position. This he did in April 1942, handing over to Captain Richard (Dick) Howe.

Ahead of the escape, a meeting is called for the Escape Committee to give the go-ahead. This is given, but it is suggested that the original team of Littledale and Stephens is expanded to include Pat Reid because of his merits as a locksmith and also because Dick will feel happier if Pat goes, 'to make sure they don't get into any trouble'. If there is a third, there will need to be a fourth, to make up two groups of two. This is an important consideration. Travelling alone across Germany as an escaping PoW is an extremely difficult prospect. Going with someone else gives you companionship in a strange and hostile land, a different perspective in situations and a source of skills to complement your own. After some thought, Reid chose to escape with Hank Wardle.

Canadian Howard Douglas (Hank) Wardle from Ontario is an accountant by pre-war profession. But when it looks like war is inevitable, he goes to England with two friends to join up and do his proverbial bit. They joined the RAF and Hank was the only one of the trio to get his coveted RAF 'Wings' insignia, denoting that he is a qualified pilot. In November 1939, he is attached to No. 98 (Bomber) Squadron at Hucknall, where he flies the Fairey Battle. On 29 November, he is transferred to No. 218 (Bomber) Squadron along with observer, Sergeant Edward Davidson, and air gunner, Aircraftman First Class Albert Bailey, commanded by Wing

Commander Duggan. Stationed at Auberive-sur-la-Marne in France, Hank flew reconnaissance flights, until it all went wrong. It is 20 April 1940, Hitler's birthday, and he receives a present he never knows he's got. One of his enemies gets into trouble with his plane and, once on the ground, is made PoW of the Third Reich by a German soldier on a bicycle.

How this calamity occurs is a bit of mystery. Hank and his crew bail out of their airplane, which has inexplicably and inconveniently caught fire, and may have been hit during one of the first night's air battles. All three get out, but only Hank lands safely, the other two are tragically killed. Once he is back on *terra firma* and before he can do anything else, Hank finds himself the captive of a bicycle-riding German soldier. He is taken to Crailsheim, an hour away, and lodged at a Luftwaffe base. After interrogation and a three-day stay in the hospital of a *Durchgangslager* (transit camp), his intended destination is Oflag IXA in Spangenberg, in a castle in Hesse, built on top of a mountain surrounded by a moat. He is ensconced there from May to August 1940, when he escapes. After being recaptured, back he goes to Spangenberg until November of that year when he is sent to Oflag IV-C Colditz, where he is the first to try to escape. He is out for 24 hours until he was reclaimed by his new carers, who promptly give him a severe beating. He ends up with an injured leg and has to walk with a stick. As further discouragement, a rifle butt to the side of his head renders him partially deaf.

Much later, during his debrief with MI9, he confirms that the mad scheme to get out through the Kommandantur was Littledale and Stephens' idea: he and Pat are merely the ones chosen to participate as the second pair.

Near where the delousing shed once stood is the window through which Littledale, Reid, Stephens and Wardle climb into the prisoners' kitchen. The window sill extends to chest height, there was a sentry plodding his beat nearby: that the four escapers proposed to leap up on to the sill and climb through the window while the sentry could turn round at any time and catch them is only the first audacious episode in an entire saga of audacity. The most difficult stretch, breaking out of the castle itself and the journey through Germany, lies still ahead of them. That they pulled it off is incredible.

The kitchen is strictly off limits to officers, but the orderlies, engaged like butlers in a stately home to look after the Allied officers, have ready access. Chief among them is Sidney 'Solly' Goldman, a 23-year-old, London-born fusilier. Solly is an extraordinary character. He has worked his way up to Chief Orderly in the kitchen and carries out his duties alongside a German NCO. He is particularly devoted to the Senior British Officer, Colonel Guy German, to whom he serves coffee every morning after shuffling across the courtyard clutching his jug of hot, brown liquid, his wooden clogs clack-clack-clacking on the cobblestones and echoing around the *hof*. That Solly is in Colditz is already remarkable, but by no means strange. He is Jewish, one of about 100 British, Dutch, French and Polish Jewish prisoners who are incarcerated in Colditz Castle. Within the walls of the castle, he is relatively safe, despite a degree of mistreatment and despite the horrors being visited upon Jews elsewhere in the Third Reich.

When Littledale and Stephens present their plan to Dick Howe, the new Escape Officer, it is obvious to him that they have not done any reconnaissance of the German kitchen, their jumping off point. Dick teams up with Solly to carry out a quick inspection when the kitchen is empty, ahead of the escape, having already made counterfeit cruciform keys to open the locked doors. According to Solly, the best time is between two and three in the afternoon, when there are no Germans about. Once inside, both men survey the place carefully. Dick suddenly enters a small office and finds a German there, fast asleep sitting at the desk. Shocked, he immediately makes to leave, but Solly says, 'No, watch this.' He roars out '*Achtung!*' at the top of his voice; Dick nearly jumps out of his skin, and the somnolent German must have had conniptions. Solly gives the startled and sleep-deprived soldier a lecture: what would Hitler think if he knew one of his most trusted guards falls asleep on duty! The German is furious, and while Solly calms him down, Dick takes advantage of the confusion to run off as fast as he can. The reconnaissance is successful, and Pat Reid can start getting things together.

Littledale and Stephens assume the identities of French workers and they need to arrange suitable clothing and fake papers that reflect their assumed circumstances. Their cover stories are that they are on leave, travelling by train to visit home. Stephens travels under the name Jean Bardet, a French electrical engineer for the Leipzig-based I. G. Farben factory. He carries an *Urlaubschein*, a leave pass, and a *Dienstausweis*, an employee's identification card complete with photograph, stamps and swastika, issued in Leipzig on 28 March 1942, a snappy reference to the date of Operation Chariot. Reid travels as Jan de Ridder, a concrete worker from Diegem in Brabant, also working for I. G. Farben. These disguises as foreign workers ensure they will not easily stand out. There were thousands of foreign civilians working in Germany while Germans themselves are at the front.

Acquiring suitable clothing is no small task. Each officer in the camp is only allowed to own one tunic. Reid has got a dark blue overcoat acquired through a Frenchman who, helped by a French orderly, gets clothes in the village. The cut reminds him of the German fashion of 1912. Underneath, he wears a fawn wind-cheater, which he has successfully kept hidden for over a year. His trousers started life as part of the RAF uniform, but alterations and adjustments have given them a fresh purpose. While all these preparations are being made, Stephens tells Littledale that it is common for train passengers to shout 'Heil Hitler' and give the customary salute when they get on or off. Ronnie says that while he does not mind sticking his arm out if he has to, he is 'buggered!' if he's saying THAT!

The cluttered little buildings in the castle's southern courtyard no longer exist. Neither do the hastily bricked buildings in the PoWs' courtyard. If historical importance alone kept things standing, they would all still be here, but it does not: they were demolished after the war. Gone too are the days when German guards stood at roll call here, or paraded under the supervision of Stabsfeldwebel Rothenberger with his striking Franz Josef moustache. A photograph taken by a US reconnaissance plane in April 1945 shows the vague outline of a shed (used for storing coal) standing in the middle of the square, with an area of burgeoning vegetation behind. These landmarks of history, so significant in October 1942, have been replaced by an anonymous, bare, sloping path with steps leading to the entrance of the present youth hotel, the old German Kommandantur building.

But in 1942, the buildings, the bushes and the shadows in the courtyard are still there, about to play their role in this drama, as Littledale and his mates lurk inside the kitchen, waiting, waiting for the coast to clear so they can emerge undetected into the Kommandantur. Over several nights, at a cross-barred window overlooking the German courtyard, Pat Reid has worked on one of the rivets connecting two crossed bars together where they meet. He saws away at the head so that on the night of the breakout, the rivet can be extracted so Pat can bend the bars back to make a hole big enough for everyone to climb through the window and out onto the roof of one of the little German buildings below.

Geology plays its part too. The renegades enter the kitchen on the PoW side through a window about chest high up from the ground. They cross the level kitchen floor to the opposite side where their bolthole window awaits them, and look out on to a flat roof beneath them, some three-and-a-half metres above the ground on the German side. How is this so? The rock formation on which the castle is built explains this strange phenomenon. It slopes down from the chapel in the north towards the dry moat in the south, meaning that the German courtyard is several metres below the Prisoners' courtyard.

The men are at the window overlooking the German courtyard, opposite where they came in, hiding in the shadows. It is time to go; Reid first, then Wardle, out of the window then down on to the flat roof below (a boiler house, according to Littledale). Littledale and Stephens will follow once Reid and Wardle had crossed the sentry's path. Slowly, quietly and in full view of nearly every window in the German Kommandantur, Reid inches down, away from safety, but towards safety. Powerful floodlights illuminate the wall, like it was a backdrop to a stage scene. But no-one was looking. Reid was astounded: doesn't anyone look out of windows at night anymore, he asks himself. Finally, he reaches the roof where he finds some shade about half way along behind the top of a ventilator. Hank is close behind. Both of them are brandishing suitcases. Suitcases! Pat insisted. An encumbrance while trying to get out of the castle for sure, but once on their way, an invaluable part of their disguises. Below them, sentries solemnly plod their beat on the slippery cobbles.

No less than the PoWs' courtyard, the German space is a hive of activity by day. There are sentry boxes, distinctively striped black, white and red and with their intended occupants never too far away; wire fences are erected, taken down, erected elsewhere. Some of these sights are recorded by prisoners like Major William Anderson: a talented artist, he has left several versions of the view from his window, each one different in some subtle way, each one the same in its basic elements. It was a view shared by his two room-mates, Littledale and Stephens.

The German courtyard has two exits, or entrances, depending on one's destination. The main gate is under the bell tower and is where Airey Neave and Tony Luteijn walked out of the castle in their fake

German uniforms in January 1942. On the east side of the square is a large arched opening to a covered passageway under the buildings that eventually leads to the park where the prisoners take their exercise. Both of these exits are guarded 24 hours a day. But Littledale and his companions, dressed as they are in civilian clothes, have another exit in mind. They have focused on a door in a building next to the bell tower. This door (the entrance to a carpentry workshop according to a later statement by Littledale) is significant: it leads to an attic with windows overlooking the dry moat and is a tried and tested way out. A month earlier, a small British RAF officer, Dominic Bruce, was smuggled here in a tea chest, and climbed out of a window using bed sheets tied together in the classic manner. It is not until he is in the ports of Danzig that he is arrested. Pat Reid, the lockpicker, is along to open this door.

The next stage, getting past the guards unseen and across the courtyard, is the hardest part of this venture. The escapees cannot see the sentry whose path they need to cross. To do it, they will need a signalling system. Littledale's idea that the guards will not think of such the brutal venture the four escapers have in mind, and that their attention is therefore slackened, may be reasonable, but if they hear anything at all when the four cross the cobbled square, the attempt will fail. Above the kitchen, to the left are the senior officers' rooms in the gable end of the Saalhaus, from which the entire German courtyard can be seen, along with everything in it. In one of these rooms, a musical ensemble has gathered and is practicing diligently, under the watchful gaze of their conductor, as they have done for several nights, so as not to raise suspicions. The mini-orchestra serves a purpose. When the conductor sees that the sentry has his back turned and it is safe to cross, they stop playing. One at a time, the renegades can cross the courtyard safely to the shed and bushes on the other side. But they have to wait for the signal each time.

The conductor has an important part to play: the escapers are relying on him to keep alert to the sentry's movements and signal at the right time. They need someone whose reputation is beyond reproach: a go-to kind of guy. So who better than Douglas Bader to oversee events from the window. The famous RAF pilot may be missing both legs, but he is doing his bit for the escape attempt.

The music has been playing for some time. Reid and Wardle are ready to go. Then the music stops. Reid is just about to take off on his run across the sentry's path when it starts back up again. Reid darts back. The music stops, starts, then stops again, this time with an air of finality. Voices can be heard, then silence. They are on their own. What has gone wrong they do not know, but right now, they have a problem. Hours of waiting pass before Reid and Wardle finally make an attempt and cross over, less than ten metres behind the back of the sentry walking away from them. They hide directly behind the shed and among the shrubs.

It is time for Littledale and Stephens to get into action. They lower themselves down to the roof with their suitcases, making so much noise that Reid is amazed the guard did not hear them. Littledale thought he was probably thinking about his girlfriend.

The sounds of the night determine the men's actions. They are sheltering in a pit just below the Kommandantur's steps, and any strange noise they make could mean they will soon be standing with their hands in the air. In the shadows of the buildings, Reid creeps silently to the door leading through to the attic. Just as Reid is working on the lock, he hears Hauptmann Paul Priem, the security officer born in Posen and one of the few Germans the British consider to have a sense of humour. Priem has a habit of turning up when it is least convenient. Reid stops fiddling with the lock and quickly returns to the pit. Once Priem has left the scene, Reid goes back to the door and tries for another hour to get the thing open, but without luck. They cannot get in, they will have to think of something else.

Further into the pit and through a small, unlocked door, the men find a cellar, built under the Kommandantur building. Right at the end, they see a flue that slopes up to an opening to the outside. It is a squeeze though, through which a 'pygmy could not yet pass', according to Reid, 90 cm wide and 22 cm high, but it is the only way out. Reid will manage, and for once, Littledale will benefit from his slim physique. Hank and Bill, though, with their size and height, will find it much more of a struggle. Reid has to partially undress before he gets through, with his suitcase, head first and on his back. Hank and Billie are next, helped through by Pat on the outside and Ronnie pushing from the rear. Littledale is last, helped by someone hauling him through from the outside. Still, it takes him ten minutes to emerge on to the terracing above the dry moat.

It is half past three in the night. Using sheet rope, braided like cords, they carefully and silently descend the three-tier terrace. A German

Shepherd dog, one of the camp's *schnuffelhunden* (sniffer dogs), barks furiously twice, but as with the racket Ronnie and Billie made when clambering over the roof earlier, the nearby German guards seem not to hear a thing. Given the outcome, is this the difference in luck that separates Littledale from his friend Sinclair? The Devil's luck.

The diarist Padre Ellison Platt reports that Wednesday, 14 October 1942 was 'A very quiet but busy day. An intense, exciting evening.' Captain Platt, a Methodist chaplain who chose during the Battle of Dunkirk to stay with his wounded men and go into captivity with them, keeps a diary during his four-and-a-half-years in Colditz, but has to be discreet about what is so 'exciting' that day, as his diary is subject to German censorship. The next morning, ten men turn out to be missing from *appell*. The Germans count and re-count, but it still comes back, ten men short. Captain Priem is convinced that the ten men are hiding somewhere in the castle. That is quite possible given that there are 700-plus-rooms in the PoWs' side alone. After much deliberation, it becomes clear who the prodigal sons are. That much established, the prisoners are kept in the chapel while the Germans are busy looking for their lost property. One of the rascals among them short circuits the lighting in the British section to cause further inconvenience. Six of the ten prodigals are eventually revealed to have never left home at all, but the others have definitely flown away.

It is the schnuffelhunden who reveal how the refugees got out of the castle; it is the German guards who strenuously deny that it happened like that. Meanwhile, Security Officer Reinhold Eggers is on his way back from a meeting in Dresden on 15 October and extensive checks on the train lead him to suspect that something is amiss at the castle. Sure enough, four officers are absent. The sniffer dogs do their work, and show particular interest in the southern area of the Kommandantur. Footsteps are discovered in flower beds, and the sheet rope the four escapers used to descend into the dry moat has been found.

Diary-keeping is not confined to the prisoners: German guard Georg Martin Schaedlich, nicknamed 'The Ferret', also confides in a journal. He reports that:

> A woman found four fitted sheets in the park, which were obviously from the castle. After it is revealed during the Appell that four men are missing, a search is carried out for hours to

find where these four men broke out, but nothing is found.

What is found, however, are English sweet wrappers in the cellar where the four found their exit. A bent bar in the opening at the top is more tangible evidence. The only logical conclusion is that the escapers somehow walked across the courtyard, unseen, in the full glare of the floodlights and under the watchful eye of German guards! No wonder this theory is dismissed as ridiculous. The sweets were probably eaten by a guard who got them from one of the prisoners. According to Reid, the only trace they left were several pieces of cardboard cut into particular shapes, that convey a message to Dick Howe, the Escape Officer, telling him how they got out on to the terrace and down to the moat. Other than that, Pat says, they left nothing.

On 15 October 1942, at the bottom of the walls of the mighty castle shrouded in the bright glow of the floodlights, there are handshakes as Reid and Wardle say goodbye to Littledale and Stephens. Just over 30 years later, on 14 February 1973, Pat Reid, now a retired major, and Reinhold Eggers met again. This was for the filming of the Thames Television episode of *This is Your Life* which focused on Reid's life. Together, they share memories of that particular night back in October 1942, when they were each other's friends, the enemy. Amicably, the former enemies shake hands.

In October, 1942, four men manage to escape from the castle specifically set up to stop them, that was set aside to keep seasoned escapers and *Deutschfeindliche* within its walls; that boasted more guards than prisoners. These same four men successfully run across a floodlit square, dodge behind German sentries, spend an hour or more fiddling with a door that won't open, and finally end up outside the castle by crawling through a hole in the wall of a potato cellar and down some high terraces, leaving only 650 km between them and freedom in Switzerland? How is this possible? Is it indeed 'the devils luck' as one of them said?

Shortly before a remarkable event in the history of Oflag IV-C takes place that may have influenced the perceptiveness, or lack of it, of the guards. On 13 October 1942, the day before the four officers got out, SS troops enter the castle to pick up an important consignment. Under heavy guard, seven British commandos are collected in two groups to be taken to Berlin for interrogation at the *Reichssicherheitshauptamt* (Security Service Main Office) by Heinrich Müller, head of the

Gestapo. After interrogations that are, indubitably, not gentle, commanding officers, Captains Graeme Black and Joseph Houghton, along with Privates Miller Smith, William Chudley, Reginald Makeham, Cyril Abram and Eric Curtis, end up in Sachsenhausen concentration camp. On Friday 23 October, just before dawn, the seven men are executed with a shot in the back of the neck. They have the dubious honour of being the first victims of the *Kommandobefehl* (Commando Order). In a concerted effort to punish attacks on his empire, Hitler declares this Befehl on 18 October 1942:

> Henceforth, in so-called commando operations in Europe or Africa, all opponents of the German troops—even if, judging from their appearance, they are uniformed and armed or unarmed soldiers or extermination forces—must be killed to the last man. And this regardless of whether they are soldiers fighting or fleeing.

The story of these Commandos begins on the Orkney Islands. Captain Graeme Delamere Black, a Canadian from Ontario, born in 1911 in Dresden, and Captain Joseph 'Joe' Blundell Houghton, also born in 1911, are part of No. 2 Commando stationed in Ayr, a town in Scotland some 70 km south-west of Glasgow, in the summer of 1942. With eight other men, those named above and Lance Sergeant Richard O'Brien, Guardsman John Fairclough and Private Fred Trigg, along with two Norwegians, Erling Djupdraet and Sverre Granlund, a commando raid, Operation Musketoon is set in motion. The objective is to sabotage a hydropower plant in Glomfjord, Norway, vital to supply power to a nearby aluminium factory.

Raids like this are mere pinpricks. A way for Churchill to test his country's own power to strike, to test his opponent and above all to fight back in a war, which so far has been disastrous for Britain. The Germans, though, do not care, whatever these raids achieve has no bearing on the direction the war is taking. Equally, the men engaged in this mission are extremely motivated as they set off from Orkney on 11 September, in a French submarine named *Junon*, heading for the dark Norwegian fjord coast. Their submarine closely resembles its German sisters and is excellent camouflage for when the men are deployed four days later in the dark on a rubber boat. At nine o'clock at night, they land in Bjaerangsfjord south of Glomfjord. Their first attempt to get into action fails on 17 September when they discover a boat in the fjord and are worried their cover is blown. After a while, with the weather deteriorating and supplies beginning to run low, Black decides that they have delayed long enough. The group splits off into two and plant explosives around the pipes and in the engine room of the power plant. Although both groups manage to get out, they are not so lucky in getting away, despite their frantic attempts. Seven of them are captured, trying to escape to neutral Sweden. They are probably unaware that their action has been extremely successful. When the explosives go off, they cause enough damage to the power station that it cannot be used for the rest of the war.

From prisons in Trondheim and Oslo, the heavily guarded party is put on the SS *Danube*, on 2 October, chained and bound for Aalborg in Denmark. Then via Flensburg, they end up in Lübeck where they are handed over to a General Westoff. After a long train journey, they arrive in Colditz on the evening of 7 October, still under heavy guard. The next morning, they are photographed by Johannes Lange, posing next to the guard house, against the wall close to the entrance of the courtyard where Littledale and the others make their daily rounds. Only a wooden door separates the two groups of prisoners. Direct contact between the PoWs and the commandos is out of the question, but messages are exchanged. Ultimately, MI9 is informed of the presence of the commandos in the castle via coded letter. Glaesche, the camp Kommandant, at is not happy about his unexpected guests. Extra measures need to be taken, over and above what they do already, to ensure they do not escape. After all, they have good reason to do so: although they do not know why they have been sent to Colditz, they already know what their fate is to be. Captains Black and Houghton are taken to the cells in the village. Houghton is wounded during his arrest and has his right arm in a sling. A photograph shows him in front of the town goal. He is wearing the grin of someone who values communal gain over personal loss. Black, the leader of the raid, looks impassively into the lens. He too knows what he and his men have accomplished. But also what is to come.

Colonel Glaesche, meanwhile, must have been relieved when the commandos and the SS at last take their procession elsewhere on 13 October. Guarding the usual crowd of reprobates, who keep trying to escape, is tough enough, they could do without the extra burden. So at that moment, therefore, is there a collective shrug of the shoulders, a sudden lack of urgency among the castle guards, a relaxation of vigilance that turns into negligence? Is this the last bit of 'devil's luck' Stephens talks about? The escape of Reid, Wardle, Stephens and Littledale is planned for the next day. In the false calm that has returned between the high walls of Colditz Castle, the four lie down for the last time on their straw mattresses for a restless night. They think of only one thing: tomorrow is the day, when their leap to freedom will begin.

After their handshake just outside of the castle, the two groups go their separate ways and the long journey to Switzerland begins. The route Stephens and Littledale take leads them over Rochlitz, south of Colditz. They travel on foot and it takes three and a half hours to get there. They have some food in their suitcases: Billie has corned beef and tinned cheese. Ronnie insisted on taking English sugar from his Red Cross parcels convinced it is indistinguishable from the German variety. They move through hostile territory, it is not only soldiers and policemen who are the enemy, the general population are not their friends either. Half an hour in Rochlitz, then there's a train to Chemnitz, and after that, another one to Nuremberg. They are questioned by the railway police but their fake papers and cover stories work their magic and they get through. That afternoon, they wander around Hof to pass the time and drink beer in the station restaurant, the train to Nuremberg does not leave until 7.30 pm. In Nuremberg, the two spend the night in a restaurant.

On the morning of 16th, they arrive in Stuttgart where they catch yet another train, this time to Tuttlingen, travelling through a motley collection of towns and suburbs like Esslingen, Plockingen, Reutlingen and Tubingen. They even travel on an electric train at one point.

The word is out. The hunters are on the trail. The *Reichskriminalpolizeiamt* releases a special issue of the *Deutsches Kriminalpolizeiblatt* on 16 October. Issue Number 4409a of the 15th volume announces the escape of PoWs from 'Lager Colditz in Saxony'. The direction in which they are traveling, as well as what they are wearing, are not known. But they do have photographs and additionally, their names, rank, places of birth, or just country in the case of Patrik (sic!) Reid (Indien), prisoner number, previous camps, their height, stature, hair and eye colour are given in detail. Prisoner number 811, petite, with dark blonde hair and blue eyes looks at the camera when he was still a prisoner of Stalag XXID, Posen. It is

Littledale, who like the others must be tracked down and detained, and all possible means must be used to prevent his crossing the border. The birds have flown and from today, this poster will be displayed at all police stations, and manpower will be engaged to hunt them down.

Littledale and Stephens have gone well out of their way; it would have made more sense to travel directly from Stuttgart to the Swiss border, but a Polish officer in Colditz told them that this route is heavily guarded. They arrive in Tuttlingen at 10.30 pm and have to spend the night in a nearby forest after taking a wrong turn. 6 km out of Tuttlingen, they are forced to spend the night under sky and foliage.

October 17. They walk to Immendingen using a small map of the area and a compass manufactured in Colditz. They stay until darkness has fallen and then continue south to Engen. Other than an occasional hunter shooting at rooks, and a harmless terrier, they encounter neither man nor beast that could threaten them or betray them to the authorities. Again, they elect to stay until nightfall, when they are once more on their way. They cross several fields that run parallel to a railway line, and it is midnight when they finally get close to Singen. They are passing a bridge when a sentry stops them. It is late to be out, he is suspicious. Once again, their fake papers pass muster, and the excuse that they are trying to get to the train station and have lost their way is enough to convince the sentry to send them on their way. They are lucky: another time, another companion, it could have been so different.

Their relief is doubled when they finally locate the forest they are looking out for on the Helsingen to Singen road. This will take them directly over the border. Not far now. But then, they realise they have gone wrong somewhere. But where? Time to stop and try and figure this out once and for all. Which way?

The moon has gone, along with its revealing glow. It is dark, pitch black in fact, in the midst of all these trees. The forest wraps them in its cloak, drawing them on, rendering them invisible as they carefully pick their way through its eastern edge, their path forward revealing itself as they go.

It is now morning, three o'clock, it is 20 October 1942 and at last, they cross the border and are in Switzerland, near Ramsen. Thanks to the quality of their forged documents and the naivety of a border guard, they are free. They have made it, 24 hours after Reid and Wardle.

Meanwhile, back in Saxony, on 9 November, Padre Platt reports that news is slowly trickling through that Hank, Pat, Billie and Ronnie have reached Switzerland. It took them four days after their escape from the castle and they have joined Hedley 'Bill' Fowler, who escaped from Colditz in September along with Dutch officer Damiaen van Doorninck. The names of the four new home runners can now be added to the List of Honour that hangs in one of their rooms.

When daylight breaks, Stephens and Littledale hand themselves in to the police in Ramsen. They are taken to Schaffhausen where they spend the night in a hotel. Someone approaches Littledale, a man saying he is a journalist and he wants to know how Ronnie got across the border. Before Ronnie can answer, the hotel manager takes him aside and tells him not to say anything. This man cannot be trusted. The hotel manager thinks so and so do the police.

On 21 October, they are taken to the Military Barracks in Bern. An official from the Swiss General Staff asks them a few things about military affairs in Germany and then they are taken to the British Embassy. Littledale stays with the military attaché for ten days, and then in a hotel.

The Swiss enclave of Colditz escapers is growing. Around Christmas 1942, Fowler and Littledale's group are joined by Don 'Tubby' Lister and Walter 'Wally' Hammond, two Royal Naval petty officers sent to Colditz before convincing the Kommandant that they did not belong there because they are not commissioned officers. They are two submariners, engine room mechanics: Hammond on HMS *Shark* and Lister on HMS *Seal*. In 1940, they are captured and sent to a PoW camp. After escaping alongside some naval officers, they are re-captured and sent to Colditz on 1 September 1942. Initially, the Germans informed Wally and Tubby that seeing as they escaped with officers, they could now live with officers. They put their time at Colditz to good use, learning the intricacies of the Colditz escape method. In return, they happily share their mechanical expertise with their new colleagues. For instance, Hammond designed and made a tool that enabled rivets to be silently withdrawn from window bars. Pat Reid uses this tool in his escape from the kitchen onto the storeroom roof in the Kommandantur.

When Lister and Hammond figure out that it should be easier for them to escape from a troops camp, where guards outnumbered prisoners, they decide to make a formal complaint to the Germans in the hope of getting themselves moved. They claim that their imprisonment in Colditz is unjust on the grounds that they are not officers, they are petty officers, NCOs. Their complaint is accepted and the two men transfer to a camp near Lamsdorf. It does not take long for their Colditz escape education to be put to good use. They join a work party and get away fairly quickly. On 19 December 1942, they are free in Switzerland after a riotous journey through Germany.

After the excitement of their escapes and travels, things settle down. The ex-Colditzers throw a reunion party that will be long remembered by the participants. Switzerland offers freedom, but not constancy: they rarely stay very long in one place: Montreux, Wengen and Saanemoser in the Bernese Oberland, they call all these places home. They take the opportunity of relatively deserted mountains slopes to learn to ski, first on Kleine Scheidegg and later on Hornbeg. A couple of months of rest and restoration and the men have largely regained condition, feeling much more like their former selves. They could have remained in this island of calm while the turbulent sea of war churned around them. But only one of them did. One man clearly felt the call to elsewhere, Ronald Bolton Littledale.

15

SWITZERLAND

Back in Colditz, Rupert Barry gets a postcard from Lucerne, dated 23 November 1942 with Mount Pilatus in the background. He reads the following:

> This is to wish you and all your friends a very happy Christmas and all the luck in the world for the New Year, You've no idea how sorry we are that you are not with us. Things are moving fast these days. Give our dear love to your friend Dick. We are having a holiday here. Love from Harriot & Phyllis Murgatroyd.

Barry knows immediately the card is from Pat Reid, and it is telling him that he and Wardle have arrived safely in Switzerland! The H and P are written in bold letters signifying Hank and Pat. He recognises Hank's nickname, Murgatroyd, and the greetings for Dick are of course meant for Dick Howe, the new Escape Officer.

The very moment Littledale, Stephens, Wardle and Reid slip from behind the delousing shed in the courtyard into the German kitchen on their way to freedom, they know which route they will take to Switzerland and how they will cross the border. One year earlier, two Dutchmen also entered the neutral Alpine country using this very particular route. Hans Larive and Francis Steinmetz crossed over to Switzerland near the southern German town of Singen. Curiously, there is a salient in the Swiss-German border west of the German mountain Rosenegg, and north of the Swiss hamlet of Hofenacker, where Switzerland has poked its way into Germany. This is known among PoW circles as The Ramsen Salient, after the Swiss town of the same name. This is the spot where 19 Allied officers eventually make it to freedom.

It is an interesting vignette, how this essential nugget of information found its way into the survival kit of many successful PoW escapers, all thanks Hans Larive. On a previous escape attempt, Larive is arrested quite literally within sight of the Swiss border. He is taken to the German town of Singen and interrogated by the Gestapo. During this process, he has a very strange and revealing conversation with the local Gestapo chief. The interrogation itself is conducted in a villa on the outskirts of Singen, once inhabited by the director of GF, a firm producing cast-iron fittings that was named after one Georg Fischer. Since Villa Welzhöfer was requisitioned by the Nazis, the building has been the headquarters of the Gestapo in the region. While a young man sits in a corner behind a typewriter tapping out his notes, a huge gentleman carries out Hans' interrogation. This man makes such a lasting impression on Hans that he is referred to as 'The Bull' in Hans' book, *The Man Who Came In From Colditz*.

After establishing his identity, Hans continues his story that he is a naval officer, lost all his papers when his ship sank in Rotterdam and is on his way to the Far East. The Bull gradually becomes friendlier as the conversation continues. He was once a cook in a Dutch hotel for a while and regrets that the Netherlands did not remain neutral. As if the Netherlands could do anything about that! When Larive tells him which route he took and that he got off the train in Singen, the Gestapo agent tells him that this was the only sensible thing Larive did. According to him, Larive could have simply walked across the border, as easy as you like. There are no defences at all in this stretch between Germany and Switzerland: the Germans do not have enough troops to spare for that. The officer even goes so far as to pull out a staff map and goes over the route with Larive. At a bend in the road, he points to a building. If he had walked straight on from the bend there, he would have reached Switzerland within a few hundred metres. The building the Gestapo agent is referring to is café-restaurant Spiesshof. Remarkably, the building itself is already in Switzerland.

Larive was not stupid. He knew that he had not just been given the Golden Egg, he had been given the Golden Goose which lays them. He tucked all this knowledge away in his head, along with any other trade secrets the Gestapo Bull was happy to divulge. Back to Colditz on a one-way ticket Larive goes. He coalesces all he had been told, draws a map as illustration, and pretty soon any interested Allied parties are in the know. Consequently, when he and Francis Steinmetz escape via a manhole in the Colditz recreation park on 15 August 1941, reaching Switzerland safely is no longer a problem for either of them. The route he discovers turns out to be worth its weight in gold. On 19 August that year, Larive is interrogated again. But this time in Schaffhausen by Swiss police after his successful escape.

On 27 October, he leaves Switzerland to return to England via France, Spain and Gibraltar, where he resumes his role in the fight against the Germans. In September 1941, two more Dutchmen enter the country through the same route: Major Cornelis Giebel and Lieutenant Oscar Drijber. In January 1942, the first British officer shows up at the now famous (only to the Allies) border crossing. Lieutenant Airey Neave, together with Dutch Lieutenant Tony Luteijn, cross the border on 8 January. They only get stopped by a border guard once they are walking to Ramsen. The border guard was Swiss.

The Germans see little reason to mount a permanent guard on the border with Switzerland. Apart from having no fear that any of their own countrymen will defect to the south because they are fed up with the war and the regime, the number of refugees such as deserters, Jews, French soldiers working on farms or in factories in Singen or even expatriate PoWs seeking to get over the border is small. Only a few cases a day occur. Both sides of the border are patrolled, but usually by soldiers who are no longer fit for frontline service, and may be struggling to keep up their morale. The *Hitlerjugend* (Hitler Youth) is also sent out to track down any passers-by who want to cross the border. It remains a moot point whether their fervent zeal is enough to cope with the intransigence of the soldiers and officers determined to reach free Switzerland.

On 20 October, Littledale is interrogated at the *Polizeidirektion* (Police Directorate) in the canton of Schaffhausen. The brief report with his impeccable signature at the bottom introduces him as a professional officer living in Bunbury, Chesire. His father's name is John, his mother's is Klara geb. Stevenson, he is single, belongs to the *Englische Kirche* (Church of England) and is a major in the motorised infantry. As he crosses the border, he wears civilian clothes. He is not in possession of an *Ausweise*. His story is short:

> I grew up in County Chesire. I attended school in Rottingdean and Eton. When I was 18, I attended the Military Academy in Sandhurst for two years. I then served with the King's Royal Rifle Corps in India, Palestine, Ireland and England. At the

outbreak of war, I found myself in England. On 22 May 1940, we went by ship to Calais where we fought for four days. On 26 May 1940, I was captured there. I ended up in a transit camp in Trier, then one in Mainz. Then I was interned in the Laufen camp near Salzburg for ten months. In early March 1941, we and 400 officers were taken to a camp in Posen as a retaliatory measure. On 28 May 1941, I escaped from this camp with two more officers. We held out for about six months in Poland, Hungary and Yugoslavia. The moment we tried to cross the border into Bulgaria, we were arrested by a customs officer on 17 November 1941 and taken to Sofia. I then spent six weeks in a military prison in Vienna. On 17 January 1942, I was transported under escort presumably to Colditz, that is, I was to be transported there. During the transport, the moment we were in Bohemia, I jumped off the train. I managed to stay hidden in Bohemia until 27 May 1942. On this day, I was caught and sent to Colditz. On 15 October 1942, at two in the morning, the four of us escaped from this camp. Outside the castle, we split into pairs. My comrade Stephens and I went on foot to Rochlitz near Colditz. From here we went via Chemnitz, Nürnberg, Stuttgart to Tuttlingen. From Tuttlingen, we continued on foot to the border, which we crossed at Ramsen-Hofenacker at 2 am on 20 October 1942. We spent the night still near the border and in the morning made our way to Ramsen where we reported to the police.

Littledale signs his statement with a signature that betrays no emotion. The tight handwriting, impeccable and so English, shows no trace of the thoughts going through his mind, irrevocably thinking back to that other statement he made almost a year earlier under completely different circumstances to the Bulgarian authorities.

Over a week later, on 28 October, the *Armeekommando Gruppe Id, Abteilung Sicherheitsdienst* (Army Command Group Id, Security Service Department) of the Swiss Army sends an interrogation report to Dr Jezler of the Police Department of the Justice and Police Department in Bern concerning the English subjects, namely officers Ronald Littledale, born 1902, and William Lawson Stephens, born 1910. According to the covering letter, both escaped from German captivity and entered Switzerland illegally at Ramsen on 25 (sic!) October 1942.

They are then transported to Bern, interrogated and introduced to the British military attaché. The letter further informs that the two men are in Bern under the control of the *Pol.Of.Ter.Kdo.3* and will remain here until their fate is decided. It is proposed that they be assigned a mandatory residential location.

One day earlier, on 27 October 1942, the district chief of Konstanz sends a message to police stations in the region, namely Konstanz, Allensbach, Reichenau, Radolfzell, Wangen, Gailingen, Gorrmadingen, Rielasingen, Singen (Hohentwiel), Hilzingen, Beuren a.R. and Engen, reporting a significant increase in border crossings. It is noted that measures taken so far have not proved adequate to reduce illegal border crossings. To halt the crossings, all officers of the Gendarmerie and the police are urged to increase their watch for suspicious persons, and also involve the population in support of this vital work.

On 2 November 1942, *Kriminalkommissar SS-Hauptsturmführer* (Criminal Commissioner SS-Captain) Josef Stange of the Geheime *Staatspolizei-Staatspolizeileitstelle Karlsruhe* (Secret State Police Headquarters Karlsrhue), *Grenzpolizei-Kommissariat Singen* (Border Police Commissariat Singen) sends a letter to Herrn Krim. *Obersekr.* Fischbacher, the chief of the administrative district including Constance, Donauschingen and Vilingen. It is reported that three English and one Dutch officer crossed the so-called Green Border into Switzerland on 18 October, and two other English officers on 20 October. The Gestapo reports that they were captured near Ramsen. The border crossing reportedly took place between 5 am and 6 am According to the letter, which reports that the officers escaped from the PoW camp at Colditz in Saxony, some of them fled the camp as early as 9 October. The men in question were wearing civilian clothes, and were in possession of travel documents and letters of recommendation. In the documents, they pose as engineers from companies of importance to the war economy, and request free passage as well as unhindered access to rail traffic. The papers bear a company stamp as well as an unexplained SS stamp. It is suspected that the papers were forged in the camp. The refugees travel in pairs with one speaking German each time. The men who fled to Switzerland took the train from Stuttgart to Singen, crossing the border at dawn between five and six. The papers were forged so well that they passed checks on the train and overnight stays in hotels. Furthermore, following an earlier report on this on 13 October, the gendarmerie and police are asked to look out for the mentioned identification papers during checks in the streets, hotels and guest houses.

It could be a holiday snapshot from better times, but the four men looking into the camera, each holding a broom while posing at a curling gathering, know otherwise. There is a mountain with snow and pines in the background; in front are several chalets with roofs full of snow. A spectator in puff trousers in the background looks on. The sun is shining, and the men look in good spirits. But there is more going on here; layer upon layer, playing on our assumptions. It looks at first glance like a snapshot of four mates enjoying a day out at a winter sports venue, but it is ostensibly a photograph of four British officers, escapers all, from Colditz. They made it, they are free: free to enjoy the cold winter snow instead of dreading it, freezing behind stone walls. Free to wield curling brooms instead of rifles, home-made shovels or counterfeit keys. They can smile, wear sunglasses and skate on real ice, not just the thin ice of Nazi sensibilities. It is never better for them than this.

All around them, Europe is German occupied; but British and Americans fight back by air and sea, the Russians by land. Whilst war rages on in the Reich, millions are being treated as slaves, tortured, murdered. The Germans are everywhere and at the very apotheosis of their power, they are in the hot African desert as well as on the cold North Cape. They look through their periscopes at the lights in ignorant ports on the US east coast; they stand at the gates of a city called Stalingrad. SS Alpine fighters are climbing the highest mountain in the Caucasus, the 5,500-metre Elbrus, the 'holy mountain of the Aryans'. It is never better for them than this.

But all is illusory: the idyll in which Stephens, Reid, Wardle and Littledale have found themselves; the peak from which the Nazis survey all they have conquered. And they know.

One of the men in the picture is wearing sunglasses and, unlike the others, is wearing dark clothes. He looks tanned, relaxed too, and warm and friendly. The sunken cheeks and dogged look in the photo from Stalag XXID are gone. Ronald Bolton Littledale is looking good: the freedom and company pleases him. Despite the dark glasses, his eyes seem to twinkle. And with good reason. He has succeeded. After all the misery, from the fortress in Calais, the high walls of Laufen, the vermin-infestations in Posen, that months-long flight through Eastern

Europe, his arrest in Pirot, his hiding in Prague and the depressing castle in Colditz, the mission objective has almost been attained. He stands on free soil; only the journey to England separates him from the freedom of home. Strikingly, he stands apart from the others. The clothes, the glasses, the distance: a bad omen? For him, the war is not over. For him, there is always struggle, forever continuing. The outcome is uncertain.

Several photos were taken during this joyous get-together in Switzerland. The photo of the four escapees is part of a series of shots of a curling competition in February 1943 between the Saanemoser Curling Team and the Escaper's Team in Gstaad. Put together by Fritz Fieg, the Saanemoser Curling Team consisted of Fritz Jutzler, Kobi Schmidt, Robert Wehren and Rudi Wehren. In the late 1940s and early 1950s, this team are the Swiss champions three times.

Apart from the group photos, the photographer captured the prize table and the presentation of the cup, they also took individual portraits of the British officers pushing the heavy stones across the ice. Below the group portrait is the caption: '''Tubby' Lister. Watching intently is Rudolf (Rudi) Wehren of the Sporthotel.' The picture next to it shows a Wally Hammond, not the English cricketer, but of whom more later. The group photo of the four shows Stephens, Reid, Hammond and Lister. Not Stephens, Reid, Wardle and Littledale!

Is it Littledale, or is it not? The photographs need to be compared. This is tricky, not at least because the man is wearing sunglasses. Other things are apparent. Stephens and Reid are immediately recognisable when compared to other pictures of both men. But 'Wardle'? There are several photographs of Wardle taken at Colditz and they all clearly show a tall man. and the *Sonderausgabe of the Deutsches Kriminalpolizeiblatt (Special Edition of the German Criminal Police Journal)* of 16 October 1942 gives his height as 1.83 m, similar to Stephens. In the photo from Gstaad, 'Wardle' stands even smaller than Reid, who is only 1.72 m. So, it is not Wardle at all! And his face looks nothing like Hank Wardle's either. But with Littledale, things are more difficult. His sunglasses make it difficult to compare his face with any of the few photos that exist of him. At 6 ft tall, the man in the group photo could well be Littledale. Indeed, he comes between Stephens and Reid in terms of height.

There is a photograph of Littledale taken for verification purposes by the Germans at Fort VIII in Posen. There are similarities between this photo and the one from Gstaad as would be expected. Both men have exactly the same hairline, the same narrow lips and receding ears, the same pronounced forehead, the same nose and the same sloping cheek. However, a prominent spot on the upper lip in the photo from Posen cannot be seen in the photo from Gstaad, because a shadow obscures that part of the man's face in that photo. Moreover, the photo shoot in Gstaad was in February 1943, by which time Littledale is already in Spain. He cannot be the man in the photo. But on the other hand, the physical similarity between Littledale's photo from Posen and the 'Littledale' in the group portrait from Gstaad is striking. It can be recalled that Reid avers in his Colditz books that both Sinclair and Littledale were 'put through the mill and tortured' after their arrest in Prague, but Reid is wrong about that. But if it was true, it is highly unlikely that someone like Littledale would later happily compete in a curling competition in the Swiss snow.

For that matter, regarding his claim of torture, does Reid really not know better? Is he giving them, and himself, an escape clause in case something came out later after his book. Or could it be Sinclair and Littledale did not tell him the whole story? Or made one up. The answer may lie in that as Escape Officer, if he had known the truth, surely, he would have been duty-bound not to have sanctioned any escape attempt involving those two unless they went together. As it was, he accompanied Littledale himself in getting out of the castle. Sinclair never lacked for partners. But what weighs more heavily on the conscience of someone who reported his aides? That he was tortured as Reid suggests or that he voluntarily committed treason as Littledale did? So no, Littledale did not go curling in the Swiss Alps.

Hammond and Lister made a trophy cup out of old cans, which took them about four hours. Afterwards, Wally Hammond presents the prize to the winning team, handing it to Rudolf Wehren. For a long time, it remains on display in the Barengraben Restaurant of the Sport Hotel, a relic of interesting times, until 1984, when the hotel is renovated. Two years later, the new hotel is opened, the cup has disappeared and no one remembers where it went.

The autumn 2011 issue of the *Official Newsletter of the Old Caledonia Artificer Apprentices' Association* contains a feature titled *ERAs in Colditz*. It tells of the HMS *Caledonia*, a training ship used to train military apprentice engineers between 1937 and 1985. The story features Walter 'Wally' Hammond and Donald 'Tubby' Lister and tells of their riotous escape to Switzerland via the Singen route. There is a beautiful picture of the two men in Switzerland after they escaped from captivity. Hammond, in good spirits, looks straight into the camera lens. With his hairline, his narrow lips, his ears, in this picture, he looks stunningly similar to Littledale in the Fort VIII photo. This photo was taken at the curling competition.

Six weeks after the spectacular escape of Littledale's group, Mike Sinclair is making another attempt to get out of Colditz. Even without the wonderful news that his old comrade has arrived safely in Switzerland, he has not been idle. Together with Rupert Barry, he studies the German guards' routines, and the differences in them. There seems to be an opportunity in the theatre block, the part of the castle called the Saalhaus, where the senior officers reside. It was from here that Douglas Bader and his mini-orchestra tried to signal to the four back in October the moment when the coast was clear. A square shaped vertical shaft descends about 15 m inside the Saalhaus. It is sited near the outside windows so that daylight can reach the lower floors. It is known as the light well. Months of observations reveal that every day around two o'clock in the afternoon, there is a break in the continual surveillance while the guard is being changed. The plan is for the escapers to descend into the light well already wearing civilian clothes, hopefully similar to those worn by German kitchen staff, while the guards are absent, and then exit through a door into the German courtyard, where Littledale had such a torrid time back in October.

During the preparations, the British discover that some Frenchmen are also working on an escape attempt at this very spot, which they have failed to report to their escape officer, thus undermining the spirit of mutual co-operation upon which the castle escape organisation depends. Dick Howe, the British Escape Officer who has taken over from Pat Reid, is incandescent! This is diabolical! This sort of lack of coordination between the various nationalities at Colditz can have disastrous consequences for the success of a mission. In the end, pragmatism wins out and they decide that two teams of two will be formed consisting of one Frenchman and one Englishman in each team. Sinclair will therefore attempt to escape not with Rupert Barry but with French captain Charles Klein.

On 26 November, the men descend into the light well and emerge from a door into the Kommandantur courtyard. They turn left and walk through an archway that leads to the large gate on the east side of the castle. This is the same route normally taken by the prisoners to the recreation area down in the park where the prisoners exercise. Unhindered, they reach a wall, get over it and separate. Within two days, Mike is in Singen. On 30 November, in the vicinity of Immendingen, not far from Schaffhausen, Switzerland and freedom, he is arrested. Game over. Immendingen and Schaffhausen: Sinclair could hardly have followed Littledale's footsteps closer than at this very place in Germany. According to Gris's later memoirs, Mike makes a disastrous mistake. Near Immendingen, he comes to a bridge that crosses a river, this bridge is important enough to be guarded. Instead of choosing another route, or waiting until night to swim or wade across the river, he decides to cross the bridge. He is stopped. His papers are checked. The inevitable happens and kills Mike's attempt stone dead.

Gris blamed Mike's poor decision making on hunger, cold and loneliness, the three additional companions on any escape attempt. Even so, before the Germans are able to take Mike back to Colditz, he again dares to slip out of their hands, like he did in June when he pulled a similar stunt in Cologne.

On 14 December, however, he is recaptured, this time in Weinsberg. It appears he may have been traveling by train to nearby France and got off at Weinsberg to avoid the checkpoint at Heilbronn, a major railway station, just a bit further down the line. Six weeks of solitary confinement back in Colditz give him time to think through this tragedy. And to prepare for a new attempt. Meanwhile, Barry and French Lieutenant Aulard do not get further than the park.

Littledale leads an unrecorded, virtually undocumented life in Switzerland, unwittingly making yet another attempt to disappear from history. The file on him kept by the Swiss authorities contains only a few pages. One of the documents is a note from the Kant. *Polizeikommando* Schaffhausen (Cantonal Police Command, Schaffhausen) to the *Polizeiabteilung des Eidg. Justiz und Polizeidept.* (Police Department of the Federal Justice and Police Dept) in Bern dated 21 December that refers to a note of the 17th requesting the temporary issue of the identity papers of Reid (N 5341), Wardle (N 5366), Littledale (N 5415) and Stephens (N 5419). To date, there has been no reply and the documents have not been received. Urgency is requested by the *Polizeikommando*. The document is stamped 'ad acta' (considered settled) and filed away. Not until 19 February does a reply arrive from

Dr Jezler in Bern. The Police Department in the capital has no identity papers for the four English refugees. The army command has been contacted regarding this matter, but they do not know anything about any identity papers either. Shortly afterwards, in thin pencil, someone writes 'abgereist' (departed) on Littledale's interrogation report of 20 October from Schaffhausen.

Littledale is the first of the British enclave in Switzerland to leave. While Reid stays in Bern for the rest of the war and is attached to the Military Attaché, Littledale, ever the consummate professional soldier, strikes out on the path he has always taken, that of armed struggle. With the same determination that ensured his stay in Colditz was as short as possible, he soon decides to press on, the snowy surroundings of the Swiss Alps notwithstanding. He leaves on 25 January 1943, barely three months after crossing the border at Ramsen with Billie Stephens. Once again, he is in good company: together with Hedley Fowler, he is preparing for the difficult journey across France to Spain and beyond. He must surely know Fowler from Colditz. He was born in London in 1916, the son of British Commander Maxwell Thomas Bourne Fowler, Paymaster of the Royal Navy, and his Australian wife, Florence Ayers. Hedley Fowler, nicknamed Bill, shuttles between Britain and Adelaide in his youth. In 1936, he joins the Royal Australian Air Force after studying mechanical engineering. He joins the RAF in 1937 and by the time war breaks out in Europe, he is an experienced pilot. On 15 May 1940, as a member of 615 Squadron, he is forced to abandon his Hurricane when it is hit in combat by a Messerschmidt near the French town of Fumay. He tries to hide himself in a company of retreating French soldiers, but is captured by German units the next day. He is sent to Stalag Luft I, a camp near Barth in northern Germany. His escape attempt on 5 November 1941 ensures him a single ticket to Colditz in December that year.

A month before Littledale takes his leap to freedom, on 9 September 1942, Fowler get out along with Dutch Lieutenant Damiaen van Doornick and four others, by way of a daring plan. They dig through the floor in *Stabsfeldwebel* (Sergeant Major) Gephard's office, right under his desk, and into the clothing store, a side building directly abutting the north wall of the castle. Once in the store, they change into their disguises. Dressed as two Germans guards and four Polish orderlies carrying laundry in crates to be washed in the village, they make their way round to the east side of the castle and out, talking their way past the German guards on the gate there. Van Doornick and Fowler are the only ones who manage to reach Switzerland: it takes them six days. The other four are all caught. Not entirely surprising, Van Doornick and Fowler also follow the Singen route. The lucklessly unobservant Gephard, known to the prisoners as Mussolini, never recovered his soldierly armour proper. This farcical performance and his being not above taking bribes from prisoners for one thing or another, ensured he was eventually dispatched to the Russian Front and not seen in Colditz again.

Littledale and Fowler make their way to Geneva where they obtain French identity cards. A Belgian named Jacques accompanies them to the border with France at a place called Annemasse, which lies to the east of Geneva. Littledale and Fowler are not the first men from Colditz to follow this route. Earlier, in 1942, it is Airey Neave who pretends to be Czechoslovak and crosses the border after walking across a cemetery and crawling between two rolls of barbed wire. He then climbs on an elevation on the French side of the border. Seeing a small, white house, he arrives at a crossroads that points the way to the border town of Annemasse.

16

ANNEMASSE

Littledale and Fowler are too late. Too late to sneak unseen into unoccupied France from Switzerland. As a result of Operation Torch, the Allied invasion of North Africa, the Germans become nervous about the southern border of their empire. The 'soft underbelly of Europe' as Churchill calls it, in this case southern France, is controlled by the French government in Vichy, who are collaborating with the Germans until November 1942. As the military threat from across the Mediterranean grows, the Axis powers decide to lock the door. On 10 November 1942, German and Italian troops invade the unoccupied zone of Vichy-France. The German Army operates under the codename *Unternehmen Anton*. Many routes hitherto used for illegal transportation of refugees are now unavailable. This includes the French town of Annemasse, a small municipality on the eastern side of Geneva.

In the afternoon, a German car drives into the border town. The Head of the Customs Committee simply announces that from then on the border between Switzerland and France is closed. Two days later, 300 German troops of the 99th Battalion Reserve-Gebirgs-Jäger-Regiment 1 take up residence in five hotels scattered around the city in the Avenue de la Gare and the Place Nationale. The staff billet themselves in private homes. A few days later, they are followed by 600 German customs officers, there to guard the border. However, the German occupation lasts only briefly. On 10 December 1942, it is relieved by units of the Italian Army's 5th Alpine Division Pustéria, which will eventually occupy the whole of Haute Savoie. Two companies consisting of 300 Alpine fighters commanded by Captain Gandolfi take possession of the town on 18 December. The Italians maintain their presence here until the Germans finally takeover in September 1943. Littledale and Fowler are on the other side in

Switzerland, eager to set off for Spain and eventually England, while right before their eyes the border is hermetically sealed.

The Italians are on the ball when it comes to making the border tightly secure. They limit the number of crossing points, they disrupt or cut off telephone connections. In a building next to the Hotel Du Pax, a prison is set up in the cellars. People with Gaullist tendencies or those with knowledge of illegal border crossings are tortured here for intelligence on their contacts.

This is not new. Even during the Vichy period, before the Italian occupation, efforts were made to keep the border closed and prevent illegal passage. Hedges are erected, as well as barrels; farms are isolated, roads are diverted. They installed electrified barbed-wire fencing. But still, the border is anything but secure. The smuggling of goods and foreign currencies is rife, despite the counter-measures. The Swiss are also concerned: they fear a massive flow of refugees coming over from Vichy-France. As a consequence, patrols increase and a second barbed-wire fence is erected. But still, people get across.

The first ones to take the plunge do so without help from the local population. They do not have much choice. They try both with or without valid papers at customs, or they try to find an unguarded section where they can cross unseen. Former PoWs try to reach the southern part of France through Switzerland. Some 3,000 of them are reported in 1941. Between January and October 1942, 1,397 former prisoners pass through the Moillesulaz border post west of Annemasse.

One of the ex-PoWs crossing the border in January 1942 is Airey Neave. He is the first British officer to escape from Colditz and successfully reach Switzerland. In his attempt to finally make a home run from Switzerland, a police car takes him to a cemetery near Lake Geneva. Behind it are rolls of barbed wire, which form the border with Vichy France. Neave, along with a fellow fugitive answering to the name of Hugh Woollatt, crawls his way over, between the graves. When he is on the other side, he notices a patch of material from his trousers is hanging off a strand of barbed wire. Woollatt cannot suppress a laugh and lends him his mackintosh to cover the tear. From this point on, Neave has no control over his escape and depends on Resistance fighters and helpers to get him to England. Eventually, he succeeds in his mission. The route through the cemetery is used more and more. Small groups accompanied by smugglers regularly pass the graves of those who think they would be left alone for good.

As the war continues, and Italian troops come to occupy the Haute Savoie, concern rises on the Swiss side of the risk of German reprisals. As a result, the Swiss intensify their surveillance. The door is now permanently locked on both sides and attempting to cross the border has become extremely dangerous. But still the illegal crossings persist. The Belgian Resistance helps Jewish children over. There are Christian organisations taking part in smuggling activity. Through the boarding school *Juvénat de Ville-la-Grand*, the school of the Congregation of the Missionaries of Saint-François de Sales, 1,000 to 2,000 refugees penetrate the safe Swiss port.

Using the same spot as Neave, Littledale and Fowler are accompanied by a 20-year old French girl. They have to cross a shallow river, and they end up with soaking wet clothes. A French customs officer helps them out of the water, and they have to dry their clothes before they can continue. They then get taken to Annemasse, and they are handed over to a man wearing a ski suit, who lets them spend the night in his house. They are taken to a garage the next day, where a car is waiting to take them to La Roche. On the way to the garage, they pass Italian soldiers.

Billie Stephens, the St Nazaire commando who escaped from Colditz with Littledale, remains behind in Switzerland. He was originally to lead a group through France in January 1944, but due to a leg injury his departure was postponed. Finally, on 5 June 1944, a most propitious date, he and RAF Sergeant Edwin Worsdale cross France on a trip organised by Françoise Dissard. In Toulouse, they are joined by RCAF Flight Lieutenant Adolphe Duchesne and the three men cross the Pyrenees via Cier in France to Bausen in Spain. On 10 July 1944, Stephens and Worsdale fly from Gibraltar to Whitchurch in England.

Howard Wardle leaves Switzerland earlier, on 9 December 1943. After several false starts, he eventually manages to cross the Pyrenees along with a group of Dutchmen. Finally, on 18 December, they arrive in Spain. Where they are all subsequently arrested! On 5 February 1944, Wardle flies to Whitchurch.

Unlike most British PoWs who reached Switzerland, Pat Reid stays behind in this free port until 1946. He will not say much about his time in the Alpine country. What is certain is that he joins the British legation in Bern on 9 March 1943, as assistant to the military attaché.

He is aware that the repatriation of escapees from Switzerland through France to Spain is sluggish at best, and he knows it is because the routes are clogged with downed air force personnel from France. So he decides to try and do something about this sorry state of affairs. He works under Colonel Henry Cartwright, himself an escapee during First World War, who is Military Attaché and Head of Intelligence MI9 in Switzerland from March 1943 to December 1946. Reid interrogates escaped prisoners of war arriving over the Swiss border from Germany. The information he gleans from them, which includes routes taken, help received and what checkpoints and bottlenecks they encountered on their journey, is helpful for future escape attempts. Both PoWs in camps and Resistance organisations in occupied countries benefit from the information acquired through Reid's interviews. Shortly after taking up his post, Reid is given diplomatic status despite his illegal entrance into the country. He is promoted to major on 1 November 1945. In August 1943, in Thun, he marries Janey Cabot from Boston, who received her education in England. In Switzerland when the war broke out, she had to remain.

Years after the war, the cup that Wally and Tubby made for the curling tournament in Gstaad, is found in the barn of a local farmer, Ernst Hauswirth. It is none other than Jane Cabot, by then divorced from Pat and living in Zurich, who is informed by phone of the discovery of this lost treasure. In 1993, she meets Billie Stephens at the Imperial War Museum in London, who receives the cup, decorated with fresh ribbons. Four years later, he died. Thus, the last member of the quartet who escaped from Colditz in October, 1942 and who could have confirmed whether or not the fourth man in the photo with the sunglasses is actually Ronald Littledale was gone.

17

VIA SPAIN TO ENGLAND

In La Roche, Littledale and Fowler spend most of the day in a hotel, where their guide has lunch with them. In the afternoon, they both receive 100 francs for the train to Chambery. The guide takes them to the station, and in Chambery they are transferred to Perpignan. On 27 January at 9 am, they arrive, and catch the tram to Hotel Sainte-Antoine. Photos are taken of them the next day, in a room at the back of a small shop nearby. The following day, their guide hands them over to a Spaniard. This new courier takes them by bus to the town of Elne, just north of the border with Spain. He tells them to sit separately so they are less conspicuous. The party is joined by a young Frenchman called Albert Cortes, who is about 19-years-old. Leaving the bus at Elne, they continue on foot, heading south, keeping to the rails. They pass the Tech river and walk into the foothills of the Pyrenees. Along the way, the guide gets lost, but using the stars they get back on the right route, before sleeping for a few hours in a cave.

The next morning, on 30 January at six o'clock, they cross the border with Spain and by noon they are on the main road from La Junquera to Figueras. Their guide wants to drop Cortes off at his house in Agullana. At around four o'clock that afternoon, Littledale and Fowler, and their guide, are picked up by a Spanish patrol. The soldiers have become sufficiently accustomed to there being so many refugees in this region who have crossed the border, that they even drive their truck through the area unarmed.

At La Junquera, the men are put in a cell and later interrogated in French. The Spanish officer thinks they are Canadians. But as instructed, Littledale and Fowler indicate that they are British who were captured in France. Littledale manages to maintain his sense of humour. While Fowler gives John Parsons as an alias, Littledale calls himself Bighill. Their guide is beaten up when it turns out he has fought on the side of the communists in the Civil War. Littledale and Fowler end up in the inevitable cell, where they burn the papers they are carrying. During further interrogation, the two 'confess' that they think Franco is a great guy. It does not help them to get in touch with the British consul.

Littledale and Fowler have an unpleasant time being held in various cells before being taken to the British consulate in Barcelona. In Figueras, their heads are shaved and they are vaccinated. The circumstances under which the latter happens are remarkable to say the least: Fowler is given an injection with a needle that has been used nine times before him. They have to share a tiny locked room with 14 other men, two of whom are criminals waiting for their death sentence to be carried out. There is no furniture and very little light. The sanitation arrangements are grim, a single slops bucket emptied every 24 hours. No wonder the men are constantly sick, and two of them do not survive. The two corpses remain lying there for two days before guards take them away. The nights are cold, they have no blankets, vermin crawl across the floor, and the food is disgusting. Fowler sells his watch to buy something decent from the guard.

Finally on 22 February, they are taken to Barcelona by a Spanish sergeant where they get in touch with the British consulate. In a hotel, they sleep in real beds after weeks of suffering. They are given civilian clothes. On 18 March, they are interned: Littledale in Jaraba, Fowler in Alhama de Aragon, both in the province of Zaragoza. This is not an arbitrary separation, allied ranking officers are dispersed among various camps according to their unit and arm of service. Littledale is in the army and therefore goes to Jaraba, while RAF pilots like Fowler get exclusive treatment, stay in hotels and go to Alhama de Aragon, where a quieter stay awaits them.

The moment Littledale and Fowler cross the border between Switzerland and France on their way to Spain, Portugal and freedom in England, they enter a maelstrom of crowds heading for the unknown. Many tens of thousands will cross the Pyrenees during the years of the Second World War, preferring an unknown fate in Spanish hands to the all-too-obvious rule of the Nazis and their allies occupying all but a single spot on the map of Europe. When the captured Littledale is tramping his way on foot from Calais to Laufen, more fortunate British and French troops, who were not caught but failed to make it across the Channel at Dunkirk, begin a similar footslog, only in their case, southwards, heading for Spain.

The flow of refugees to the Iberian Peninsula increases over the years and varies in composition. Soldiers and officers from British and French army units, illegal workers and Resistance fighters, escapees from PoW camps, artists and intellectuals: they all take the risk and like migrating birds in winter, head south. In addition to the mountain range separating France and Spain, they have to get past German border guards and the Guardia Civil. In mid-1942, French Jews, recognising a pogrom when they see one, also try to leave occupied Europe before it is too late. Increasingly important are the so-called pilot lines, which run scattered through the Netherlands, Belgium and France, aiming to bring Allied air force crews safely back to their own lines.

In Spain, by the time the first shots fall on Danzig's Westerplatte, Generalissimo Francisco Franco has been in power for several years. After the Spanish Civil War, numerous opponents of his regime, as well as fighters from the International Brigades who tried to fight the Spanish fascists, are locked up in various camps scattered around the country. One of the largest camps is located in Miranda de Ebro, south of Bilbao. The camp consists of monotonous rows of barracks with sloping roofs, interrupted only by a camp street. The Nazis, who supported Franco during the civil war, the dramatic low point of which was the bombing of Guernica, advised in the construction and organisation of these camps, along with rehearsing their blitzkrieg tactics in combat. Of the more than 40,000 people who fled to Spain in the years between 1940 and 1945, some 37% ended up in Miranda de Ebro, 29% in prisons, 14% in spas converted to house prisoners, and 20% in hotels also converted to house the refugees.

Many British and Americans end up in Miranda, but stay there for a relatively short time due to the intervention of the British embassy. This camp is extremely adept at differentiating the officers from the men. Despite poor conditions in the camps, poor food, lousy sanitary conditions, and the soldiers' frustration at not being able to take part in the fighting going on in the countries around them, the British enjoy a greater degree of freedom than most, especially in Alhama and Jaraba, where the senior officers reside. This is partly due to their remaining aloof during protests over the poor conditions and not participating in escapes and other activities directed against the camp leadership.

Spain is not part of the Axis powers, and is not a formal ally of the Nazis either, though her rulers, thanks to close co-operation with them during the Civil War, share a similar political outlook, countenancing similar ideals. Spain is also under a high degree of economic pressure. Her need for raw materials like petroleum, cotton and phosphates forces Spain to make particular choices in defining their neutrality, and this is reflected in the accelerated release of British prisoners in particular.

Two members of the Guardia Civil accompany Littledale on the train to the officers' camp in Jaraba. Fowler leaves for England via Gibraltar shortly afterwards. In Jaraba, Littledale finds himself in a spa, where about four large hotels have been converted to house officers. Compared to Miranda de Ebro, and certainly to the conditions in which he and Fowler stayed in Figueras on entering Spain, the situation here is incomparably better. He sleeps between real sheets, and can bathe in a marble bath, and probably best of all, he is not locked up all day. The officers in Jaraba can walk freely through the town, the food is good and 'the Rioja flows richly'. When an officer leaves, a farewell party is held. After all his harsh and bitter experiences, capture in Calais and the feeling of defeat, the hike to Bastogne, the penal camp in Posen, 14 months on the run in Europe, being treated to the Gestapo's hospitality, Colditz Castle 'from which escape is impossible' and then doing exactly that, his short-lived joy on reaching Switzerland, and finally his miserable reception in Figueras, all the luxuries of the moment will probably not be wasted on the ascetic Littledale.

On 27 March, Fowler flies to Hendon. Littledale is not due until later. On 12 May, he leaves by car for Madrid, where he reports to the British Embassy. He stays with a staff member of the Military Attaché until 15 May when he goes by train to Gibraltar. He arrives the next day at two in the afternoon. On the morning of 23 May, he flies to Lisbon. Finally, on 24 May 1943, at Whitchurch, near Bristol, he walks again on his native English soil.

At home in Bunbury, the return of the prodigal son is reported in the Parish Magazine of St Boniface's Church in July 1943:

> We have been quietly but prayerfully awaiting the event and now at last it has happened. Major R. Littledale D.S.O. returned to his home some days ago. It is to be hoped he will at some convenient date publish his experiences from the Calais epic till

his return to Bunbury about three years later. For stirring episodes as the result of an inflexible determination to escape the clutches of the enemy, such an account should render the ordinary tale of adventure rather tame reading. He is to be congratulated on his decoration, but one confidently feels that with a soldier of his stamp even this is only an earnest of greater things to come.

Bunbury is curious about Littledale's experiences in the previous three years, but it is doubtful he has divulged anything at all about them, except at his debriefing at MI9.

Questions, always questions. What is the next step? The war is not over, not by a long chalk. His future is defined by the colours on the current map of Europe. His determination knows only one goal, back to the mainland of Europe, until the battle is over.

Hedley Fowler will not live to see the end of the war. On 14 December 1943, it is announced that he will be awarded the Military Cross for his successful escape. The recommendation for this award reports that:

> This officer displayed great skill and daring in his attempts to escape. Despite being caught on his first attempt this did not deter him from trying his luck a second time, and this time successfully. This escape was made from a camp specially reserved for officers who had either previously attempted to escape, or otherwise inconvenienced the Germans. The initiative and daring he displayed deserves recognition and I strongly recommend the War Office's proposal to award him the MC.

Back in England, he is promoted to squadron leader, and is stationed at Boscombe Down, an aircraft test facility near Amesbury. Here, Fowler becomes a test pilot. On 26 March 1944, over Crichel Down in Dorset, his Hawker Typhoon Ib JR307 disintegrates in mid-air as he attempts to emerge from a dive. Hedley is 27 when he dies.

'The real heroes and heroines were those who despite the barbarities of the Germans gave no useful information.' Airey Neave is clear in his definition on what constitutes a hero: those who do not give valuable information to the Germans despite the horrific torture to which they are subjected once they fall into the hands of the

Gestapo. He makes the statement in his 1969 book *Saturday at MI9*, in which he describes his experiences after becoming the first British officer to escape from Colditz, wearing a fake German uniform, along with Dutchman Tony Luteijn. 'Saturday' is Neave's codename given to him when, after his escape in January 1942 and his safe return to England in May that year, he is asked to take up an important position in British military intelligence, MI9.

Officially, Neave is assigned to I.S.9(d) Room 900 of the War Office, a ministry of the British government, responsible for directing the British armed services between the 17th Century and 1963, when it was reconfigured as the Ministry of Defence. One of Room 900's aims is to provide assistance to various aid lines in occupied Europe. These aid lines, which run from the Netherlands or Belgium through France to Spain, are intended to bring back safely to England escaped prisoners of war and more importantly the valuable crews of shot-down aircraft, who have managed to stay hidden. Indeed, aircraft crews can be immediately redeployed back into combat assignments upon their return, unlike ground troops.

The support Room 900 provides is broad and diverse. It is a hub, a nerve centre from which tendrils of help and materiel reach over occupied Europe. It is responsible for the co-ordination and delivery of money for food or to pay the guides, weapons for the Resistance, radio operators with transmitters to establish the necessary contact between the line and MI9, plans to help prisoners escape from guarded forts, and plans for nocturnal evacuations carried out on the beaches of southern France.

Its success can be gauged by the number of men returned. The O'Leary Line brought back some 600 men; the Comet Line 1,200. The Germans make numerous attempts to infiltrate the escape lines in order to destroy them. Agents posing as Allied refugees are rigorously interrogated by members of the helpline, with questions whispered to them by the British side of the line, answers only known to someone who is who they claim to be: Which base did you take off from? Where in London is this or that pub? What was your last meal before you went on a mission? No wonder that it was not long before this method of infiltration lost its popularity and died out. The Germans devised another plan: posing as a helper to support the line.

Returning soldiers and officers or Resistance fighters who had crossed over end up at the Royal Victoria Patriotic School in Clapham.

The building was erected in the 19th Century for girls orphaned after their fathers were killed in the Crimean War. During the Second World War, the building takes on a very different function. MI9 interrogates those who made the crossing from occupied Europe to the still unoccupied island on the other side of the Channel. Anyone could claim to have worked for the Resistance, their claims need to be tested by experts. Lengthy interrogations follow for these men and women who think they are free after escaping from the clutches of the Nazis. Army personnel seem easier to check: the unit someone belongs to, the base where someone was stationed, friends, colleagues, superiors; there are plenty of opportunities to check whether someone is who he says he is. But it is harder finding out what a man thinks, or how he will behave once he is living in complete freedom. The possibility must be taken into account that someone who fought for the Allies has changed tack and has now become a Nazi supporter.

Officer of the Dutch Security Service, Oreste Pinto, is a master at unmasking spies. Voluntarily or under duress, he interrogates thousands of escapees and manages to disprove various stories, detecting and eliminating attempts at infiltration. He has a famous colleague who also conducts interrogations: Airey Neave.

They never met at Colditz, but it is very possible that Neave spoke to him after returning from seeing Littledale in England. Neave is the first Briton to escape from Colditz, six months before Littledale is recaptured and transferred to the castle in Saxony. Littledale reaches England a full year later than Neave and as the second man back home from of Colditz. Of course, that he is Littledale is easily ascertainable. But standard procedure dictates the interrogation to which Littledale is subjected. In answer, he pours out the tale of his three years of adventure, suffering and struggle. Keen ears are listening; ears that have heard this kind of story countless times before, ears belonging to interrogators no longer even bothering to look up with surprise or alarm at what he says. Not that it is any less serious, the purpose of the questioning is not to find out if this man really is Littledale. What they really want to know is does Littledale have anything useful to tell them. Does he have information that could benefit the intelligence community? Information that can be used for other escapes? Military information of relevance to any future operations? Names of unknown secret agents doing work that could be useful in saving valuable lives?

That Littledale was at Colditz is something MI9 and perhaps Neave can easily verify. After all, he was there himself. Ronnie's partners in escape, though, cannot confirm that part of his story: all three are still in Switzerland. Gris and Mike are still in Colditz and therefore unavailable to them. Fowler might have something useful to contribute. But has Neave even spoken to him? He writes nothing about it in his memoirs as 'Saturday'. Only that prophetic sentence perhaps: 'The real heroes and heroines were those who despite the barbarities of the Germans gave no useful information.'

Of course, he was referring to the brave men and women who risked their lives to maintain the flight line across Europe and who were seized by the Gestapo, tortured and wrung out for information about other members and hideouts where soldiers might be hidden, only to end up in a camp themselves in Germany or executed. Neave knows from experience what it means to be interrogated by the Gestapo. He too was seized and interrogated during an earlier escape attempt, although he says he did not experience even a fraction of the terrible treatment meted out to civilians in the pilot line. Pat Reid writes in *The Colditz Story* that both Sinclair and Littledale were 'put through the mill and tortured' after their arrest in Prague. Did Neave hear from the mouth of Littledale himself or through his associates what that 'putting through the mill' ultimately meant for the Germans, and whether it was damaging? In *Saturday at MI9*, he is completely silent on Littledale.

Littledale's interrogation report, which will eventually be archived by MI9 under number Wo 208/3311 and almost in danger of being forgotten, consciously or unconsciously, is explosive. As the sentences are tapped onto the paper, and the dry staccato sounds of the typewriter echo through the walls of the interrogation room, the implications of his confession that he has written 'a statement truthfully [-] about our routes and helpers' are not yet known in England. By then, far away in Poznań, Lódz and Berlin, tragedy has already unfolded.

18

CONFESSIONS

Littledale's statement that he drew up a list of the names of his aides and the routes Sinclair and he followed must be regarded with some scepticism. The British are notoriously bad with languages other than their own, so it follows that it would have been hard for Littledale to cope with the complexities of the Polish tongue sufficiently to remember the names of everyone he encountered, and everywhere they went. It is also highly unlikely that the Poles used each other's real names whilst in the presence of the escaping officers: aliases only.

After his successful escape from Fort VIII, Littledale states during his interrogation that:

> We stayed at night in different neighbourhoods in Poznan. I slept in the flat of a young Pole whose address I had forgotten. The next day, the young Pole took me to a house where I met Sinclair. Davis-Scourfield came later. We stayed with a widow called Markiewicz. I don't know the address. We were not allowed out. After three days' stay, we moved to a small room where we stayed for nine days. There we were visited many times by a man who was preparing our onward journey. Our intention was to go to Russia. This man, the 'Doctor', was wounded during the war; he had a long Polish surname, which I cannot remember. After ten days of preparation, we went by car to Lódz to a man called Wolf, who lived in Böhmenlinienstrasse. In Lódz, we stayed with Wolf and waited for the opportunity to travel to Warsaw. A Pole called Nikodem accompanied us from Poznan to Lódz, and in Lódz we were joined by another Pole called Roman; I don't know the real names. Ms Kaller provided us with clothes and food. About a week after our arrival, Davies-Scourfield, Roman and I were driven by a lady to a town on the

border with the General Government. We got there at about 8 am and then we were led one by one across the border to a house on the edge of a border town near Koluszki. Sinclair and Nikodem arrived the next day. At noon, we went to the village of Lubochnia, about 30 kilometres away. We arrived there at 8 pm.

Sinclair also gives a detailed account of his wanderings after his outbreak in Poznan.

We stayed here for nine days, and in the meantime the Doctor arranged everything for our trip to Lódz. We travelled in a car with a young, almost 23-year-old Pole we knew as Nikodem. The car was driven by a Volksdeutscher who knew something was wrong with us, but he did not know we were English. For our route, the Doctor provided us with fake passes and an identity card issued by a German mining company, formerly owned by a Pole, Marian Klimczak. I gave this name in Pirot as my own. We arrived in Lódz without a problem, without being asked for proof on the way, and Nikodem took us to Mr Wolf in Böhmischlinienstrasse 9. Here we met another Pole, Roman, who was a friend of Nikodem's, and who came to Lódz by train. Wolf's cousin called Teze stayed here, and a young Polish woman, Mrs Kaller delivered cigarettes and clothes.

Sinclair added that the civilian clothes they were currently wearing were given to them by the Doctor in Poznan, replacing what they wore when they escaped from the camp.

Sinclair continues:

We waited in Lódz for eight days. On the eighth day, my two friends went to the border with Roman and a Polish woman. The Polish woman worked in a pharmacy in Lodz. The Polish woman knew the border between the Wartheland and the General Government very well, as she had friends and relatives on the other side of the border. On the ninth day, I crossed the border with the aforementioned woman and Nikodem. In the evening, we went by horse and cart to the border village, where we had dinner with a friend of our Polish woman, whom we knew as 'the pharmacist'. At home, we waited until dark and then left for another house about a kilometre from the border. I waited there with Nikodem and 'the pharmacist' while a 12-13 girl and a Polish woman whose name I can't remember watched the border guard; when he came, they gave him a bottle of vodka, which is hard to buy, and persuaded him to drink. After drinking the vodka, the guard was completely drunk. Then we went to the border. The drunk guard walked ahead, supported by both Polish women, and Nikodem and I about 30 metres behind. When we crossed the border, the guard turned around and lit a cigarette, and 'the pharmacist', Nikodem and I started looking for the house of a Polish friend. Unable to find the house in the dark, we spent the night at the edge of a small forest. In the morning, it turned out that we were staying very close to the house we were looking for. At 6 am, we had breakfast and arrived at an inn, where I expected to find my colleagues, but they were no longer there, but we were told they were in the nearby forest. By chance, we met Roman on the street near the forest. We went to a restaurant in Koluszki, where Roman soon brought both my friends. It was Sunday, when the German-Russian war broke out, we first heard about it in this restaurant.

The mention of 'a woman from a pharmacy in Lódz' is a huge clue for the Germans. This seems to confirm an earlier reference to a 'Frau Apotheke', who is listed in a document at the start of the investigation. All the Gestapo has to do is to focus their gaze on all-female pharmacists in Lódz. Even without knowing Maria Jasińska's name, they soon arrive at the pharmacy owned by a Baltic German from Riga, Nilson Storacky, 'Pod Łabędziem'. This establishment is subjected to an investigation lasting over a month, during which all the employees are interrogated. When one of them, Tadeusz Kotynia starts talking, things start falling into place for the Germans.

Kotynia, born in 1919, Catholic, married, states that in the lead-up to the events of 1941, he met a certain man called Jurek in early June in a flat belonging to a school friend named Henryk Jagiełło. After about an hour, they left the apartment and walked to the tram stop on the corner of ul.Gdanskciej and ul. Gen. Litzmanna. Here, they go their separate ways. A few days later, Jurek comes to the pharmacy to buy a bottle of cod liver oil. During this visit, Kotynia explains, he has the impression that Jurek wants something else from him beyond cod liver oil. This turns out to be true: Jurek suddenly asks if Kotynia knows anyone who knows how to get across the border. Kotynia says while he does not know, maybe his colleague Maria could help. She sometimes crosses the border to go to the cinema in Koluszki, he says.

Kotynia calls over Maria, who gets into a conversation with Jurek, but Kotynia stays out of it. He says that Jurek comes by several more times, but he always keeps out of the way whenever he finds the two of them talking: he wants nothing to do with the man. Nothing else happens, until one day Maria tells Kotynia that the border crossing was a success. At this point, Kotynia starts complaining that Maria's time-keeping at work is not good (a suggestion for her absence during the illegal crossings?). He further adds that he did not see Jurek again after that, including with his friend Henryk. Finally, he says that Maria heard from Jurek saying that he had made it to Warsaw at the first time of trying and was happy with how things had turned out. With these incriminating statements, he handed Maria over to the Gestapo on a plate, but it was not plain sailing for them at all as she proved very resistant to their charms. Kotynia will eventually become the pharmacy manager. Aged just 40, he will die in 1959.

Bernard Drozd, The Sailor, is arrested by the Gestapo on 10 November 1941, and is interrogated in the prison at ul. Młyńska in Poznań. The brutality these interrogators subject him to have one result: he talks. And the consequences are dire. This is in direct contrast to the stubborn silence of Maria Jasińska, the brave pharmacy assistant.

Kriminalpolizeisekretär (Criminal Police Secretary) Albrecht Giebelhausen, who leads the investigation in Lódz, can see that Maria is a particularly difficult nut to crack. He describes Jasińska as exceptionally secretive, admitting to something only if she cannot deny it otherwise. The only time they start to make any headway towards getting a confession out of her is when she's confronted by Drozd's incriminatory statements over her role in getting fugitives over the border illegally.

The Nazis have long known about the activities of the Poznań Resistance group who helped escaped British prisoners of war from Fort VIII, but it is only with Littledale and Sinclair's incriminating statements following their arrest in Pirot that they start finding out who was who and who did what. Littledale it is who names Bernard Drozd as one of the helpers. However, the Germans require more than names and addresses. They need to know how the organisation works, who does what and how it all fits together. If they can get a confession from someone who then points fingers at one or more of the others and what they get up to, they can cross reference everyone's statements and by comparing them all, the Gestapo can complete the jigsaw. Drozd's statements in particular will allow the Gestapo to penetrate deeper into the network that helped Littledale, Sinclair and Davies-Scourfield.

In a session of the *Sondergericht* (Special Court) in Poznań, on 13 February 1942, Bernard Drozd received the ultimate sentence for his part in aiding the enemy. From now on, as the weakest link in the chain, he will be regularly brought out to add further flesh to the bones of the Gestapo's investigation.

An undated statement from 1942 mentions that Drozd was interrogated by the Gestapo on 27 March 1942. The Gestapo are aware of the contact Drozd had had with Maria Jasińska regarding the British officers and their border crossings, and they need this confirmed in a statement so they can, in turn, present it to Maria and see how she gets on with denying that little lot. Just to refresh his memory, he is shown a photograph of Maria. Drozd says he is not sure that the person in this photo is the same Maria whose name was brought up during the interrogation in March. He acknowledges some similarity between the Maria he was talking about and the person in the photo, maybe, in the eyes, but the Maria he described had a narrower face and a different hairstyle.

He reads back his typed statement and signs it to confirm that it follows on from his earlier testimony. It is not known which photograph Bernard saw, but the confusion is understandable. Of the cheerful-looking Maria, posing with a generous smile in the pharmacy a few years before her arrest, all that remains is a world-wearied woman with lifeless hair combed harshly backwards, with bags under her eyes, a sad look and bulging puffy cheeks: mute testament to months of detention and torture by the Gestapo.

On 16 June, the Gestapo transfers the defendants Mieczsałwa Kierczyński, Maria Jasińska, Bronisław Wieczorek and Józef Połczynski to the *Sondergericht*, a special court at 152 Buschlinie in Lódz, for sentencing. In an accompanying letter, explicit reference is made to the statement made by the defendant Drozd in which he makes accusations against Maria Jasińska with regard to helping fugitive PoWs.

A letter dated 14 August signed by Steinberg, Gestapo Łódz, addressed to the Attorney General's office in Poznań, follows a request from the state police in Łódz. The letter concerns the criminal investigation under Art.I Abs.III and the resulting charges against Maria Jasińska and several others. It confirms that the files concerning the investigation have been sent to the State Police in Łódz for further investigation. Steinberg considers it necessary that the accused Jasińska, who denies any involvement in helping escaped English PoWs, be confronted with the statements of a Pole sentenced to death by the Poznań court (Drozd).

Moreover, it is important to interrogate this Pole further in order to identify other Polish girls and peasants involved in the crossing of English officers across the General Government border. In order to do this, the police in Łódz suggest taking Drozd to the border area in question where he can locate and identify the farms in which the British had hidden, and in particular to ascertain the role of the Nowak sisters. For this to happen, they need to transfer Drozd from Poznań to Łódz.

It is also reported that the police in Łódz have been asked to arrest and question a certain Mrs Kaller for her involvement in this affair. This is Christine Kaller. Her Polish name is Krystyna Kallerowa, and she supplied Littledale, Sinclair and Davies-Scourfield with cigarettes, playing cards and magazines in Czesław Wolf's flat at Böhmische Linie 9 m. 49 whilst they were hiding out in Łódz. Her name floats to the surface after 'the English lieutenant Sinclair during the investigation [pointed out] a person in Łódz, Mrs. Kaller [Kaller, Kallerowa] who supplied the refugees with cigarettes and clothes,' according to a report from Steinberg dated 7 July 1942. The same report also mentions a Pole named Jerzy Szczepowski. According to the statement made by Sinclair after his arrest in Bulgaria, apart from Christine Kaller, he, Gris and Ronnie are also helped by a cousin of Czesław Wolf, whom he knows as Teze, the phonetic sound of Jerzy Szczepowski's name.

On 9 October 1942, in a note signed by a certain SS-*Hauptsturmführer und Kriminalkommissar* Kauter, the Gestapo in Łódz informs the Chief Prosecutor in Łódz in the trial of Maria Jasińska that the planned confrontation of the accused with Bernard Drozd cannot now take place because the local unit handling the case are unable to provide the necessary transport for him at the moment, though they will be able to sort this out at a later date. It is finally rearranged for 4

November 1942. When the confrontation with Bernard Drozd finally takes place, Maria Jasińska discovers she has been checkmated. She finally admits that she was involved in transporting British officers to Gałkówek and Koluszki, a town near Zakowic. She explains that she came into contact with a young man named Jurek through Kotynia, a pharmacist working in her shop. According to her, this young man is a friend of Kotynia, and wants to accompany a stranger across the border. Since Maria herself will soon be visiting family near Tomaszów, she should be able to point out to Jurek the best way to get across the border illegally. She does not remember exactly when she met Jurek, just that she did. One day, Jurek shows up at the pharmacy with his friend Niko. After saying hello, Jurek and Niko are keen for Maria to meet three men they know. These men, who keep very much to themselves, are the ones wanting to cross the border and Maria is introduced to them. She then describes how the journey over the border was disrupted when a guide and his driver refused to take everybody because there were too many of them. Such a large group would draw attention to itself and increase the risk of all of them being checked and discovered by the authorities. As a result, accommodation has to be arranged for the men. At that point in her statement, Maria mentions the name of Drozd, who stays overnight with one of the Englishmen in the flat they have arranged. Since Maria herself has to go to Gałkówek to visit the Nowak family, she agrees to take one of the men with her. The other two men will follow later.

Together with Drozd, Maria leaves for Koluszki where she goes to church. She has also arranged by letter to meet up with her brother-in-law Stanisław Ogórek, who arrives while she is in Koluszki. According to her statement, she wants to see him because she wants to give him a jacket and blouse for his wife. She does not deny having spoken to Niko and her brother-in-law there. But does not remember what the conversation was about. She says it is possible that her brother-in-law told her how the group should continue travelling to Warsaw. After more than an hour, she leaves for Gałkówek, and then returns to Lódz. She states that she had no idea that there were Englishmen in the company.

On 5 November 1942, Drozd signs a statement giving his side of this story, and also the role played in it by 'Maria working in a pharmacy' and the Nowak family. Drozd begins his statement with the contact he has in Poznań with 'Doctor':

In Poznań, I received from Mr Verbno-Laszczyński ('Doctor') the address of Czesław Wolf in Lódz, where I was to meet the Englishmen who had arrived from Poznań. While we waited in the flat for further transport, a certain Mrs Kaller regularly dropped by to bring cigarettes, playing cards and other items. After four days, Jerzy and Nikodem arrived at the flat and told us they were in contact with Maria who worked in a pharmacy. On 18 June 1941 around six in the evening, Jerzy, Nikodem and I and two Englishmen took the tram to the terminus of line 10. At about twenty past eight, Maria arrived and we introduced her to the people in our group. We were to set off for Gałkówek with two more women.

As nocturnal travel is subject to strict control, the party decides to spend the night at a safehouse, except Maria who has already left for Gałkówek by then with one Englishman. Two girls serving as couriers lead the English and Poles to Gałkówek the next day, where they meet up with Maria and the other Englishman. The group travels on to Żakowice, where they stayed for two nights. Halfway through the trip, the 'young lady Nowak' joins the party, taking two Englishmen with her to stay with her parents. At the time, Drozd is staying in a building opposite the Nowak family's farm. He continues his story:

I was supposed to wait until the border guard returned from his round, he was supposed to pass in front of the houses. When the patrol returned, I pretended to be at the Nowaks' house. The two Englishmen then left with two girls. I followed the party to the border and passed a barrier on the left side of the road. At Żakowice, we passed the border. As told, after passing we arrived at a restaurant in Żakowice whose owner had left for Warsaw. When he returned the third night, we were forced to seek shelter elsewhere in the countryside. We then slept on straw in the kitchen of a worker's house. A woman unknown to us told us that the customs officer on duty at the time had the nickname 'Czekolada' (chocolate) and that she wanted to invite him 'for a pleasant evening'. At that moment, the third Englishman arrived. When I was in the house opposite the Nowak family, the said customs officer arrived on a bicycle with a dog.

The customs officer is accompanied by two other officers on bicycles. The woman who remained unknown to Drozd tells him that only 'Czekolada' would go on patrol. He stops for a while at the Nowaks' house, then rides on. At that moment, the border crossing takes place. Drozd takes the two Englishmen into the forest and then looks around to see if, as agreed, Maria would arrive with the third Englishman. Finally, he meets her in the middle of the village, together with Niko. They tell him they had been hanging around this place since the previous evening, but could not find the restaurant in the dark, so they had to spend the night outside. They also told him that Maria went ahead with the customs officer nicknamed 'Czekolada' and that Niko and the Englishman followed them.

In Koluszki, the group meets Maria's brother-in-law, and after a brief conversation with Niko, he shows them the way to Lubochnia where he will give them somewhere to stay. After saying goodbye to Maria, Niko, Drozd and the three Englishmen set off. At Lubochnia, they meet up with Maria's brother-in-law again, who takes them all to his flat. The next day, the group continues to Piotrków to meet people who will take them further to Warsaw. But then it breaks down. These people fail to make contact, so the Poles return, leaving the Englishmen to stay at the address for a second night. Drozd decides he wants nothing more to do with any of this, and while Niko leaves for Warsaw and the Englishmen go off on foot to Warsaw where they are subsequently taken care of, Drozd decides to go back to Poznań.

Every word of this testimony, Drozd declares, is the truth. By his own action, he has compromised Maria and delivered himself to the wrath of the occupier. On the statement, under Drozd's name, is the name of *Kriminalpolizei-sekretär* Giebelhausen. Two days after Drozd's statement, Maria Jasińska makes an additional statement and again, it is Giebelhausen whose name appears on the bottom. She can no longer ignore the facts and gives a supplementary statement to her earlier statements. Maria states that she came into contact with Maria Zrobek from Gałkówek through a former colleague from a previous job. This woman is willing to help her smuggle English servicemen across the border. She further acknowledges spending a night in the woods with one of the officers. While two Englishmen remain behind in the border region, Maria shuttles back and forth to Łódz to pick up the third man. As the party of six (the three Englishmen, the two Marias and Nicodemus, who has since joined the group) are about to leave, a border guard, known to Maria Zrobek, passes by and is called 'Czekolada' by her. Once it is dark, the group crosses the border. Maria concludes her account.

Both Bernard Drozd and Maria Jasinska speak of a border guard nicknamed 'Czekolada' in their statements. As the Gestapo's investigation continues, the identity of this customs officer with the remarkable name becomes clear. He is a friend of Maria Zrobek and is called Johannes Fehlau. He was born on 21 October 1905 in Elblag. A customs assistant, Fehlau was once sentenced to two and a half years in prison for smuggling. He does not really take his job seriously, and on the day when Littledale, Sinclair and Davies-Scourfield made their illegal crossing, he was busy with a bottle of vodka, getting drunk. According to Sinclair's statement, the man charged with keeping the border closed to fleeing PoWs had to be supported by a number of Polish women in order to stay upright. This was the second time that the English are aided by rogue Germans. He pays a high price for his drunken helpfulness. He gets locked up in a special prison in Bernau in Upper Bavaria, where lax SS men, under-performing members of the Gestapo and other discredited officials are subjected to a heartless regime. Czekolada's fate is not to be envied.

On 4 January 1943, less than two months after Maria Jasińska finally admitted her involvement in the PoWs' escape, Bernard Drozd is executed in the prison of the Untersuchungshaftanstalt Posen at ul. Młyńska, the Gestapo having no further use for him. The countdown for Maria begins now. There is no longer any uncertainty about her fate.

19

THE GALLOWS

On 4 February 1943, five Poles are indicted before the National Court in Łódz. The extensive file on which the indictment is based has been compiled by *Oberkriminal* Assistant Bodenstein in cooperation with Captain Wenz, *Abwehr* (Security) Officer of Stalag XXID in Posen. The accused are Miecsysław Kierczyński, merchant; Maria Eugenia Jasińska, pharmacy assistant; Józef Połczynski, transporter; Bronisław Wieczorok, worker and Henryka Nowak, seamstress. They have been in pre-trial detention since 19 June last year, except for Henryka Nowak, who joined her fellow accused on 2 November. They have been detained in the *Erweitertes Polizeigefängnis Radegast* (Radegast Extended Police Prison), located on a former factory site in Radogoszcz, a village on the north side of the city now swallowed up by Łódz.

From the Gestapo police prison for women on Danziger Strasse, Maria is transferred to the same location, a former Carmelite monastery on Senkeweg, after six weeks of preliminary investigation. The charge in the indictment is that the five harmed the interests of the German Reich through collaboration and helping English officers escape. The outcome of this trial has already been decided in advance. The charge in the indictment is that the five harmed the interests of the German Reich through collaboration and helped English officers escape. The outcome of this trial is already known in advance. The indictment continues by describing the escape on 28 May 1941 of three English officers from a camp in Poznań. How Jasińska meets the Englishmen as well as Drozd (the Sailor) and Kaliszan (Niko). How the driver who was to provide the transport broke off the journey for fear of being discovered during an inspection on the road to Gałkówek. How the party splits and the journey continues. The overnight stay in a forest with an officer accompanying them (Gris).

The meeting Jasińska has the next day with her friend Maria Zrobek. How later, Drozd arrives at the farm together with an Englishman (Littledale) and two unknown women. How Maria Zrobek's sister-in-law helps with the temporary hiding of both Englishmen and the continuation of the transport. This also involves Henryka Nowak, 15-years-old at the time. How after crossing the border and continuing the journey to Żakowice, the journey ends at the inn where Ronald and Gris wait for the arrival of their fellow fugitive Mike and the continuation of their journey. How Maria Jasińska has returned to Łódz to accompany Sinclair along the same route past Widzew to Gałkówek, until he arrives at Maria Zrobek's farm. How Maria, Niko and Mike then cross the General Government border after which the young lieutenant is reunited with Ronnie and Gris at the inn in Koluszki, where a certain Stanisław Ogórek is also present, a brother-in-law of Maria Jasińska. How while Maria goes back to Łódz, this Ogórek explains to Ronnie, Gris and Mike how to get to Warsaw. Further guidance is then out of the question when it turns out that Germany has invaded the Soviet Union.

Initially, Maria says she does not know the nationality of the men she has accompanied, and only after spending the night in the forest does she find out that the man with her at the time is English. Both Jasińska and Nowak are confronted with their actions by the information from Drozd's confessions.

The indictment goes on to describe the second group of four PoW officers who manage to escape from Poznań in June 1941. How they, like Ronnie, Gris and Mike, are taken by car to the flat of Czesław Wolf at Böhmische Linie no. 9 in Łódz, from where the further escape route is prepared. How defendant Mieczysław Kierczyński is repeatedly asked by his brother Bolesław from Poznań to help transport the four to the General Government. How Mieczysław eventually declares his willingness to help the four British officers and establishes contact with co-accused Józef Połczynski and through him with Bronisław Wieczorok. How the Polish man named 'Józef' approached by Bronisław Wieczorok for the illegal border crossing ends up taking the four to a certain Dolniak in Warsaw.

At the time the charges are formulated, this 'Józef' is still unknown.

Accusations against Mieczysław Kierczyński are piling up. Apart from his attempts to negotiate the border crossing for the fugitives, he also regularly gives them food during their stay in Wolf's flat. He flatly denies knowing that they are English, and has no idea that they are escaped prisoners of war. But he then says he recognised their English accents. At this the prosecutors think they have hit the jackpot: if Mieczysław Kierczyński recognised English accents, he must have known they were English and by helping them on their way, that he was helping enemies of Germany. They further argue that it is almost certain that his brother Bolesław, who got him involved in all this in the first place, had already told him all sorts of details about them, including their nationality. Józef Połczynski and Bronisław Wieczorok have since admitted helping the men.

While the group in Łódz await the start of their trial, the proceedings against Bernard Drożd, Bolesław Kierczyński, Klara Dolniak and six other Poles have come up at the Special Court in Poznań, the Sondergericht Posen, in late 1942. They have already been convicted and sentenced to death for aiding and abetting escaped English servicemen. In February 1942, the arrest of a large group of Poles involved in helping at least 30 fleeing servicemen follows. The group consists of Witold Verbno Łaszczyński (Doctor), Klara Dolniak, Maria Duszyńska, Michalina Gorczyca, Bolesław Kierczyński, Bronisław Sobkowiak (the Polish electrician from Fort VIII who helps Gris, Ronnie and Mike), Maria Klichowski, her husband Bolesław and their sons Zbigniew (Sobkowiak's 15-year-old assistant at Fort VIII) and Zygmunt, Irena Markiewicz, Praksed Michałowska, Karol Salewski, in addition to several others. In the end, seven of them will receive the death penalty.

On 23 February, Witold Verbno Łaszczyński (Doctor) is arrested in his flat at ul. Matejki 57. He is badly beaten during the interrogation after his arrest, losing an eye as a result. One cannot help but conjecture if this was deliberate: he had already lost one eye when fighting the Germans in 1939. He spends his days in captivity at Fort VII in Poznań and at the prison on ul. Młyńska. On 13 July 1942, the Sondergericht passes judgement on his case. On 15 December that year, the sentence is carried out. He is executed in prison.

Michalina Gorczyca, nicknamed *Kapitanowa* (Captain), was born in 1904 into the family of a clergyman. She joins the ZWZ in 1940 and is the close associate of Doctor, with whom she helps to establish the local Dorsze cell in Poznań. She is heavily involved in organising accommodation for the men who flee during the Dorsze campaign. Her name appears on the list Ronald Littledale hands over to his interrogators after his arrest in the Balkans. During the trial in which Doctor is convicted, she is particularly harshly addressed by Judge Dr Schwab. After which he passes sentence. She is executed on the same day as Doctor.

Irena Markiewicz was born in 1900 in Kaczkowie in a peasant family. She works in a tailor's shop making underwear in Poznań. In April 1941, she is sworn into the ZWZ and nicknamed *Krawcowa* (Seamstress). Her flat at ul. Garbary 18 is the first address used in the Dorsze Campaign to shelter refugees. When the Germans shut down the Dorsze Campaign and Doctor is arrested, she too cannot avoid the long arm of the Nazis. She is interrogated at length and sentenced to death on 13 August, despite denying all allegations during the trial. All attempts at a pardon come to nothing. Irena Markiewicz is also executed on 15 December in the same prison as Doctor and Captain.

Maria Elżbieta Klichowska, nicknamed Czerska during her initiation into the ZWZ in 1941, acts as liaison between Doctor and Bolesław Kierczyński (Sława or Fame). The Abwehr arrests her and her husband Bolesław on 21 February and hands the couple over to the Gestapo in Poznań on 27 February 1942. She undergoes brutal interrogation sessions in the Dom Żołnierza, the Soldiers' House, the seat of the administrative office that houses the *Geheime Staatspolizei* (Gestapo: Secret State Police) *Staatspolizeileitstelle* (State Police Headquarters) Posen. This is where Irena Markiewicz is also interrogated. Boldly, she takes all the blame, and this is possibly why her husband is subsequently released. He is not totally free. He is forced into factory labour for the Wehrmacht, the police and the SS. Maria's life also ends on that grim 15 December. Shortly before her death, she writes a last letter to her mother from the *Stammlager Untersuchungshaftanstalt* (Remand Centre, Main Prison) Posen.

> Dear Mother,
> I must leave this world today and once again I send you many warm greetings, asking you to remember me in your prayers.
> Your daughter
> Maria

That same day, she is beheaded.

A few days before Maria's arrest, her sons, Zygmunt and Zbigniew, are arrested. Both deny the allegations being thrown at them. But they do not get off that easily. Zygmunt Klichowski has a long tale to tell to the Gestapo:

> On Saturday 21 February 1942 around 1pm, the Gestapo raided the house. First they took me, then brother Zbigniew when he came home, and finally mother and father. I was transported by car to the Gestapo building, on the spot where the Soldiers' House stood before the war. Even at the first stage of the investigation, I realised that the Gestapo knew in detail the whole course of the escape of the British. I wondered who could have betrayed all this. I adopted such defensive tactics that I knew nothing about the case, because although I initially worked in Fort VIII, I was later transferred to Mosina near Poznan and did not even make it home. As I later discovered, the Gestapo checked Mosina's work cards, confirming my testimony. The Nazis initially persuaded me to cooperate and when I refused they took me to the basement. There was a Gestapo officer leading the investigation, a clerk and two torturers. I was tied up and interrogated, and when I answered that I knew nothing, in between swearing and insulting Poland, I was beaten until I lost consciousness. Then they poured water on me, followed by a question and then clapping again to the point that I lost feeling. How long it lasted I don't know. At one point, the interrogator told me to get dressed. This went very slowly because I could hardly move, and every movement was excruciatingly painful. A tall SS man came in and asked the interrogator if I had said anything. Hearing that, he did not tell me to come near him. When I approached, he hit me in the face so hard that I flew through the cellar like a ball, bounced against the opposite wall and fell. An SS man ran towards me, kicked me a few times and then shouted at me to get up and come to him. When I did, he hit me again like with a hammer.

The torture is ongoing and persistent. When he is brought back upstairs, he briefly considers jumping out the window to end it himself, but being on the first floor in the building, he doubts the usefulness of such an action. He denies all knowledge of Doctor, when questioned about him. He is forced to stand facing the wall. Someone is brought in to the room. It is his brother Zbigniew. Zygmunt is led away to his isolation cell, where he can hear his brother, his mother and other suspects involved in the action in Fort VIII being tortured.

Several days later, missing his front teeth thanks to the Gestapo's heavy-handed interrogations, he is transported to Żabikowo concentration camp near Poznań, a Jewish Labour camp named Poggenburg was set up here. From 1943 until the end of the war, it is also used as a Nazi prison, replacing Fort VII. More than 20,000 prisoners will be interned there. Later, Zbigniew ends up at Mauthausen, a camp many times bigger and more infamous than Żabikowo. Both brothers will survive the war.

On 18 July 1942, the *Ostdeutscher Beobachter* (*The Eastern German Observer*), an organ of the NSDAP in Poznan, posts the following *Verkündungsblatt des Reichsstatthalters und seiner Behörden* (Reich Governor's Announcement):

> On Monday, the special court in Posen tried nine Poles who helped English officers escape from a PoW camp in the summer of 1941. The accused Bronislaus Sobkowiak, Michalina Gorczyca, Irena Markiewicz, Witold von Verbno-Leszczynski and Marie Klichowki, all from Posen, Boleslaw Kierczynski from Starachiwice (Radom District) and Bernhard Drozd from Polajewo, Scharnikau District, were sentenced to death. Sixteen-year-old Zbigniew Klichowski was sentenced to six years and defendant Klara Dolniak to three years in prison camp.

Apart from members of the Polish Resistance, there are also casualties from within the German war machine's own ranks. On 13 March, Captain Wenz arrests a key figure from Fort VIII. Otto Devant is serving with the 10th Battalion of Domestic Riflemen at the time of his arrest. Three days later, Wenz apprehends Karol Geerdts of the 662nd Battalion of Domestic Riflemen. In his report, which forms the basis for their indictments, *Oberkriminal* Assistant Bodenstein outlines the escapes from Fort VIII and the subsequent events. Over 17 pages, he details everything, from the provision of clothing and false identity papers, to the chain of couriers who enabled Littledale and Sinclair to travel 2,000 km from Posen to Pirot without once being apprehended. Bodenstein elaborates on Devant's role in preparing the escape, and blames the Abwehr for failing to establish whether Devant actively helped the British escape from Fort VIII.

Guilt rests firmly on the shoulders of Devant, who, once informed of a planned escape attempt, not only fails to prevent it, but offers the English his explicit friendship and cooperation. This is compounded by the contents of a letter from Devant to Captain Hanken found during a search of Zygmunt Klichowski's house, which leaves no ambiguity as to where Otto Devant stands. The German soldiers are condemned and executed. When it comes to any of their number helping the enemy, the Nazis make no exception.

In mid-February 1943, a letter is delivered to the Office of the National Court addressed to the Special Court that was created to hear the case against Resistance fighters involved in helping escaped British officers from PoW camps in Poland. The notice, dated 13 February, is requested by the High Secretary of Justice in Łódz in order to pass information to Maria Eugenia Jasińska concerning the lawsuit filed against her and four others. At the time, she is still confined in Radogoszcz prison. On 8 March, she is required to appear at the *Kreisgericht* (District Court) at Hindenburgplatz 5, Litzmannstadt (Special Court No. 1 at present-day Place Generala Henryka Dąbrowskiego 5 in Łódz). The letter states that should she be at liberty at that time, she is to be arrested and forced to appear. Apparently, not everyone is aware that Maria has been detained since late April last year.

A report written by Inspector of Justice Kersten, dated 15 March, details the trial on 8 March of Mieczysław Kierczyński, Maria Eugenia Jasińska, Bronisław Wieczorok, Józef Połczyński and Henryka Nowak. The President of the National Court, Dr Beyer, acts as chairman during the trial. Dr Jehlen is the prosecutor. Two generals and ten German officers are also present. This indicates the seriousness with which the occupying forces view the whole affair. The report states right at the beginning that the sentences imposed at the trial are final and binding. Appeals against the verdicts are no longer possible.

Defendants Połczynski, Wieczorek and Nowak are being shown leniency by the court because it cannot be proved with certainty that they knew that the people who crossed the border illegally were British. Henryka Nowak cannot even be blamed for having had contact with the British. However, for Kierczyński and Jasińska, the situation is considerably different. They know exactly the nationality of the soldiers and in any case, they have all been involved in one way or another in aiding enemies of the Reich. The court stresses in the ruling against Kierczyński that his contribution is limited to finding a contact to arrange transport and sorting out food for the escapees. Moreover, he was put under great pressure to do this by his brother, even to the extent of being threatened by the involvement of their mother in the affair. These factors constitute mitigating circumstances, which are therefore reflected in the sentence issued against him.

Mieczysław Kierczyński is sentenced, a few days before his 37th birthday, to eight years' imprisonment in a camp for his part in helping escaped PoWs. Józef Połczyński and Bronisław Wieczorok are both given one year in a labour camp. Henryka Nowak, now nearly 18, is given a sentence of nine months in a labour camp for her part. Her youthful age at the time of the 'offences' is taken into account in determining the punishment. And to add insult to misery, those convicted will also pay the legal costs incurred.

Finally, it is Maria Eugenia Jasińska's turn. She is considered extremely active in helping the British, even to the point of escorting them across the border and is therefore regarded by the Nazis as very dangerous. She listens to the verdict with dignity. Maria receives the most severe sentence possible: death. Until the very end, she remains obstinately resistant, proudly standing her ground. She does not respond to the prosecutor's request to make statements about her co-accused, even for sentence reduction. Her mother hears her telling the judges, 'You were looking for aces. That ace is me.' She has nothing left to lose. It cannot be any worse than during the past year in which she was tortured so severely that she was often brought back to her cell in a blanket because she could no longer move. Her reaction to her sentence is stoic, dignified and strong. 'I accept the punishment with peace,' she says simply, though she cannot possibly in her heart and mind do so. She did nothing wrong, she is not a criminal, and she tells the court she does not deserve this verdict. She did what she did from her heart, with compassion for her suffering, unfortunate, fellow man.

On the same day that Kreisgericht Litzmannstadt's final report is completed, Anna Szczygielska Jasińska, Maria's mother, receives a short note from Berlin at her address at 80 Kleingärtnerstrasse in Łódź. Although an appeal against the verdict in the case against her daughter Maria is out of the question, it is still possible for Maria to apply for a pardon. However, according to an 18 March communication from Artur Greiser, *Reichsstatthalter und Gauleiter* (Reich Governor and Gauleiter) der NSDAP in Reichsgau Wartheland, the district under which Litzmannstadt falls, Maria declines this opportunity for freedom.

> Maria E. Jasinka: *ich mache von dem mir vom Führer übertragenen Begnadigungsrecht keinen Gebrauch.*

> (Maria E. Jasinka: I will not make use of the right of pardon granted to me by the Führer.)

Her sister Helena applies for a pardon instead, on behalf of their mother. In addition to Artur Greiser, this request goes right to the top: Adolf Hitler and Hermann Göring. The letter that reaches Anna Jasińska in response to her daughter's request comes from the *Neue Reichskanzlei* (New Reich Chancellery) on Voßstraße in Berlin. The office of *Der Staatsminister und Chef der Präsidialkanzlei des Führers und Reichskanzlers* (The Minister of State and Head of the Presidential Chancellery of the Führer and Reich Chancellor) reports on 15 March:

> *Ihr Gnadengesuch für Ihre Tochter Maria ist hier eingegangen. Auf Anordnung des Führers habe ich es dem Reichsminister der Justiz, Berlin W 8, Wilhelmstr. 65, zur Bearbeitug zugeleitet. Etwige weiters Eingaben in der Sache sind unmittelbar dorthin zu richten.*

> (Your petition for clemency for your daughter Maria has been received here. By order of the Führer, I have forwarded it to the Reich Minister of Justice, Berlin W 8, Wilhelmstr. 65, for processing. Any further submissions in the matter are to be sent directly to this office.)

The manager of pharmacy 'Pod Łabędziem', Baltic German Nielsen-Storackge, writes a good character reference for his assistant:

> I confirm that Maria Jasinska worked in the pharmacy I managed from 1 April 1940 to 30 April 1942. She performed the duties entrusted to her diligently and conscientiously, to my complete satisfaction.

It is highly doubtful that these the words have any effect whatsoever on Maria's fate. What is beyond doubt is that by giving such support to a person convicted of crimes such as Maria's, he has exposed himself to the whims of the authorities: the Gestapo. Their dangerous gaze could well alight on something as simple as the company's letterhead, which uses the word 'Lodsch' as a place name, the Germanised variant of Lódz. He should probably have used the Nazi name: Litzmannstadt.

Whilst Maria awaits the outcome of the application for a Pardon, she uses the time to write letters, which she is allowed to do once every four weeks. On 21 March, she notes in poor German and occasionally illegible handwriting to her family (translated to English below):

My dearest parents and whole family!!!
    The word is nothing. I want to give you all my heart today. I have never been with your dearest mum, dad, sister, brother [...] (sic)
    I ask God for health and happiness for you every day. Please, very please, don't be sad and don't cry. For me this [...] is very difficult.
    If you do not cry, I will be better. Everything is very good for me, and for me it was very good together. Now I must go on. How easy that is better.
    Not long my dear parents will be your 40th wedding anniversary. I wish you all the best and good luck, I wish you many more sweet years together, and long love.
    My dearest sisters! And family
    Parents and family are the biggest and best treasure in this world. Don't forget that!!! You [...] also must know that you are not [...] but good man. Don't have much, but good friend. Love well all my family! I don't have much to say, then I'll give you my little heart once again. Many kisses and greetings also for the whole Kalniowskich Ciezielskich family at the first place for Aunt Maria and her whole family, for Aunt Jozia and family, for Celine and [...] all relatives and acquaintances, for Lodzio, [...] for my comrade, comrade for [...] Andreas and Elisabeht that are my dear children
    Your Marie

On 20 April 1943, she writes her last letter to her closest family. Shortly before, she had been told that Helena's application on behalf of their mother for Maria's pardon has been rejected and that her sentence has been confirmed: all that awaits her is death. She is not allowed any visits from her priest, she cannot go to confession or receive the last sacrament. All she is allowed to do is write to her family. And wait.

> Dear mother, father, brothers and sisters,
>
> These are my last wishes I write, I don't have much time left. I will die without having been able to confess. I apologise for everything, please pray for me. I trust in the grace of God. I know God is the most beloved Father and will accept me. Always I have hoped that things will go well for you. Today I will leave and ask God for favours for you. Just before death, you see many things more clearly, and I see a lot of my mistakes. Daily I prayed for happiness for my family, not based on increasing prosperity, but on mutual love, understanding and respect. Oh, most beloved Jesus, let them live according to Your commandments give them Your blessing!
>
> My beloved ones! Most beloved and my beloved, do not despair, destiny is there, apparently it had to be so. Strangers came to me [in her cell], after all I didn't care about anything, it's just a coincidence, but that happens in life. Now I know I will be executed tonight at 6 o'clock.
>
> Beloved brothers and sisters, respect each other and love each other. Honour father and mother. Say goodbye to everyone and apologise to anyone I have done anything wrong.
>
> Your Marycha
>
> P.S. Mother, make confession for me and ask God for mercy for my soul and body.

The German Eagle With Swastika spreads her wings above a *Bekanntmachung* (Announcement) dated 20 April 1943 and signed by *Der Oberstaatsanwalt* (Chief Public Prosecutor) in Litzmannstadt. Her shadow hovers menacingly above the names of five Poles convicted by *Das Sondergericht* for their acts against *Das Deutsche Reich*. At the bottom of the list is Maria Eugenia Jasińska.

On 12 March 1943, the *Sondergericht* pronounced:

Wegen Schädigung des Wohles des Deutschen Reiches durch Unterstützung entflohener Kriegsgefangener zum Tode verurteilt. Die Urteile sind heute vollstreckt worden.

(Sentenced to death for harming the welfare of the German Reich by supporting escaped prisoners of war. The sentences were carried out today.)

A translation in Polish is placed below in a smaller font.

On the morning of 20 April, as Hitler celebrates his 54th birthday, Maria Jasińska is picked out of line during morning exercise. She is given a black apron and her picture is taken. At the *Gerichtgefängnis* located on Friedrich Goßler-Strasse (now ul. Kopernika 29), she is escorted to the garage in the courtyard. It is the only place where capital punishment is officially carried out in Lódz. Present are Prosecutor Heble, Clerk Krahn, Head Guardsman Scheibler, Dr Wannagat and scribe Schorzek, who draws up the protocol of the execution of the sentence against convict Maria Eugenia Jasińska. It is with these representatives of the occupying force's officialdom that she spends her last minutes. The party enters the execution chamber located in the prison courtyard where Prosecutor Heble introduces her to the prison staff, who then bind her hands and escort her to the gallows. Once she's climbed up and is standing on the trapdoor, her feet are bound together. The Prosecutor confirms her identity and at two minutes past six he orders the execution to be carried out. The noose is placed around Maria's neck and the trapdoor opens.

At five minutes past six, the prison doctor pronounces Maria Eugenia Jasińska dead.

Her body is handed over to the prison authorities for further processing. Although Maria requests before she is executed that her body be handed over to her mother, despite all efforts to find out, the family does not know where she will eventually be buried.

Emil Brunclík (Public Domain).

Maria Brunclikova (Public Domain).

Gertruda Šašková (left) (Public Domain).

Plaque commemorating the murder of the Bergauer couple (Author's Collection).

Colditz, 2015 (Author's Collection).

Mike Sinclair in Colditz, middle row second from right, 1942 (Sammlung Schloss Colditz).

Mike Sinclair in Colditz (Sammlung Schloss Colditz).

Prisoner's courtyard in Colditz, 2015 (Author's Collection).

The author in Colditz trying to enter the 'Pat-Reid-Keller' (Author's Collection).

Cellar under the Kommandantur building, Colditz Castle (Author's Collection)

The flue in the cellar, Colditz (Author's Collection).

Terraces on the southside of the Colditz, 2015 (Author's Collection).

Olga Kamińska-Prokopowa (Public Domain).

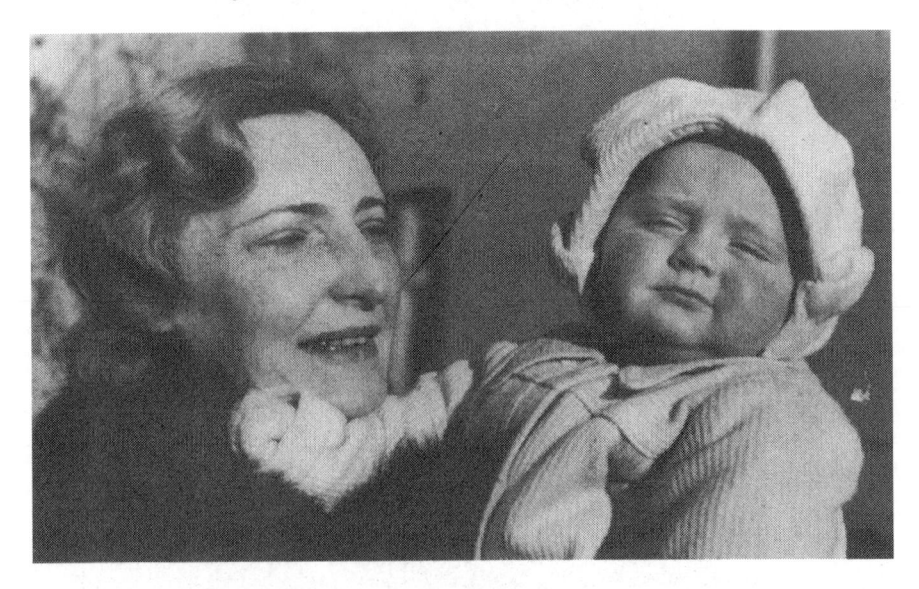

Marek Prokop as a child with his grandmother Irena (Public Domain).

Marek Prokop, Olga's son (Public Domain).

Cemetery in Airaines, France (Author's Collection).

Gravestone of Ronald Littledale in Airaines, France (Author's Collection).

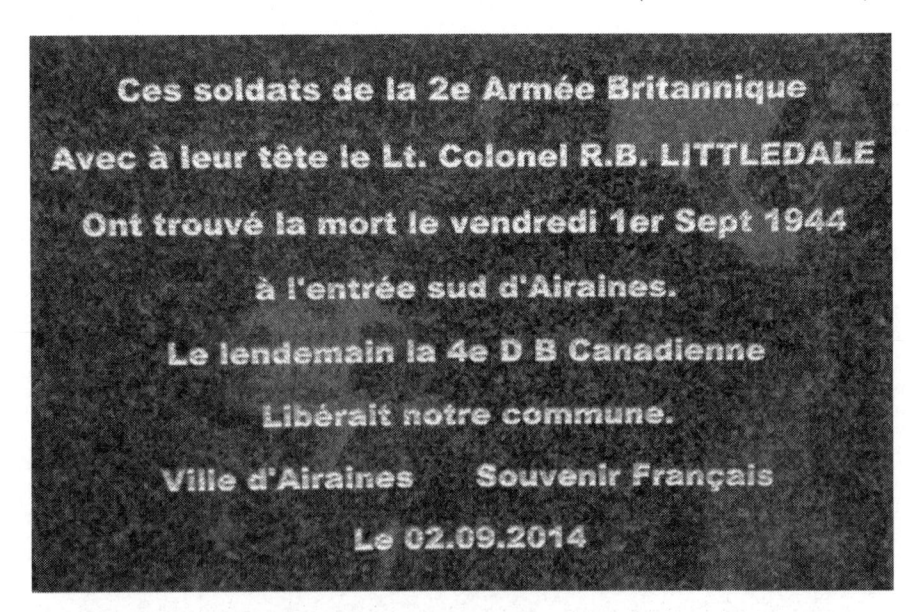

Commemorative plaque, Airaines Cemetery, France (Author's Collection).

Gravestone of Mike Sinclair in Berlin (Author's Collection).

Dorotheenstädtischer Friedhof cemetery, Berlin, plaque commemorating the victims of Hermann Stieve (Author's Collection).

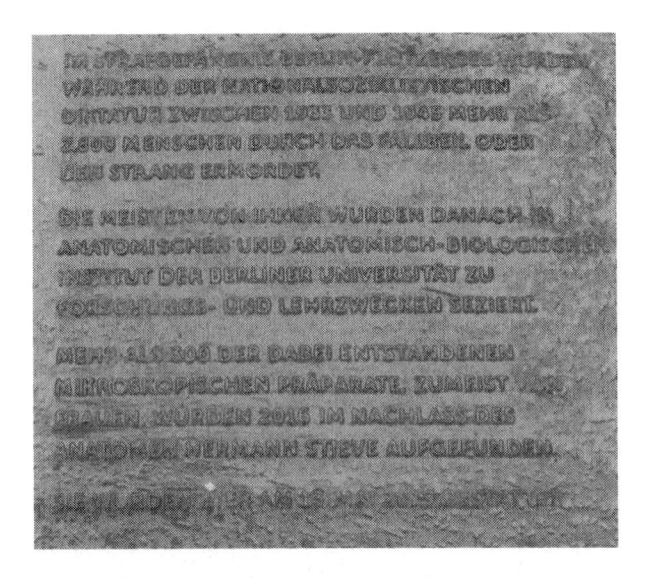

Closer view of above plaque (Author's Collection).

20

MIKE

The London Gazette of 4 May, 1943 contains the following announcement:

> War Office, 4th May, 1943
> The KING has been graciously pleased to approve the following awards in recognition of gallant and distinguished services in the field:-
>
> The Distinguished Service Order
>
> Major Ronald Bolton Littledale (25378) The King's Royal Rifle Corps

'For gallant and distinguished services', indeed. The Distinguished Service Order (DSO) is a high decoration and Ronald is one of only two people who escaped from German captivity to be so honoured.

On 9 April 1944, he accepts the award at Buckingham Palace. At the same time, he rejoins his regiment. In May 1944, the Parish Magazine in Bunbury reports:

> On April 9th in Buckingham Palace, His Majesty the King, decorated Major R.B. Littledale with the Distinguished Service Order medal, 'for' [to quote the citation] 'gallant and distinguished service in the field'. We recollect how his host of friends and admirers were thrilled when it was known how, through unexampled bravery and dash, he had successfully outwitted the whole pack of Himmler's Gestapo and secret police and emerged triumphantly in neutral territory. We tender our heartiest congratulations, and our best wishes go with him.

The truth has not penetrated the Bunbury community, the Parish Magazine awaits its presence still ere long. Littledale has apparently said nothing that might induce the thought that it is not he who 'outsmarted the entire platoon of Himmler's Gestapo and secret police', but that they outsmarted him, when he was persuaded to be more candid than he might have been. This must have been a huge burden for him to bear: how did he keep a secret like that, knowing he had talked? At a time when he should have been recovering his equilibrium, enjoying the official recognition, being treated like a hero.

In the same column of *The London Gazette*, another name appears: Lieutenant (temporary Captain) Patrick Robert Reid (58974) Royal Army Service Corps. He is awarded the Military Cross (MC). By convention, officers receive awards according to their rank. Senior Officers (Major and above) like Littledale, receive a DSO; Junior Officers (Captain and below) an MC.

Littledale's DSO was awarded while he was still en route from Spain. MI9 had yet to speak to him, which may have been fortunate, as would they have awarded his medal after the incendiary revelations he had given them. But his mind is elsewhere. After three years on the run through Europe with a dramatic twist, he receives sad news on his return home. His father had died on 24 December 1942 at the age of 74, and was buried on 28 December that year. Ronnie was still in Switzerland. When was the last time father and son saw each other? The moment the KRRC was sent to France to help quell the German onslaught in Calais?

Meanwhile, Mike Sinclair languishes back in the castle at Colditz. Are his dreams or waking thoughts haunted by the ghost of Christine Kaller? Or those of Maria Jasińska, Olga Prokopowa Kamińska or Maria Klichowska? What motivates his obsessive need to attempt to escape his guards again and again? Belligerence, soldier's honour, an officer's oath? Or is it remorse? He would have realised the repercussions of the confessions he and Littledale made back in Pirot. Repercussions not visited upon them. He and Ronnie lived to fight on, that was not the fate for those whom they named. Is it atonement is he looking for? Some kind of redemption?

In November 1942, he escaped from Colditz. It was through the Light Well in the theatre block alongside the French Captain Charles Klein. After getting clear of the castle and the town, they separated to travel their own paths. Sinclair made it to Immendingen, but that was as far as he got. Within sight of the Swiss border, he was arrested and taken back to Colditz, again trying and failing to escape while on the way. So while Littledale catches his breath in England, coping with the loss of his father and receiving his DSO, Sinclair is back in the castle just southeast of Leipzig. A different world away.

In 1953, following from the huge success of *The Colditz Story*, Pat Reid published a second volume, *The Latter Days At Colditz*, this time covering the period after his escape in October, 1942 up to the castle's liberation in April 1945. He wrote this account based upon interviews he carried out with former prisoners. It is largely through events described in this book that the name and reputation of Michael Sinclair, *Der Rote Fuchs*, The Red Fox, gets a wider introduction to the reading public. One of these events took place in 1943.

As ever with Oflag IVC, what happened is steeped in ambiguities. According to Pat Reid in 1953, Sinclair's singularly spectacular escape attempt took place on 19 May 1943. However, 30 years later, in his third volume, *Colditz: The Full Story*, Reid gives the date as 3 September 1943. In the steady flow of Colditz memoirs that followed Reid's accounts, is a book by former Prisoner Jim Rogers entitled *Tunnelling into Colditz*. In this, he talks about 2 September, nearly four months and a complete season apart.

On numerous internet sites, both dates are given. Is it one? Is it the other? Is it neither? Definitive clarity is only provided by Padre Ellison Platt's diary, (published in an edited form in 1978 as *Padre In Colditz*) when he writes on 2 September:

> A day of suppressed excitement, and a very busy day for the team concerned. The director has a nasty fear that fate will somehow close in on the scheme.

What is meant by 'fate' is evident from his September 3 diary entry:

> Mike Sinclair was shot through the body, two inches wide of his heart.

On the night of 2 September, Mike Sinclair ventures a spectacular escape attempt with near-fatal consequences for his life. The attempt is certainly spectacular.

There are three ways out of a prison: over the wall, under the wall, or through the wall. Through the wall means through a door, window or gate, and this is risky because one can never be too sure of what is on the other side, likely a suspicious sentry on the lookout for any prisoners being outside when they shouldn't be.

Even before Mike gets to Colditz, there have been several successful and unsuccessful attempts to get out of the castle in a fake German uniform. On 5 January 1942, Airey Neave and Tony Luteyn walk out of the gate dressed as German officers and manage to reach Switzerland safely. Neave has previous experience with a fake uniform when he walks out disguised as a soldier on 28 August 1941. Unfortunately for him, the colour of his uniform, so convincing during the day, is somewhat less so under the lamplight at dusk, when he makes his attempt. He is immediately grabbed and with a rueful smile that only sporting losers can exhibit, he then poses for Johannes Lange for security officer Eggers' photo collection. A day after Neave and Luteyn, Dutch Lieutenant Herman Donkers and British Lieutenant John Hyde-Thomson follow the same route but they are arrested at the railway station in Ulm. Hedley Fowler and Daemian Van Doornick also dressed in the enemy's vestments to get out successfully. Over time, the Germans amass a whole collection of confiscated fake uniforms. The ingenuity of the Prisoners in making these is not lost to history. There is a photograph of Germans posing in these fake jackets and caps, and cardboard pistol holsters.

Merely walking through the gate in a German uniform is not enough. This plan, with Mike Sinclair in the starring role, is bolder, and if it succeeds it means that dozens of PoWs will soon be fanning out across Germany. Together with two fellow officers, Mike, who is dressed as the striking Stabsfeldwebel (Sergeant Major) Fritz Rothenberger will relieve the guards on the east side of the castle. That gives a waiting escape party several minutes to run through a gate in the barbed wire fence and off into the night, unhindered. The choice of Rothenberger is not arbitrary. Mike bears a strong resemblance to the man nicknamed 'Franz Josef', after the former Austrian emperor, because of his distinctive moustache. As early as April, they start their preparations. Uniforms have to be tailored, gun holsters made of cardboard, wooden rifles. Mike has to study Rothenberger's behaviour and gait. He has to become Rothenburger in a sense, so his impersonations of his gait, facial expressions, manner, behaviour and accent are second nature to him and convincing enough to the real German guards so that they follow his orders. The language is no problem for Mike, but whether he ever thought his studies in Modern Languages at Trinity College in Cambridge would come in handy in this way is doubtful. Fourteen moustaches are manufactured until the right one is found to complete the fake Franz Josef. Mike's seconds are John Hyde-Thomson, who, once again, dons a fake uniform in a bid to escape and Lancelot Pope. They too speak excellent German.

On the night of 2 September 1943, the men descend onto the terrace on the north side of the castle from a window in the infirmary. John and Lancelot successfully relieve the sentries they encounter on the way. At the main exit, though, things start to go wrong. The guard standing there refuses to comply with the fake Rothenberger's demand to leave. Mike tries again. The guard still won't budge. Why not?

Again: ambiguity. Why won't he go? Is Mike's pass the wrong colour? Is Rothenberger's first name wrong ('Fritz' instead of 'Gustav'), or is it the wrong number? Does Mike give the wrong password, or make the wrong gesture, or not at all, or does the sentry find it strange to be relieved after only 15 minutes?

Mike decides to continue playing his part instead of fleeing with John and Lance. The verbal tussle that ensues with the rigid guard gets louder and louder, finally attracting the attention of other guards elsewhere in the castle. And then the real Rothenberger appears. He and his doppelganger go at it verbally at each other. Who's who? The guards aren't sure anymore. No-one trained them for this. Suddenly, in the confusion a shot is heard and one of the Rothenbergers falls to the ground. The moustache comes loose a little, it is Sinclair. The Germans leave him lying there for ten minutes, while the prisoners on the other side of the bars loudly identify the shooter as the overzealous Corporal Pilz, nicknamed 'Big Bum' among the prisoners. The ill-feeling persists into the emergency *appell* (roll call) that follows every discovered attempt. The Kommandant, Prawitt, has to intervene personally, assuring the prisoners that Mike is 'only wounded' and not dead, '... a shot through the body, two inches wide of his heart...'

Again, Mike fails. He is, however, lucky to be able to recount the tale. In a statement, he describes what happened:

> His [Pilz] whole attitude was one to provoke and increase the tension and excitement instead of taking charge. Pilz drew his

pistol and brandished it in a reckless and gleeful manner and obviously enjoying the possibility of using it. He screamed at me, 'Hands up.' I put my hands up. He screamed at me again, 'Hands up,' and I shouted back at him, 'My hands are up, they are high enough.' He then repeatedly shouted a word which sounded like '*absehnalen*' to which I replied, 'I do not understand.' Owing to the state of confusion I do not remember exactly when I was shot, but I do remember being extremely surprised that the shot should be fired, there being no reason for it. The shot was fired into my chest from a yard in front of me, and slightly to the left.

It was Mike's forged ID pass that gives them away. The pass Mike is carrying is a copy of a real pass obtained from a German guard. The latter insists that his pass was stolen in the castle, thus avoiding the possibility of execution for helping the enemy. Captain Eggers only reveals this years later, in his contribution to the canon of Colditz literature, *Colditz: The German Viewpoint*. He writes that just a few days before the escape, and unbeknownst to the prisoners, the German passes issued to the Colditz guards undergo two essential changes. On each card, in tiny print, an additional number is added to the bottom right corner, unique to the holder of the card. The prisoners believe that the number on each card is identical. It is not. The number on Mike's fake card does not belong to Rothenberger. Furthermore, the colour of Mike's card, yellow, is incorrect. Rothenberger carries a grey pass. Moreover, years later, Hugh Bruce is told by a former guard that Rothenberger's Christian name is not Fritz as indicated on the forged pass, but Gustav. Any observant and diligent guard can easily foil the cleverly devised escape attempt.

That same month, on the 30th, Gris ventures out. Although he witnessed the dramatic outcome of Mike's attempt shortly before, he is not deterred. He tries a repeat of his attempt at Fort VIII. In the same manner as before, two orderlies smuggle him out through the gate in a dust crate of diminished proportions. Like before, Gris is covered in trash. He has a few anxious moments when the crate is temporarily set down in the courtyard by the two Scottish orderlies carrying it when a German corporal calls the men away for another job. A crack in his putative coffin allows him to see his assistants walking across the square where not long before he himself had been wandering around and attended *appell*. After an unnervingly long time, the coffin is lifted up again, and he is dumped, rubbish and all, into one of the buildings in the German part of the castle. He is relieved, his muscles were aching, and now he has to fend for himself. He is thickly dressed, over a civilian outfit is a stolen German uniform that has been given the right colour at the last minute. Looking in a mirror, he neatens himself up, so as not to stand out when he steps through the storage room door. With some sweat on his back, he walks across the courtyard of the Kommandantur to the large gate on the east side of the castle while around him German soldiers are milling about.

Once he is out of the castle, the hike can really begin. And this time, he has a huge advantage—he is not missing. Someone takes his place for the various *appells*, allowing Gris to travel across Germany while the count remains correct in the castle he hopes to leave behind forever. The secret is a ghost, one of whom is Lieutenant Jack Best. These ghosts are very special in that they are still of the living. Months earlier, Best is hidden in the castle, and the Germans think he has escaped. The usual hue and cry goes up and when the officer does not get recaptured or shot, it is assumed he has made it to neutral territory. In reality, the officer has gone to ground, quite literally. To preserve the deception, he is not allowed to write home anymore, so his family have no idea what has happened to him and therefore fear the worst. He has to stay hidden except during *appells*. He cannot be seen. As far as the Germans are concerned, he has successfully escaped, or dissolved into air it seems.

It takes enormous stamina for the men who sacrifice themselves in this way to keep the deception going. Of course, they get fed, and they do not have to go out for *appell*, but exercising or getting out into the fresh air are not among the options open to them. They spend most of their time in their hidey-hole. One is under the pulpit in the Chapel. Thus, when someone escapes, like Gris, the ghost emerges and takes the place of the real escapee, hoping that at *appell*, his pale and gaunt, sunlight-deprived visage does not stand out to the guards.

Gris buys a train ticket to Leipzig, but not with the intention to go there. There are too many soldiers in the city who could pick him up, especially if it becomes known that someone has escaped from Oflag IVC. On the way, he tries to be as inconspicuous as possible by pretending to read. Was he reminded, at that moment, of the train journey to Teschen with Weekes the year before that ended so fatally? At Hildescheim, near Hannover, whatever reverie he was enjoying was brought to a swift conclusion. Some soldiers thought him suspicious, interrogated him and that was that. Back to the high walls of Colditz.

And Ronald Littledale? According to *The Eton College Chronicle* of Thursday 2 December 1943, he is drafted into the KRRC football team to play in a match against a team from the Brigade of Guards. The match is played on St Andrews Day and is won 1-0 by the Guards. The match report ends with the sentence:

> The game, however, ended with a terrific attack by the 60th who, to borrow military parlance, captured all the heights but failed to dislodge the enemy.

'Dislodge the enemy'... drive out the enemy. It will be another six months before the invasion force, currently being built up on the south coast of England, will storm the beaches of Normandy, to drive out the enemy once and for all. Littledale, a major of the 60th Rifles of the 2nd Battalion King's Royal Rifle Corps, can do nothing but wait and play football. But he is not the only one.

The International Red Cross Committee visits the castle in Colditz in July for their regular inspection of the conditions of the PoWs and to check whether the Geneva Convention is being adhered to. After the departure of the Dutch, Polish and French residents, the camp has become populated entirely by British officers. At the time of the inspection, there are 220 officers and 50 orderlies, or servants. The empty rooms left behind are being prepared for any influx of British officers and the hope is expressed that there will be no more than 450 all told, so that there is no overcrowding and suitable sanitary conditions can be maintained. It is reported that the water supply is still inadequate and that the camp is also still short of cutlery and crockery. Since the departure of the French, the German doctor has been in charge of the infirmary. A British medical officer has been transferred to the camp as well as a British chaplain. Dental care is given by a civilian in the town who has a reputation for being very slow. Some improvements in recreational opportunities for the prisoners have been made, however. For instance, officers are allowed to play football on the town's fields from time to time, swim in public pools and attend special cinema screenings. All under guard, all on parole not to try and escape. Littledale is not the only one playing football in the middle of the war, his erstwhile colleague Mike Sinclair also joins a group that can be found on the green turf with some regularity. It seems any remorse he might have felt about the events in Pirot does not prevent him from getting rid of his energy and perhaps his aggression and anger in a sporting manner. It is no different for Littledale back in England.

Still recovering from the near-fatal gunshot wound he received when escaping as Franz Josef, Sinclair is already brooding on a new plan. In the north-west corner of the castle, there is a tall watchtower set up on a terrace that overlooks the immense castle's striking west side, the town and the River Mulde. At the same time every evening, the guards change shift and just after that, while the fresh sentries are settling into their posts for the night, the flood lights that illuminate the entire west side of the castle come on. In the summer, it does not matter, but during the winter months, dusk has already fallen before the night shift takes over and before the lights are switched on. Strangely, no adjustment to the lighting up time is made to take account of this: they come on at the same time every evening, without fail, no matter what, all year round. Therefore, there is a brief window of opportunity when there are fresh guards on duty, but who are unable to see much because the lights have not come on yet. Sinclair has been observing this phenomenon for a month or two with the forensic precision and attention to detail that has become his trademark and worked out that the average time between the arrival of the night shift and the switching on of the lights is some 60 seconds. Sometimes it is slightly more, sometimes slightly less. Sinclair wonders if this is a possible mouse hole to crawl through.

But until it turns out that there are indeed possibilities here, he, like Littledale, has a lot of time to think things over: Sinclair on a bunk under a 'bag of donkey feed', Littledale in barracks or with his mother Clara at Bunbury House. Reflections on what happened after their arrest nearly two years before in Pirot. The interrogations by the Bulgarian police, their confessions and the consequences. About the 'experience during his interrogation [he] had gone through that I did not have' as MI9 report Littlewood saying when talking about his comrade-in-arms Sinclair. About the war. That still rages on and is far from over for both of them.

21

NORMANDY

On the evening of Friday 9 June 1944, the 2nd Battalion of the King's Royal Rifle Corps led by Lieutenant Colonel William Heathcoat-Amory lands on the French coast, and somewhere in his wake, so does Major Ronald Bolton Littledale. Is this the same Heathcoat-Amory with whom he played football in Calcutta at Fort William in 1932? It is a different game now, with a bigger prize.

The 2nd Battalion forms part of the 4th Armoured Brigade led by Brigadiers John Currie and Richard Michael Carver. The Brigade further consists of the following:

- The 44th Battalion Royal Tank Regiment, under Lieutenant Colonel Hopkinson,
- The Royal Scots Greys, under Lieutenant Colonel Readman,
- The 3rd County of London Yeomanry (Sharpshooters), under Lieutenant Colonel Anderson, who were joined, from 1st August, by the 4th.

Littledale has spent more than a year preparing for this day, since he returned to England after his three years of wandering around Europe like a hunted animal. Now he is marching with an army of liberation, making prey of his old hunter.

But where exactly does Littledale land? And on what day? Was it 9 June at Gold Beach? Or earlier, perhaps on Sword Beach? Once upon a time, you could only answer questions like these by delving deep into regimental libraries, blowing the cobwebs off of dusty tomes to find the secrets held on crinkly, fragile pages. Now, one can sign up to any number of internet forums where one can join like-minded folk in nick-named anonymity and discuss various aspects of the Second World War with them. On one particular forum there is a fascinating discussion that touches on the very issue of when and where the 2nd Bat. of the KRRC landed in Normandy.

Derrick recently buried his uncle Frank, who served in the '60 Regt Kings Royal Rifles' and inherited five medals. In June 1944, Uncle Frank was a 19-year-old boy who had never left Essex before being thrust into Second World War history on a cargo ship bound for occupied Europe. On 13 June 2013, Derrick writes:

> Hi All,
> Firstly I may be in the wrong area here, please advise and I will repost.
> My Uncle Frank sadly passed away recently and I have inherited his regular army Certificate of Service and medals (please see pictures enclosed), I am beginning a research project on his Army service and hope to fill in some details.
> I had sat and chatted with him over his Army days and he recalled that he was at Sword Beach on D-Day, now if you take a look at his handwritten note he has his army no and a reference to D-Day with the '60 Regt KRRC'… (wrong year I know but he was well into his eighties)… does anyone have any thoughts on if this is accurate? … e.g. were the KRRC on Sword Beach on D-Day. If yes are any references on archives/books etc that are available ? basically I'd like to track his units progress across the span of the remainder of the period 1944-45, war diaries etc.
> The second part of the note is Aug 1945 T/14436643 CPL Wiltshire 3 Coy RASC Far East and Berlin, were his unit in Berlin at the end of the war and then transferred to the Far East, or am I way off here.
> Any pointers of thoughts would be much appreciated.
> Kind Regards
> Derrick

Derrick is looking for the landing site of the KRRC, in particular the place where his uncle Frank landed, and assumes it to be Sword Beach. It would have to be either Sword Beach or Gold Beach as they were the ones assigned to the British troops: Omaha and Utah Beach were for the Americans, and Juno is where the Canadians come ashore. So, which is it?

Derrick's question inspires a stream of opinions, facts, deductions and archive numbers, which demonstrates just how chaotic those first days from 6 June 1944 onwards must have been: units arriving at the wrong place, or at the right beach, but going back to sea to find somewhere else to go ashore where the German shelling is not so heavy. On 14 June, Ronnie's birthday, a reply arrived from someone called Mike:

> I can find no mention of a battalion of the Kings Royal Rifle Corps landing on Sword on D Day. 12 Battalion was part of 8th Armoured Brigade which did land its armoured regiments on Gold Beach on D Day. I do not think that this battalion actually landed on D Day, but did so shortly afterwards. 4 Armoured Brigade had 2 Battalion KRRC as its motor battalion. The brigade did not land on D Day but its armoured regiments landed on D+1.

So, 2 and 12 Battalions KRRC are possibilities, but not on Sword Beach on D Day. An answer from Mike alone is not enough to then assume that it must have been 'so Gold and well on 7 June'. Another participant in the discussion refers to the unit's war diaries:

> These are the two battalion war diaries covering 1944-45.
>
> WO 171/1327 2 King's Royal Rifle Corps 1944 Jan.-Dec.
> WO 171/5212 2 King's Royal Rifle Corps 1945 Jan.-July.
> WO 171/1328 12 King's Royal Rifle Corps 1944 Jan.-Dec.
> WO 171/5213 12 King's Royal Rifle Corps 1945 Jan.-Dec.

The WO figures refer to catalogue numbers under which documents are stored at the National Archives in Kew. Derrick does not benefit much from this information as his response on 20 June shows.

In the past I have looked at war diaries at Kew and it is a bit of chance to get really clear information from them! Understandably, as the poor guy typing it was otherwise engaged in other matters!

Kew, Richmond upon Thames in South-West London, is home to the National Archives, the official archive of the UK government. It covers a 1,000 years of history. With so much documentation in the house, it is understandable that Derrick struggles to find anything.

Then Derrick receives a reply to correspondence with the KRRC

Association, an association that keeps KRRC history alive. These people should know. Their site states:

> The 2nd Battalion, under the command of Lieutenant-Colonel W. Heathcoat-Amory, landed with the 4th Armoured Brigade in Normandy on 7th June, with motor companies under the command of armoured regiments, each regiment supporting one of the three brigades of the 51st (Highland) Division. The Battalion was continually in action, mostly with motor companies under their armoured regiments, the Brigade supporting various infantry divisions in turn.

On 20 June, Mike reports again:

> I don't think that 2 KRRC landed on Sword. I cannot yet find exactly where and when they did land but:
> 4 Armoured Brigade was scheduled to land one armoured regiment group on D+1 on Mike Beach, which is on Juno.
> Two more armoured regiment groups were scheduled to land on D+2 also on Mike Beach.
> Mike Beach had plenty of capacity and it is unlikely that they would divert to Sword.
> What is not clear is when they actually landed since there were considerable delays in landing on D+1. However, if they were landing from LCTs (Landing Craft Tanks), which did not suffer the same delays, and since they would have a high priority, they probably landed more or less on schedule.
> Also it is not clear if the KRRC landed at the same time.
> Juno Beach? It is possible. Juno Beach was allotted as a landing zone to the Canadian 3rd Infantry Division, the British 2nd Armoured Brigade and a unit of commandos of the British Royal Marines. On 20 June, an old veteran joins in the discussion. He was there in Normandy:
> I am not disputing that this group landed. But not on Sword. Being we were all over Normandy in small groups, we would have known, or seen them. Did they come in later on another beach? For there was no trace of them where we were. All units were under command of the Third British Infantry div. All the units are very well known, 8th brigade 185 brigade and 9th

brigade.

Being we took part in so many different operations in front of Caen, the arrival of that unit would soon be known about. They were not... Nor did we ever come across them...

How good is a veteran's memory almost seventy years later? One is more likely to solve the riddle by consulting surviving contemporaneous documentation. Fortunately, Mike turns out to be a collector, possessed of many, many documents:

- All the War Diaries for the 50 or so units which operated Sword Beach as part of 101 Beach Sub Area some of the War Diaries for 104 Beach Sub Area which operated Gold.
- None (yet) for Juno.
- The Landing Tables for all three beaches, some 1,000 pages. These generally only cover D Day. I am not even sure that tables for the period after D Day still exist, though they did once.
- The War Establishment tables for all units in 21 Army Group.
- The orders and reports for 1 Corps which controlled Sword and Juno.
- A huge amount of material relating to the naval aspects.

But despite this promising mountain of paper, the riddle is unsolved. None of the documents contained therein are of any help in identifying where or when 2 KRRC landed.

However, there seems to be some hope:

I do not have the KRRC War Diaries. War Diaries are very variable. Some include a large number of appendices with fascinating detail while others are very sparse. Still the 2 KRRC diaries are your best bet.

Then:

I have just received a copy of a page from Force Movement Tables courtesy of a forum member who is working on this. It shows the following. 593 men and 137 vehicles of 2 KKRC moved from Worthing to Southampton to embark on LSTs on D+1. These were part of a convoy of eight LSTs and one LSI(L) which were scheduled to land on Juno on D+3.

Landed on Juno on 9 June, among the Canadians, the same day Michel intervened in the debate.

> Just to make everybody happy, it might very well be that some of these LST or LSI(L) planned for JUNO actually discharged some of their load on SWORD… although the opposite was rather the norm. I've checked the Landing Tables First Tide for SWORD and First & Second Tide for GOLD and they do not contain any mention of 2 KRRC.

From Juno to Sword to Gold, to disappear altogether. Then a tip-off on 27 June from 'Drew5233' (some strange names on the internet). He refers to a book of which he is possessed: *The Annals of the King's Royal Rifle Corps, Volume VII 1943-1965*, by Brigadier G. H. Mills.

According to this, the 4th Armoured Brigade and 12th Battalion landed on 16 June with 8th Armoured Brigade. The 12th Battalion landed on Courseulles-sur-Mer. No location is given for the 2nd Battalion.

Captain Peter Gosse MC, of the KRRC writes in a brief account of the Normandy campaign that during the landing of the 2nd KRRC on 9 and 10 June, men and vehicles were put ashore, but no location was given. After the unit had moved some 3 km inland in the dark, the men came across bodies and some jeeps. Of Canadians. Edwin 'Dwin' Bramall creates some light in the darkness.

At the time of the Normandy Landings, Field Marshal Edwin Noel Westby Bramall, Baron Bramall, is a second lieutenant in the King's Royal Rifle Corps. Aged 20, he was added to the 2nd Battalion in early May 1944. He crosses the Channel on D+1 (7 June) in an American landing craft. The water was choppy and the current particularly strong. It was later in the evening when the ship finally arrives on the French coast in barely two metres of water. Amid a tremendous air raid, the men disembark at Courseulles-sur-Mer, on Juno Beach. But veteran Eric Wilfred Lawson, 2nd King's Royal Rifle Corps, who was honoured with the *Légion d'honneur*, France's highest award, in 2018 at the age of 93, also lands on the Normandy beaches on 7 June, just weeks after he joined service in April. He sets foot… on Gold Beach! Also on Gold Beach a day later, FitzRoy Somerset comes ashore along with some of the 2nd Battalion. He spends his childhood at Castle Goring, a country house in Sussex built by Percy Bysshe Shelley's grandfather. Sadly, the grandson drowns in a boating accident in Italy aged 29 and will never live in the house. FitzRoy Somerset manages to withstand the surf, though, and is eventually promoted to corporal by his platoon commander. This commander is Second Lieutenant Bramall, who, according to his own statement, lands on Juno Beach.

In the days leading up to the KRRC's landing, the occupiers and liberators fiercely contest the ground. The Allies are desperate to pierce the *Atlantik* Wall, Hitler's 'impregnable' defensive fortress that supposedly runs along the entire French coast and beyond, and work their way inland from the bridgehead on the beaches. The Americans on Omaha Beach suffer particularly badly, their traumatic experience becoming synonymous with the bloody battles that characterise D-Day in particular and the Normandy Landings as a whole. Three days later, however, things seem much calmer, but they only seem that way. The troops going ashore will find there are many more moments of fear, battle and destruction waiting for them.

The KRRC's LSTs bring ashore a mixed company of Battalion HQ, A Company, D Company transport vehicles, Royal Navy vehicles that are not completely watertight, and some Royal Marines. Quartermaster Captain Bird oversees a 'wet' landing. In the early afternoon, the men on board spot the beaches but just before landing, they get diverted to another beach, whereupon they get stuck on a reef. The air is blue with curses, swearing and much consternation as they wait for a Rhino ferry, capable of transporting vehicles and men in shallow water, to get them off. Right now, they present an ideal target for the Germans shooting at them from the shore. They hold on till just before dark, when the Rhino finally arrives. Vehicles and men start getting transferred back to relative safety. Major Littledale, though, is in a hurry: he drives his vehicle through more than half a metre of water to get to the shore. Just in time: shortly afterwards, one of the Royal Navy vehicles runs aground and sinks. Another one misses the gangway and ends up in the water, is pulled back onto the Rhino and tries a second time but again misses the gangway.

Things are going from bad to worse, as a bombardment begins and the air is thick with gunfire. Bomb fragments, shrapnel, shot fly all over the place. Then some of the bombs start landing uncomfortably close to the ferry. And then, someone already on shore chooses this moment to make the incomprehensible decision to stop the disembarkation process altogether. The men in their vehicles still floundering in the sea watch helplessly as the tide rises around them. At last, they take matters into their own hands and wade ashore through over a metre of water. The next day, finally, everyone from the 2nd is back on dry land. So here they are, the 2nd Battalion KRRC has made it to the Second Front. That much they know. What they do not know is the enemy's precise location, so they find a field and bed down. After a couple of hours sleep, the shells fall again. Somewhere in this indeterminate world, Littledale takes up arms again.

Brigadier Richard Michael Power Carver has been in command of the 4th Armoured Brigade since 27 June. At the moment, he is with his brigade participating in the campaign in north-western Europe. He is also the man who made the decision to replace Lieutenant Colonel Heathcoat-Amory, on the grounds of his being too old for this kind of thing. Carver was reluctant to do so because Heathcoat-Amory was an impressive soldier and leader with a sterling war record. Among other feats of arms, he fought in the Second Battle of El Alamein in October 1942, shortly after Littledale's escape from Colditz. It is Littledale indeed, whom Carver chooses to be rewarded with the honour of succeeding Heathcoat-Amory and leading his beloved battalion. Not only is Littledale Commanding Officer of the 2nd Battalion KRRC, he is promoted to a rank commensurate with his new position: he is now Lieutenant Colonel Ronald Bolton Littledale.

Following on from the landings, the Allies proceed cautiously inland, meeting fierce resistance from the Germans. They finally reach Falaise, which is south of Caen, where they succeed in surrounding an entire German army. At last, the Allies have a way of breaking out of Normandy and advancing north towards their main objective at this time, Antwerp. The Port of Antwerp is a vital link in the Allies' supply chain. Right now their supply lines start literally on the beaches at Normandy. As the Allies (hopefully) advance, pushing the Germans back towards their homeland, this line will be dangerously extended. If they capture Antwerp, the supplies for the advancing army can go through there instead, cutting the length of the chain from beginning to end substantially.

In the middle of all this is Lieutenant Colonel R. B. Littledale, lately almost thrown out of his jeep by a nearby shell burst. Their CO in one piece, the 2nd Battalion of the 60th KRRC are on the move, Antwerp bound. Somewhere down the road lies the insignificant town of Airaines.

22

AIRAINES

It is 1 September 1944. Exactly five years after the first shells drop on the Westerplatte north of Danzig, heralding the beginning of the Second World War. Right now, though, Littledale has no time for reflection: this professional soldier has other things with which to concern himself. He is on his way to a small town in the Somme region, Airaines. With him is Major Bernays of D Company, the commander of the anti-tank brigade, and an escort of machine gunners. Airaines is an anonymous spot on the map and it is doubtful if Littledale has ever heard of the place. It is an island of resistance in a sea of newly liberated French soil: why would he ever go there?

Back in the area between Falaise and Argentan, known to history as the 'Falaise Pocket', the Germans are desperate. They have been caught up in the middle of a pincer movement, the Poles and Canadians to the north of them, and the Americans to the south. Much of Army Group B has been destroyed and the road to Paris and the Franco-German border has opened up to the Allies. Moving out quickly, the 7th Army and 5th Panzer Division leaves behind them a trail of abandoned vehicles and weapons and a miserably gruesome tangle of thousands of dead men and horses. Demoralised, they offer little resistance and surrender by the thousands.

In late August, the Allies cross the Seine, and the 2nd Battalion moves north and northwest. Together with the 12th and 4th Armoured Brigade, they advance some 400 km to a point northwest of Antwerp, taking 12 days to get there. Three days out, Littledale is reconnoitring the area around Airaines. Reports have come in that the enemy may be heading towards this spot from the northwest. Retreating before the British advance, the battle-weary German Army stops here for a break, turning the place into a fortress. Airaines does not have any tactical significance at all, but the Germans, armed with anti-tank weapons, are determined to try and hold out here anyway. Surrounding Airaines, the Scots Greys and a detachment of Canadian troops make contact north of the village. Attempting to cross the Somme, despite being held up by some destroyed bridges, they manage to get through and penetrate as far north as Long, where two tank regiments and a company of the KRRC hold the one bridge left intact, despite fierce resistance from the Germans. Airaines is in an isolated position, and the remaining German troops there form a hotbed of resistance.

Ronnie and Bernays enter the village to assess the strength of the German defences. The Germans, they are there somewhere, but where? Maybe hiding out in the buildings on the main drag or lurking round the next corner. They also know that German relief forces could be on their way–Maybe they already are.

He steers their half-track along the main road heading south. A corner. He turns. A German anti-tank gun fires. Fate strikes. In the ensuing panic, Bernays escapes along with most of the troop. The Anti-tank Brigade commander is killed instantly, and so is Littledale. His vehicle, the half-track, remains where it is.

It is a sadly ironic twist of fate that the Somme region, that the Allies found so impenetrable 28-years-earlier, has now marked the end of the advance of the man who almost managed to break through everywhere.

The War Diary of the 2nd Battalion. King's Royal Rifle Corps contains a short note in civil service officialese, arranged in chilly columns:

Place.	Date.	Hour.	Summary of Events & Information.
CHAMPAMIE	1	1000	Bn. is moving N with Coys u/c Armd Regts.
NOIS			250 PW were brought to Bn.HQ by Maquis.
AIRAINES		1200	Lieut.Colonel R.B.Littledale went on recce with Bty Comdr 174 Anto-Tank S.P. Bty, also Major Bernays and MMG Pls of 'D' Coy. This party was ambushed in AIRAINES and both Lieut.Colonel Littledale and the Bty Comdr were killed, Bn. Task here was to prevent attack on the CL from the N. Major H.R.W. Vernon, M.B.E. took comd of the Bn. with Major E.Bernays as 2 i/c. A Company under 3/4 CLY advanced to NE of AIRAINES and subsequently took the village and 52 P.W.

That makes it official. Ronnie is gone.

It is not until after sun-down that the Allies are able to enter the village and finally rid Airaines of German forces once and for all. Lieutenant Dwin Bramall of A Company with his motor platoon and a tank squadron from the 3rd City of London Yeomanry can take the credit. After the ambush and Ronnie's tragic death, Major Dick Vernon takes over command of the 2nd Battalion KRRC. Covering distances of 130 to 150 km a day, the battalion soon arrives on the banks of the River Scheldt, to the loud cheers of liberated Belgians in Oudenaarde, Dendermonde, St Nicholaas and Beverenwaas.

Both Patrick Reid in *Colditz: The Full Story* and Henry Chancellor in *Colditz: The Untold Story of World War II's Great Escapes* tell a different story of how Littledale is killed. According to them, he was not in a half-track hit by a shell: he drove his jeep over a landmine. The true story of the reconnaissance party's sad outcome is told by the War Diary.

The next morning, 2 September, A Company sends a patrol to the village. They find the remnants of the half-track, but the bodies of Littledale and his comrade have gone. They later find out they have been taken by some of the locals to a hospital. The patrol also finds 22 enemy soldiers and takes them prisoner, the last Germans left in the village. Could these men have been thinking the same thing as the man killed here yesterday, when he was captured by a German patrol in Calais all those years ago?

The mayor of Airaines wants a public funeral to be organised for the British officers and soldiers who sacrificed themselves to liberate the town. Eyewitnesses to the funeral, which takes place the next day, speak of an impressive ceremony. Behind the procession of coffins, the entire population of Airaines walked sombrely to the cemetery. Over the coffins lies the Union Flag, including that of Littledale. The grateful villagers have gathered flowers and piled them high on the graves. Littledale fought his battle and died. He did it as a free man.

A question hangs over the events of 1 September like a very heavy cloud. What was Littledale actually doing in the village in the first place. It is ordinarily no part of a lieutenant colonel's duties to go on reconnaissance missions to fairly unimportant places like Airaines. The place is already surrounded by ground troops more than capable of getting rid of the last vestiges of resistance. It makes no sense to sacrifice a senior officer in this way. So what inspired Littledale to take on this task? He has had a year in England after his return from Colditz, time to reflect on the fact that there is a strong likelihood that people will have been executed because of his treachery. Other things too. His father died in late 1942. Ronnie's mother, Clara, is the only family he has: no wife, no children. Is it a deliberate decision to put himself at so much risk that he will be killed? Is it his chance to bid a final farewell to this world, a world in which he could not live anymore after having betrayed those brave Resistance fighters who helped him stay free? As a devout Christian, the concept of betrayal would resonate with him deeply. Only one thing left to do, in that case. Or was it that his fighting spirit got ahead of him and he became a victim of his own desperate need to act?

The official historiography reports that the armoured vehicles that were supposed to accompany the reconnaissance unit started up too slowly, and that Littledale rushed ahead in advance with his unarmoured half-track. Curiously, this goes completely against Littledale's military philosophy which states that protection by tanks is an essential condition for an infantry unit to operate under until it has dug in its own anti-tank guns. Whatever the reason behind it, Littledale makes a strange choice, one that means his 72 year-old mother, Clara Violet Stevenson loses her only son. *The Times* announces his death shortly after the fatal shell hit:

Lieut. Colonel Ronald Bolton Littledale, D.S.O., The King's Royal Rifle Corps, whose death in action in North-West Europe, was reported this week, was the only son of Mrs. Littledale and the late Captain J.B. Littledale, of Bunbury House, Bunbury, Cheshire.

The front page of *The Eton College Chronicle* of 5 October 1944 is completely covered with names of former Etonians killed in action. A large cross above the motto ETONA NON IMMEROR (Eton Does Not Forget) makes it clear what this list of dozens of names means. Somewhere in the right-hand column, Littledale is listed, citing his rank, his House during his years at Eton and his highest award:

20 Littledale R. B., D.S.O. (C.M.W.), Lt.-Col K.R.R.C

The Chesire Observer of Saturday 16 September 1944, features an article dedicated to the deceased lieutenant colonel.

LT.-COL R.B. LITTLEDALE, D.S.O.
Killed In Action In France, After Three Years a Prisoner
ESCAPED AT FIFTH ATTEMPT

With heartfelt regret, friends in Chesire heard this week that Lieut.-Colonel Ronald Bolton Littledale, D.S.O., King's Royal Rifle Corps, only son of Mrs. Littledale and the late Capt. J.B. Littledale, Bunbury House, Bunbury, was killed in action in France in August.

Lieut.-Colonel Littledale, who was 42, was born at Sandiway. He was educated at St. Alban's, Rottingdean, and was at Eton from 1915 to 1919. From there he went to the Royal Military College, Sandhurst, and was commissioned in the King's Royal Rifle Corps. He served in the Army of Occupation on the Rhine. From 1924 to 1928 he was with his regiment in India, and later served in Palestine and Northern Ireland. He frequently competed at Bisley and won many prizes with rifle and the revolver. At the outbreak of the present War he was stationed in England and went out with his battalion to the defence of Calais as a major. This was in May, 1940, and the story of the part his regiment played is one of the finest in the annals of British military history. During this action he was taken prisoner.

EFFORTS TO ESCAPE

During his captivity he never ceased in his efforts to escape. Four times he eluded his guards, but was recaptured. Of his three years as a prisoner of war in Germany he actually spent 17 months in enemy territory as a free man. On his fifth attempt he got to England, reaching here almost three years to the day he was taken prisoner. The normal decoration awarded to an escaped officer is the M.C., but for his outstanding bravery and initiative and the gallant services he rendered at Calais he was awarded the D.S.O. After a short leave he was posted again to his old regiment and went to France with the invasion forces. He was given command of his battalion during the Battle of Normandy.

A GREAT CHARACTER

Lieut.-Colonel Littledale was reserved and shy, except with a few intimate friends. He had a gentle, almost diffident manner, but that did not hide the strength and nobility of his character. No personal privation or hardship would keep him from what he considered to be his duty. He came back from his grim experiences abroad with a deep sense of responsibility and an unswerving resolve to serve his fellow men. He was a grand sportsman, one of the best rifle and revolver shots in the British Army. He rode well to hounds, and liked fishing and shooting. Bound up with his love of sport was his almost greater love of country and all the beautiful places in the world. Scotland, especially, had an abiding place in his heart. He leaves many sad friends, and among them will be many of his own men, the stalkers and ghillies of Scotland, and the country people near his own home.

    Lieut.-Colonel Littledale had a lovable personality and a keen sense of humour. All who came in contact with him felt his essential goodness and can truly say 'He was a gentleman.'

MEMORIAL SERVICE ON MONDAY

A memorial service will be held at Bunbury Church on Monday at 6.45 p.m.

From the photograph attached to the article, Littledale stares out at the reader as an early 1920s second lieutenant. At that moment, he has no idea of what circumstances can do to someone shy, bashful and a true gentleman of noble character.

Only a few years later, his mother Clara dies. An article that appears about her in *The Chronicle* on Saturday 18 June 1949, again gives attention to her son, and the grief she suffered when she learns that he has been killed in action.

A NOTED CHESHIRE HORSEWOMAN

The Late Mrs. Littledale

Friends throughout Cheshire heard with regret of the sudden death of Mrs. Clara V. Littledale, widow of Capt. J. Bolton Littledale, Bunbury, which occurred at her home on Saturday.

Mrs. Littledale, who was 77, before marriage was a Miss Stevenson, whose family lived in Scotland. Upon her marriage she came to live at Bunbury.

Captain and Mrs. Littledale were prominent figures in Cheshire Society for over fifty years. They were greatly esteemed in Bunbury and district. Capt. Littledale served for many years as a J.P. and also as a member of the County Council. Both were prominent members of the Cheshire hunt.

Mrs. Littledale, who followed hounds until the outbreak of the last War, was regarded as one of the finest horsewomen in the country. She also shared her husband's love of fishing, and frequently accompanied him on fishing expeditions to Norway and Scotland.

It was a great blow to her when her son, Major Ronnie Littledale, was killed when serving in North-West Europe. Major Littledale, who took part in the heroic defence of Calais was awarded the D.S.O. Taken a prisoner of war, he escaped on five occasions, and ultimately reached this country. He rejoined his Regiment and was commanding a battalion when killed.

Mrs. Littledale has always taken a great interest in the organisations connected with Bunbury and in the war years did not spare herself in work for both national and local efforts. She was a devout churchwoman, and a member of the Eddisbury Conservative Association.

The funeral took place today (Wednesday) when a service at St. Boniface's Church, Bunbury, was conducted by the Rev. J.R. Paterson Morgan.

In 2013, the seven gravestones in the Airaines cemetery stand against a green hedge tightly lined up and seem to stare straight ahead like soldiers at Attention. Here they rest: Arthur Christopher Spires, Ronald Bolton Littledale, Irvin Pearson, Hubert Ernest Buss, Albert Edward Rogers, George Christopher Dowell and Roger Chester Nightingale. All were killed on that first September day in 1944, most of them regimental comrades of Littledale's KRRC. On the headstones the carved memorials: 'Proud memories, dear one, At home we keep, Though in a distant land, You sleep'; 'To a beautiful life, Came a sudden end, He died as he lived, Everyone's friend'; 'While he rests, In peaceful sleep, His memory, We will always keep'; 'Years go by, But memories never fade'. The words on the headstones could almost all apply to Littledale, except those for 28-year-old Huber Buss: 'In loving memory Of my beloved husband, Sadly missed But cherished memories.' After all, Littledale remained a bachelor throughout his life.

Littledale's stone shows only rank, name, decoration, regiment, date of death and a large cross. The regimental coat of arms with the motto *'Celer et Audux'* is the only decoration on this austere commemoration. *'Celer et Audux'*, Swift and Bold. How apt.

His death is a great blow for the men of his company: they looked up to him. During the month he was their CO, he had shown himself to be a very capable leader, a man loved by every soldier in his unit. Billie Stephens, his old comrade from Colditz and fellow escapee recalls:

He was one of the finest, most loyal most selfless men I have met in my lifetime. His wonderful example and his absolute sense of purpose to his duty were a great help to us all. He died for his ideals. He would not have wished for a more dignified end.

High up in the castle, Micky Burn could hear shots. Although the room he is sitting in is lined with soundproofing material so no-one outside can hear the radio within, he can clearly hear it, gunfire. As usual, Micky is in his hiding place, listening to the BBC on the illegal radio left behind by the French for the British. Micky recalls:

> I was very, very grateful because it was exciting, of course putting on the news each night in the hole in the wall and listening to the BBC: da da da da daaaa.

In recent months, the incoming news has been extra exciting. The Russians are advancing from the east, the Allies have invaded the Nazi stronghold on the French coast. And the men who have been trapped in the castle south of Leipzig for years are beginning to hope that the end is in sight for them too. The escape attempts that once kept many an officer from sleeping in previous years are now a comparative rarity. In January of 1944, though, Mike Sinclair tries again, this time from the west side of the castle.

What has gone down in history as the Sixty-Second Escape is a sophisticated attempt that cost Mike many hours of thought and observation. As determined as his friend Ronnie to get out, Mike again defies his guards. This time, he notices that the lights in which the castle is bathed at night go out on the west side at the level of a watchtower just before the moment the guard is changed. There is a brief period of time when no-one is looking. He does not yet know why this happens, but he intends to take advantage of it.

On the evening of 19 January, 1944, at the appointed time, he is lying face down, feet first on a sanded long-table, as smooth as they can get it. Lying above him, face up, head first is Lieutenant Jack Best, a string of bed sheet rope tied together around his stomach. The table is angled downwards against a window, the bars have already been cut. The atmosphere is heavy with suppressed tension. Mike is fidgety, nervous; Best is preternaturally calm. The searchlights go out. Darkness. The moment supreme and the room explodes into action. With every muscle straining, the men by the window heave back on the bars, bending them into the room, all their concentrated energy focused on those grim strips of metal. Two others propel Mike out of the window towards the terrace, Jack right behind them. They have got to move. Terrace. Balustrade. Orchard. Wire. All in darkness, with sentries nearby within earshot. This is like Littledale's escape 15 months earlier, sneaking out behind the sentries' back. It could hardly be more striking. Another dozen metres. Descending and crawling. The rope is good. Best set off an alarm but they don't know. They are lucky and get away from the castle hovering above them like it is suspended in mid-air. At the Dutch border, their adventure ends. Mike and Jack are caught and brought back to Colditz.

As Sinclair and Best are making their way through Germany, someone else tries to get away from the castle. Canadian Lieutenant William Anderson (Dopey) Millar, captured during the Dieppe raid in 1942, makes his attempt a few days after Sinclair and Best. The route taken by this Royal Canadian Engineer is inspired by the route successfully taken by Littledale. Inspired? It is nigh on identical. Millar enters the German kitchens and saws through an iron bar in front of one of the windows overlooking the courtyard in the Kommandantur. (In *Colditz: The Full Story*, he crawls through a half-round upper window with no bars; his entire escape story is steeped in darkness.) On the night of 28 January, 1944, during an air raid, he crawls out through the window, across the low-rise building in the courtyard and lowers himself onto the cobblestones before hiding under a truck he finds parked there. When the truck leaves the next morning, it passes through the gate and is on its way. Hidden somewhere in it, on it or under it, Millar goes too, undetected. Security officer Eggers reports that a coat is later found a few kilometres from the castle, which may have belonged to Millar. Nothing further is ever heard from Dopey Millar: he simply rode that truck out of Colditz and into the aether. It is suspected that the Nazis caught him, took him to the concentration camp in Mauthausen and on 15 July 1944, they murdered him. They tried to justify it under the so-called 'Kugel Erlass' order, issued on 2 March that year. This decree is issued under the name Kugel-Erlass (also known as Aktion Kugel or Bullet Decree). This secret German order states that escaped prisoners of war, especially officers and senior NCOs, must be handed over to the SD. The SD transport these recaptured escapers to Mauthausen concentration camp where they are murdered '*im Rahmen der Aktion Kugel*' (as part of the Bullet Decree). The killing of the Fifty, who escaped from Stalag Luft III in the Great Escape, constitutes the biggest warning that '*Aktion Kugel*' can lead to.

Micky Burns' Radio Shack constituted a Public Service, as far as the company of PoWs at Colditz were concerned. There were several others involved, but Burns was already a skilled journalist and practitioner of that intricate and essential art: the taking of shorthand. He transcribed the daily news bulletins broadcast by the BBC and picked up by secret radios all over the Reich. Burns then wrote up his notes and they were copied and read out at the various messes that had formed among the British contingent.

From these daily news readings in his Mess, Sinclair would have learned that Liberation cannot be far off; that they are entering the last stages of the war. Back in April, news reaches him that his brother, John, had been killed in action after a reconnaissance at Anzio, in the Italian Campaign, in February. Word too was reaching Colditz of the fate of the escapers from Stalag Luft III. Beyond the barbarity and the tragedy of this mass murder, the rules of engagement have changed. On 23 September the Germans gave written notice to the prisoners, 'Escaping from prison camps has ceased to be a sport', this infamous document exhorts. Anyone who tries and is caught cannot expect leniency, the consequences will be grave. Mike must have felt hopeless: things were piling up. His duty, his very *raison d'etre*, his shot at redemption was now being taken away. He would have known that the Senior British Officer, Colonel W. Tod, would probably not sanction any more escape attempts under these circumstances.

Three days after Littledale is killed in Airaines, Mike is caught wearing civilian clothes under his uniform jacket as he walks to the park below the castle. It means two weeks of solitary confinement. According to his Gris, Mike has been behaving strangely since learning of his brother John's death: he wears a constant frown these days and looks old for his years. Always a lone wolf, he is now verging on the reclusive, his demeanour impregnable, his mood one of extreme introspection. And he has much to be introspective about. Is he haunted by the thought of what his and Littledale's revelations to the Bulgarian interrogators meant for those Poles who had given them help, food, comfort and shelter? Does he think about how his conduct under pressure compares with that of his brother? John died a soldier's death, he faced his end bravely in battle, Mike talked, and persuaded Ronnie to do the same.

Mike knows what the risks are if things go wrong. It is his right to decide to take them, not Tod's to decide he cannot. On 25 September 1944, he exercises that right. Before setting off to the park that morning, as part of the daily procession to get some fresh air and a change of scenery, he accosts Kenneth Lockwood in the PoW's *hof*. Lockwood looks after the prisoners' supply of German money. He asks if he can have some. Lockwood wants to know why, is he planning an escape? Sinclair simply asks Kenneth not to tell anyone. Later, according to Gris, he firmly turns down the company Gris offers him on the walk. He wants to be alone.

His attempt appears to be have been inspired by an earlier, successful escape by French Lieutenant Pierre Mairesse-Lebrun back in July 1941, who, with characteristic French bravado, sails over the barbed wire fence in the park, sent on his way by Lieutenant Pierre Odry. He sprints off under a rain of bullets and climbs over the high wall surrounding the grounds. He does not stop until he reaches Vichy France. More than three years after Lebrun's gymnastics, the Park is about to see another display.

At first, it is just another Monday afternoon exercise session down in the Park. People are milling about, a group are playing football and the guards, ever present, take up their usual posts, from where they can observe the various goings-on. Mike Sinclair, as usual these days, cuts a solitary figure in his French cloak, warm against the Autumnal cold. For half an hour or so, he circumnavigates the perimeter, his ashen grey face set, an outfit of civilian clothes concealed under his cloak. He stops to watch the football for a few minutes. He turns away and walks quietly towards the fence. stepping over a tripwire. Suddenly, he is at the wire, near a machine gun post while sentries are only a few dozen metres away. He is desperately climbing up. His movements are quick, but his progress is slow. He is at the top, hauling himself over. The sentries spot him and start shouting at him to come down. Lance Pope sees what is happening and shouts at the guards not to shoot. 'Can't you guys see he's gone crazy?'

Mike is over the wire now and has jumped off, making a hard landing and starts to sprint away past a pond and a shed standing in the grounds. This is hopeless; the terrain is too steep and he is slowing down. He has not reached the high surrounding wall. The guards are still shouting and loose off a few rounds as a warning. The Germans give him chance after chance to stop, but Mike is no longer listening: maybe he cannot now, in his desperation to get away. More shots. A bullet hits his elbow, ricochets off the bone and enters his heart. He falls forward on to his knees, then face down. He is dead.

Less than four weeks after the deadly salvo in Airaines, Mike, 26, is reunited with Littledale in death. Micky Burn, in the cracking voice of an old man recalling sad memories:

> I think I was in the wireless room up in the tower, hiding at that time. But I heard the shot. There was a lot of firing, it could only have been… that's Mike. I knew what it was, and I thought, oh no, why? You've done enough. You've been so brave and you've been insufferable the way that other heroes have been insufferable and they're all necessary, and now it's over.

For his 'ruthless dedication to escape as a prisoner of war soldier', he is posthumously awarded the Distinguished Service Order after the war is finally over. An official announcement was made in the *Supplement to The London Gazette* on 29 August 1946:

> War Office, 29th August, 1946. The KING has been graciously pleased to approve the following awards in recognition of gallant and distinguished services in the field:-
>
> The Distinguished Service Order
> Lieutenant Albert Michael Sinclair (75265),
> The King's Royal Rifle Corps (Winchester) (since deceased)

He is the only lieutenant to receive this honour for an action whilst held in captivity.

The award was on the recommendation of Major General Victor Fortune, who knew Mike from his time in Laufen and who at the time, was the highest-ranking PoW in Germany. Military Intelligence had requested him to write a recommendation for nomination in June 1946. Of 21 recommendations received, 17 served with Mike at Colditz, three others were members of his regiment.

It is extremely unlikely that anyone was aware of what happened in the interrogation room in Pirot, or indeed, the consequences of the confessions made there for the Polish Resistance organisation that accompanied Mike and Ronnie so far on their journey to Turkey. Even so, the possibility cannot be ruled out that both MI9 and the senior officers of Mike's old regiment wanted to set an example for others by acknowledging the inspirational bravery of a young officer, who was utterly focused on escaping from his PoW camp.

The Germans called him *Der Rote Fuchs*, the Red Fox. Of all the prisoners in Colditz, he was one who had their respect, even some affection possibly.

On the morning of Thursday 28 September 1944, Mike is buried in Colditz in the cemetery of St Nicolai Kirche. In attendance are ten prisoners from the camp including Padre 'Dickie' Heard, Lieutenant Colonel Tod, the SBO (Senior British Officer), Captain Martin Gilliat, his regimental colleagues Philip Pardoe and Gris Davies-Scourfield, Jack Courtney, and Peter Parker. Also in attendance is a German contingent, led by a *Feldwebel* (Sergeant), to accompany the procession. A moving service is held in the chapel near the Colditz cemetery. Mike's coffin, like Ronnie's, is covered with the Union Flag, and his uniform cap is placed on it by Padre Heard. The padre will also pronounce the first part of the service. Martin Gilliat will read two pieces. The first is from the 17th Century book *The Pilgrim's Progress* (*'Once Christ's Journey to Eternity'*) and is titled 'The Death of Mr Valiant-For-Truth'. It is followed by Chapter 14, Verses 1 to 6 from the *Gospel of John*. Six pall-bearers dressed in black carry Mike's coffin to the churchyard after the service, closely followed by the bareheaded company of officers. When the coffin is next to the grave, the Padre reads the conclusion of the service. The coffin is lowered into the grave and Senior British Officer Tod lays a wreath at its head, given to him by the Germans. The PoWs salute, and step back. The Germans are represented by Captain Püpcke and ten other ranks. Finally, the Germans fire three rounds in salute over the grave.

A memorial service is held for Mike later that afternoon in the castle. The Chapel is packed as Padre Heard delivers the service. He has lived in the same room with Mike for a year. In a letter to Mike's mother written the next day, Phil Pardoe recalls, 'There was an atmosphere and reverence in the air that I have rarely experienced like this before.' At his request, the hymn *Abide With Me* is sung, followed by *The Lord Is My Shepherd*. Tod reads the 21st chapter from the *Book of Revelations*. Padre Heard gives a moving speech in tribute. Then the whole assembly sings *For all the Saints*, and a horn player in the gallery sounds the *Last Post* and the *Reveille*. The spirit of Littledale is present in the chapel as a comrade is bidden farewell. Mike and Ronnie have become Colditz Ghosts. Now they can rest easy.

Three years and a day pass after his burial in the churchyard at Colditz. On 26 September, 1947, he is reburied by the Americans in the Charlottenburg War Cemetery in Berlin under grave number 10.1.14. His determination to escape, rivalling that of Ronnie Littledale, will probably enable him to escape from here too. In his death, he achieved his goal. He may have died, but he died like Littledale, a free man. On his tombstone reads the text from the *Book of John 14.4*: 'And wither I go ye know, and the way ye know'. It could well have been a text from Rupert Brooke: 'If I should die, think only this of me, That there's some corner of a foreign field, That is forever England'.

Mike's parents posted an In Memoriam in *The Times* on 3 November:

> Passed into the Greater Life on September 25th 1944, whilst a prisoner of war in Germany, Lieutenant Albert Michael Sinclair, The King's Royal Rifle Corps, very dearly loved younger son of Colonel and Mrs. T. C. Sinclair, aged 26. Undaunted in the service of his country.

Fearless or not: what motivated Sinclair to make that mad dash through the Park and past the pond? Was it suicide? What gale-force winds stormed through that restless mind of his? Was it that interrogation room with Ronnie after their arrest in Pirot? It is a compelling image: two men of faith knowing they betrayed their fellow fighters, the Polish men and women who helped them. They must have understood that they would have been arrested en-masse and executed as a result of their betrayal. How could they live with that knowledge? Mike attempted escape many times, and they all made sense except that last one, ill-considered, strange and unnecessary.

Gris said this:

> No one knew about his very last escape. Not even me. It was very risky, and if he had told anyone they would have tried to stop him. But it was a calculated risk, he always calculated everything down to the minute. I was in the castle when I heard the shooting. There was a lot of shooting as Mike ran away. He was unlucky to be hit, and even more unlucky not to be merely wounded.

That is true. If Mike had intended suicide, he would have made sure he did it right and left as little as humanly possible to chance, exactly like how he managed his escapes. Suicide by Sentry held no such guarantees. Moreover, he asked Kenneth Lockwood for German money, which Kenneth gave him. Why would Mike ask for money if he knew it would not be needed? Why say anything at all? But still the thought persists. According to Philip Pardoe, in his book *From Calais to Colditz*, the consensus of opinion is that he engaged in a gallant form of suicide whilst the balance of his mind was disturbed. But Pardoe is emphatic that this is not true, adding that only a handful of people, ten at most, know the true reasons why Mike made his last, desperate bid for freedom. He went on to say, cryptically, that Mike's story must remain untold 'for the time being'. Has Pardoe heard the truth from Sinclair?

23

THE LONG WAY TO TIPPERARY

An icy wind is blowing through Europe from the East. At least, that is the forecast according to the West, which sees in the Eastern Bloc a danger it has long felt threatened by, its worst nightmare come true. If there is a crisis, an emergency situation of the worst kind, the Iron Curtain separating East and West may not prove so strong after all. In the East, the feeling is mutual. It is not the first time the hordes from the West have thundered into the East and caused death and destruction, the last time was not so long ago. The Iron Curtain is a metaphorical, double-sided shield, protecting both sides from each other's rockets and guns and each other, keeping us in and them out, or us out and them in. It also keeps both sides from knowing both sides of a long story that involves both sides.

The *Teatr Polskiego Radia* has a march on the BBC. On 6 August 1972, the Polish radio station *Teatr Polskiego Radia* broadcasts the second part of the radio play *Daleka jest droga do Tipperary*. A couple of months later, on 19 October, 1972, BBC One broadcasts the first episode, *The Undefeated*, of a 28-part series, *Colditz*, a co-production by the BBC and Universal Studios. It was exactly 30 years after Ronald Littledale and Billie Stephens cross the German-Swiss border at Ramsen. It will be 25 January 1973 before this crossing is re-enacted in an episode entitled *Gone Away Part II-With The Wild Geese* is broadcast. Only it was not Littledale and Stephens or even their dramatic equivalents on screen, it was Grant (Reid) and Carrington (Wardle). A week earlier, *Gone Away Part I* had been aired, which concentrates on the escape of Littledale and the others from the castle itself. This what the Iron Curtain really does: it divides cultures, people and the stories told in different parts of Europe. Does the British viewer know anything about Zbigniew Klichowski, Bronisław Sobkowiak, Maria Klichowska, Bolesław and Mieczyslaw Kierczyński,

Maria Jasińska, Olga Kamińska-Prokopowa, Bodenstein and Giebelhausen? Does the Polish listener know anything about Reid, Wardle, Stephens or Colditz? Both have one overriding connection that unites them even after the stories have been hurled into the ether: Ronald Bolton Littledale.

A year earlier, in 1971, Polish radio journalist and publicist Edmund Odorkiewicz, politician, member of the National Council and fighting in the ranks of the Radwan unit during the Warsaw Uprising, publishes the book *Kryptonim 'Dorsze'* (Codename Cod) about the Polish line helping escaped PoWs to neutral territory. And in 1974, a documentary by Krzysztof Szmagier titled *AKCJA DORSZE* (Action Cod) was made, that dealt with the same theme. While the British aired a catchy and engaging series about the adventures of PoWs in a medieval castle, the Poles focus on their own history, reporting on the Polish Resistance. Littledale and Sinclair play pivotal roles in both histories, yet tragically, the curtain that separates Europe from itself also divides these stories.

Littledale and Sinclair never quite managed to complete the long road to Tipperary. Littledale is killed at Airaines, Sinclair is tragically shot just three weeks later during his last attempt to escape from Colditz. Even after their deaths, their story and that of the Polish Resistance heroes is ongoing. Both before and after the fall of the Berlin Wall, stones are added in east and west on the long path to that imaginary Tipperary from the radio play.

***

Liverpool, England, 1945.

When Ronald Littledale is killed at Airaines on 1 September 1944, he leaves a fortune of £76,248 (equal to £4.2m in 2024) to two heirs. They are retired Lieutenant Colonel Benjamin Arkle MC (Ret) and Maud Thackeray Schwabe, described as an 'old spinster'. Ronald himself inherited much of this capital from his father after the latter's death on 24 December 1942. On 14 April the following year, he received a sum of £52,975 (equal to £3m in 2024). Benjamin Arkle was commanding officer of the Liverpool Scottish, a unit of the British Army, part of the Army Reserve (formerly the Territorial Army), from 1930 to 1932. Maud Thackeray Schwabe, the 'spinster', is Ronald's cousin. Her mother May was born on 11 July 1875 in Sandiway Bank and was the younger sister of John Bolton, Ronald's father. May's marriage is announced on 18 July 1913.

A marriage has been arranged, and will take place very quietly in August, between May, youngest daughter of the late J. B. Littledale, and Clifford Schwabe, of Arden House, Ashley, Altrincham.

May and Clifford marry on 12 August 1913 in St John's Church, Chester. The couple have two children: Betty and Maud. Clifford Schwabe dies on 9 November 1947 at Cuddington Grange near Northwich in Cheshire. When Maud comes into her share of Ronald Littledale's inheritance, she does not remain an 'old maid' for long. A year after the ship of gold has docked, Miss. M. Schwabe becomes engaged to Mr A. R. Legard. Again, apart from an advertisement, little publicity is given to the marriage.

Mr. A. R. Legard and Miss. M. Schwabe The marriage arranged between Antony Ronald, second son of Brigadier General D'A. Legard, CMG, DSO, and Lady Edith Legard, of Maes Court, Tenbury, Worcestershire, and Maud, elder daughter of Mr and Mrs Clifford Schwabe, of Cuddington Grange, Northwich, will take place very quietly on 28 May.

Major Antony Ronald Legard is born in Sialkot, Punjab, in India in 1912 and is educated at public school Winchester College, like Mike Sinclair, and Trinity College in Oxford. He is a cricketer, good enough to play 36 first-class matches in the 1930s, mostly for Oxford University. His nickname is Loopy, an appellation that can refer both to bowling a cricket ball with a sinuous curve, and to a character trait best described as 'not well-worn', naïve. Given the dowry Maud brings with her, the latter is not appropriate it seems. In 1954, Maud and her sister Betty inherit a sum of £3,717 (£127,000 in 2024) from Edith Maud Littledale, an older sister of their mother. Loopy must have been delighted.

***

London, England, 1945.

A special committee of MI9's escape organisation is responsible for compiling a list of non-UK civilians who have rendered meritorious assistance to British servicemen in their attempts to escape from German captivity in Western Europe. The chairman of the committee is Donald Darling, former head of MI9 in Gibraltar, codenamed

Sunday. Airey Neave, the first successful British escaper from Colditz also worked for MI9, under the codename Saturday. In two years, more than 35,000 claims are processed by the organisation. Those who successfully filed, or had their claims filed for them, may receive financial compensation in addition to recognition and a corresponding certificate. It was originally planned that Prime Minister Winston Churchill would personally sign the certificates. However, as the majority of the recipients of this help are RAF personnel, the RAF absolutely insists that its Commanding Officer, Air Chief Marshal Sir Arthur Tedder, after whom the certificates were named, sign them instead. He must have realised all the work involved in initialling these Tedder Certificates, so he has a rubber stamp of his signature made and uses that. Sadly for him, it does not lighten the load.

Somewhere from a pile of paperwork, the name of a Polish Resistance fighter comes up. Who made the claim is unknown, as is the identity of the person who receives the Tedder Certificate, but presumably it is her family. The pharmacy assistant from Lódz is not forgotten. Under the UK Royal Crest of the with the motto *Dieu et mon Droit*, (God and My Right) she is honoured:

> This Certificate is awarded to
> the late Maria Eugenia Jasińska
> as a token of gratitude for
> and appreciation of the help given to the
> Sailors, Soldiers and Airmen
> of the British Commonwealth of Nations
> which enabled them to escape from,
> or evade capture by, the enemy.
>
> Air Chief Marshal,
> Deputy Supreme Commander
> Allied Expeditionary Force.

Arthur Tedder's stamp underneath makes it mechanical. He does not know who Maria Eugenia Jasińska is. That knowledge is reserved for MI9. He just rubber stamps the document.

***

Warsaw, Poland, June 1945.

Mieczysław Kierczyński, indicted along with Maria Eugenia Jasińska for his role in helping escaped PoWs and subsequently sentenced to eight years' confinement, survives the war. Initially sent to a prison in Sieradz after his conviction, he then ends up in a prison camp in Mirów in the Czech Sudeten. When the war is over, and he is freed, he sets out to investigate how he got there and why. Everything that happened: his arrest, torture, trial, conviction, punishment. That so many of his friends were murdered, and the suspicious death of co-accused Bronisław Wieczorok in prison: it all demands explanations. Who is responsible for what happened? Who betrayed him?

His quest for answers takes to the British Embassy in Warsaw in June 1945, where he speaks to the deputy military attaché there. By sheer, dumb chance, it turns out to be Peter Winton, one of the officers who escaped from Fort VIII in Poznań. When Winton asks Mieczysław who betrayed them, the latter is hugely surprised. Mieczysław was unaware that the British officers he helped to escape from Łódz to Warsaw (Kit Silverwood-Cope, Kenneth Sutherland, Peter Winton and John Crawford) were also arrested by the Gestapo and, like the Polish Resistance fighters, were brutally interrogated. On his return to Łódz, Mieczysław is given access to the files pertaining to his case and thus finds and reads the testimonies of Littledale and Sinclair.

He takes copies of these documents back to the British Embassy and gives them to Winton, uttering these ominous words: 'I think this is where you will discover who betrayed us', Mieczysław leaves the building. He did not say goodbye.

***

Sydney, Australia, Tuesday 21 October 1947.

A report in *The Sydney Morning Herald* about the arrest of Mr Charles Whitehead is the beginning of a story that will lead to questions to the Secretary of State for Foreign Affairs in the UK.

Police Action in Poland
London, Oct. 20 (A.A.P.)

Polish security police last Friday arrested and questioned two employees of the British and American Embassies in Warsaw, says the Warsaw correspondent of American Associated Press. They still hold the assistant commercial attaché at the British Embassy, Mr Charles Whitehead. It is understood that he is a Polish citizen. The British Charge d'Affaires in Poland, Mr Philip Broad, has lodged a protest against the arrest of Whitehead, says Reuters correspondent in Warsaw. He has also asked for an opportunity of contacting Whitehead.

Although of British origin, the Whitehead family has lived in Poland for many years. Mrs Whitehead is descended from the well-known Wedel family from Warsaw. Charles Whitehead adopted Polish citizenship several years before the war. After the Germans invaded in September 1939, Whitehead fought in a Polish unit during the six-week battle. Once the fighting is over and Nazi Germany and the Soviet Union have occupied and split the country, Whitehead returns to work at the Wedel chocolate factory. Here he deals with personnel matters, among other things, and becomes head of the fire brigade. The special passes provided by the Germans for this brigade make their surreptitious way to the Polish underground via Whitehead. He is increasingly involved in Resistance work. For a time, he plays a role in the underground press, collecting news broadcast by the British and anti-German broadcasters. The factory is now obliged to work for the Germans, but thanks to Charles Whitehead's efforts, Jews in the city's ghetto are helped out with the factory's products. And not only them. Escaped British PoWs can also turn to him for food, clothing and shelter. In October 1947, he is arrested without any prior warning or explanation when he is involved in important commercial negotiations that a British Delegation is conducting with the Polish authorities at the time. No official charges are made against Whitehead, but he is suspected of collaborating with the Nazis during the war. This information comes from General Grosz, Director of Press Information at the Polish Ministry of Foreign Affairs, and is all the more remarkable since Charles was injured during the Warsaw uprising against the Germans. After the war, he left for Katowice and started a small clothing business, working there until January 1946, when he joined the British Embassy, where he was eventually arrested.

It is a Major Lloyd who, during questions in Parliament to the Foreign Secretary, Mr Ernest Bevin, asks if he can make a statement on the recent arrest of Charles Whitehead by the Polish authorities. His statement leaves nothing to be desired in terms of clarity. Charles Whitehead and his father most assuredly helped Allied PoWs in Poland, during the war and received certificates for doing so. One of these prisoners is Major R. B. Littledale, DSO, KRRC, who managed to escape from Poland and return to England. Another name brought up is Lieutenant Davies Scourfield, KRRC, who knows Charles by the name of Karol, and is currently with his regiment in the Middle East. Mr Silverwood-Cope, who works at the British Embassy in Rome, also provided testimony highlighting the unconditional help and protection from the Gestapo that the Whitehead family gave to British PoWs of which Silverwood-Cope had first-hand experience of this in 1941 when he was seriously ill at his hideout with Mrs Walker. Charles Whitehead rushed to Mrs Walker's aid as she was diligently seeking a doctor and nursing care for Silverwood-Cope. Walker and Whitehead will continue to work together a lot. Anyone engaged in anti-Gestapo activities was in danger of betrayal or discovery, as several of Whitehead's colleagues tragically found out. According to Mr Ernest Bevin, it is therefore very unlikely that Charles Whitehead provided any support to the Germans at all. This may be so: Whitehead disappears into prison for eight years. Gris Davies Scourfield visits Poland again in 1991, looking for the people who helped him in the war half a century earlier, this time under more peaceful conditions than half a century before. He meets up with Karol again, two years before Karol's death. Together they stand on the great bridge over the Vistula, Poland's largest river that winds through the capital. The bridge is close to the Saska Kępa district, and Gris thinks back to the moment he stood here before: at war and abandoned by God and everyone. What about Ronnie? Did they think of him?

***

Łódz, Poland, 10 November 1944.

Colonel Michał Stempkowski, nicknamed Grzegorz, commander of the *Armii Krajowej* of the Łódz district posthumously awards Maria Jasińska the Silver Cross of the War Medal *Virtuti Militari*, 'for military virtue'. It is Poland's highest military decoration for bravery in wartime and the award testifies to Maria's active participation in the fight against the German invaders and the courage shown in doing so.

Having died for the freedom of her homeland, she is posthumously awarded the War Cross. On the 30th anniversary of the country's liberation in 1975, Jasińska is awarded the Cross of Bravery 'for her courage and bravery'.

***

Lódz, Poland, 1979.

The Apteka Calendula is still there, on the corner of 6 Sierpnia and Wólczańska. Nicknamed Pod Łabędziem, it is the former workplace of Maria Eugenia Jasińska. Against the wall on the Wólczańska side, a plaque funded by Lódz pharmacists and the Polish Scouting movement, is unveiled by Maria's closest relatives, her sister and her brother. The large rectangular slab of black stone features, on a grey-coloured cross, an esculape in the form of a snake coiling around a cup with a slender stem. Below it is a war cross with laurel wreath with a fleur-de-lis in the centre alongside the text *CZU WAJ*: Be Alert. It is the emblem of the Scouting Movement.

W tej aptece pracowala
Farmaceutka Bohaterska Harcerka
Maria Jasińska
Zamordowana Przez Hitlerowskich
Ludobójców w dniu 20 Kwietnia 1943 R
za niesienie pomocy jeńcom wojennym
Farmaceuci Harcerze

(She worked in this pharmacy, Heroic Pharmacist Scout, Maria Jasińska, Killed by the Nazis, On 20 April 1943, For helping PoWs, Pharmacist Scouts.)

The plaque was unveiled in 1979, 40 years after the outbreak of the Second World War. In 1993, 50 years after Maria Jasińska's execution, an exact copy was made and fixed to the wall in the same place. At another time, in another country, a similar plaque commemorating the fallen of both world wars is also stolen from the entrance gate of the parish church in the town of Bunbury in Cheshire. The parish is deeply disappointed, according to *The Chester Chronicle* in September 2017:

Community 'heartbroken' and 'disgusted' as thieves steal war memorial plaques from outside church

Metal plaques listed the names of Bunbury's fallen men during both world wars.

A community has been left heartbroken after callous thieves stole metal war memorial plaques from outside a church. For decades, two bronze plaques containing the names of all the men from Bunbury killed in both world wars have been displayed on sandstone pillars outside St Boniface Church in the village, as a respectful tribute to the local fallen heroes. But over the weekend, heartless vandals prised off the metal memorials; leaving the village with no official war memorial, less than two months before Remembrance Sunday.

Church warden David Kendrick said the village has been left 'extremely distressed' as many families of the men named on the plaques still live in Bunbury. 'It is just so sad that people feel they could desecrate a memorial which would provide them very little monetary gain,' he said. 'We are just so upset. The plaques were very secure and have been there for years. There is damage to the sandstone pillars too. The plaque was our War Memorial for the village and obviously with Remembrance Sunday coming up soon we are very concerned about what will happen but sadly this kind of thing is happening all over the country.'

Revd. Tim Hayward, vicar of St Boniface, said his telephone hasn't stopped ringing, with members of the community expressing their 'upset and disgust' at the thefts. 'These plaques provide a point of remembrance for the village to pay respects and remember those who made the ultimate sacrifice so that we can live in an open and free society. Maybe this is the price we have to pay for such a society by suffering these indignities from people who have no respect for the endeavours of others and display a callous disregard for what so many people hold dear,' he added.

Callous disregard.

Mike Rogers, president of Bunbury's Royal British Legion, said it was a 'vain hope' that the thieves might find it within themselves to return the plaques but 'one would like to hope'. 'The community and British Legion are deeply saddened that anyone could sink so low as this. We are not a million miles away from Remembrance Sunday and that will be particularly poignant without these plaques,' he added. 'But the fact that the plaques aren't there doesn't mean the men are forgotten. It will take time to replace them but by hook or by crook, we will.'

A Cheshire police spokesperson said: 'Police were called at 6.10pm on Sunday, September 17, to reports of brass memorial plates having been stolen from gates at a church on Bowes Gate Road in Bunbury.' Enquiries are ongoing and anyone with any information is asked to call 101 quoting incident 698 of 17 September.

One of the names on these panels: Ronald B. Littledale.

***

Colditz, Germany, 1980s.

It is a grey day. Hugh Bruce is wearing a green rain jacket over a white shirt and black tie and standing on the terrace on the north-west side of the castle. This is the same Hugh Bruce, who, as a 21-year-old lieutenant of the Royal Marines, pulls his film of the fighting in Calais out of his camera on being taken prisoner of war in May 1940. He makes the same march and train journey to Laufen and Poznań as Sinclair and Littledale, and like them, winds up in Oflag IV-C, Colditz. Many years later, he is in Colditz again, this time hosting a documentary on this most famous Oflag of the war. In a quintessential English accent, he describes what happened on the night of 19 January 1944; how in total darkness, his compatriots Mike Sinclair and Jack Best are catapulted out of one of the upper windows, land on the first terrace, quickly get to the edge and descend to the terrace below. The position of the sentries and the risks taken by Mike and Jack are revealed in great detail. How long has it been since Bruce himself was imprisoned here? He tells the story matter-of-factly, with typical British reserve, his upper lip stiff at all times, like it does not affect him. But it must do: how can you live through that and not be affected?

In the courtyard of the former Kommandantur, the viewer also follows the escape of Pat, Hank, Billie and Ronnie through Bruce's telling. In 2015, a large, wooden, hutch-like structure was put into place over the basement entrance, blocking it off. A sturdy plastic sign on the wall tells the story of the escape in October 1942, complete with a photo of Pat Reid taken at the British consulate in Switzerland, wearing his civilian clothes and carrying a suitcase. There is no photo of Stephens, Wardle or Littledale. As ever, Mr Colditz has 'worked his way into the picture'. The phrase 'So called Pat-Reid-Keller' is printed above the photo. The man with the plan for this successful escape is ignored: the man with the pen who wrote at length about it is not.

***

London, England, 9 August 2005.

Lord's Cricket Ground, home of the Marylebone Cricket Club (MCC) in St John's Wood, is dotted with numerous war memorials, commemorating MCC Members and cricketers who died in various conflicts down the years. Field-Marshall Lord Bramall, who landed almost simultaneously with Ronald Littledale and the 2nd KRRC in Normandy, unveiled one of the memorials on 9 August 2005. It hangs at the top of the pavilion steps at Lord's, the wooden sign with gold lettering that lists the 282 names of MCC Members who died in the service of their country during the Second World War. Below the club's logo, an M intertwined with two Cs, reads

> To the memory of
> Members of the MCC
> Who died in the service of their
> Country during World War II

There are many names, but two stand out in particular. They are 'Lt.-Col. R.B. Littledale, D.S.O.', and 'Lieut. A.M. Sinclair, D.S.O.' Sinclair played cricket for his school, Winchester, and he also played for the college cricket XI at Lords. In the 1930s, senior public schools often played an annual match at Lord's. It was a means of introducing the boys into the ways of their future lives in the Establishment, of which Lord's Cricket Ground and Membership of the MCC was and remains an important part. Although Littledale, in his Eton days, only occasionally played cricket, being more inclined towards football, he was still a Member of the MCC. Even after his death, he was not forgotten by this august body: a wooden cross with a poppy and the braided MCC symbol adorns Littledale's grave in Airaines on the day of our visit in 2013. On the memorial near the pavilion at Lord's,

Littledale and Sinclair are finally reunited.

***

Lódz, Poland, June 2010.

On the facade of a three-storey tenement on ul. Przybyszewskiego 9, a plaque is unveiled. Below the memorial plaque is a metal tube to which a metal rose is attached. There is also a war cross with laurel wreath bearing a *fleur-de-lis* in the centre and the text *CZU WAJ* to the side. Under this it is stated in Polish that here on this spot 'on 11th June 1941, the first group of English pilots arrived who had escaped from Fort VIII of the Poznań citadel during the action code-named '*Dorsze*'. The street in which the building stands has had various names in the past, including Zarzewska Street and later Napiórkowski Street. At the time Littledale, Sinclair and Davies-Scourfield crossed the threshold, the street is called Böhmische Linie, and at number 9 is the flat of Czesław Wolf. The unveiling is performed by 'a son of the family' who dedicates the memorial carved in stone to his mother, to Mieczysława, a scout from Poznań who, together with the Dolniak family, took care of the men and set up an operation to help them further.

These three Britons' being identified as pilots rather than army officers is a persistent misconception in the Czech Republic. Prague-based Czech historian, Jaroslav Čvančara, is the author of a thoroughly researched trilogy on the 1942 attack on Heydrich and its impact on the Czech people. He has also researched and published works regarding Czech anti-Nazi resistance, the repression of the Protectorate of Bohemia and Moravia during the German occupation and the extermination of Lidice. He also acts as a consultant and co-author in the creation of various documentaries, radio programmes, films and exhibitions. Littledale earns a mention in one of his works as he hid with several people (the Bergauers, Zdenka Pakova, the Bruncliks and Gertruda Šašková) murdered in the aftermath of the attack. Čvančara also makes the mistake of referring to Littledale as a pilot.

***

London, England, 18 May 2011.

Littledale's medals are Lot 717 at auction house Dix Noonan Webb in 16 Bolton Street, Mayfair, who specialise in the sale of coins, medals, military paraphernalia, jewellery and banknotes. In the auction catalogue they are described thus:

- Distinguished Service Order, G.VI.R., 1st issue, the reverse of the suspension bar officially dated '1943', with its Garrard & Co. case of issue
- General Service Medal 1918-62, 1 clasp, Palestine (Capt. R. B. Littledale, KRRC)
- 1939-45 Star
- France and Germany Star
- War Medal 1939-45, together with original Army Council condolence slips in respect of his Palestine and 1939-45 War awards, both in the name of 'Lt. Col. R. B. Littledale, D.S.O.'

The set of medals forms part of the Bill and Angela Strong Medal Collection, a project of former Brigadier W. E. Strong and his wife, who not only take great pleasure in collecting themselves but also feel it is important for future collectors to tell the stories of remarkable people who might otherwise be lost to posterity, through the artefacts they once owned. Conservative estimates of the collection's value range from £10,000-£12,000. Ultimately, the precious pieces of iron are bought by a private collector, fetching £33,000. This has piqued the interest of several UK media outlets and military-oriented web sites, who report this latest achievement in Littledale's life. *The Daily Mail* and others print the photo taken at the curling match in the Swiss snow under an article about the auction. The mysterious 'man in dark clothes with the smile and sunglasses' is referred to as 'Lt-Col 'Ronnie' Littledale', a rank he does not hold at the time. A reminder of the names of the people who helped him during his escape from Posen and the consequences they suffered is reason enough to consider that the plaudits he received once he was back in England were wholly undeserved, especially in the light of Airey Neave's conviction that 'the real heroes and heroines were those who, despite the barbarities of the Germans, gave no useful information.' Ronnie's alma mater, Eton, seems to have had its doubts. While *The Eton College Chronicle* seems happy to report that Ronnie had been awarded the DSO, matters appear to have been reflected on when it came to adding his name in remembrance on the walls in the Cloister. Any trace of his DSO is missing.

***

Airaines, France, 2 September 2014.

In the Airaines cemetery, against a misty backdrop, local residents and dignitaries are gathered for a ceremony to mark the 70th anniversary of the town's liberation from the Nazis. To the right of seven military tombstones, is a monument, currently veiled by a Union Flag. Another proud Union Flag hangs motionless from a mast behind the graves. Speeches are made, a band plays a suitable musical accompaniment, and under the watchful eye of five flag bearers adorned with the French Tricolour, the veil is slowly lifted from the monument. The text, inscribed in gold letters on the dark grey granite stone, gradually becomes legible. It commemorates the seven soldiers killed on Friday 1 September 1944 during an attempt to liberate Airaines and buried here.

Ces soldats de la 2e Armée Britannique
Avec à leur tête le Lt. Colonel R.B. LITTLEDALE
Ont trouvé la mort la vendredi 1er Sept 1944
à l'entrée sud d'Airaines.
Le lendemain la 4e D B Canadienne
Libérait notre commune.
Ville d'Airaines Souvenir Français
Le 02.09.2014

(These soldiers of the 2nd British Army
Led by Lt. Colonel R.B. LITTLEDALE
Died on Friday 1st September 1944
at the southern entrance to Airaines.
The next day the 4th Canadian D B
Liberated our town.
City of Airaines Souvenir Français
02.09.2014)

A temporary sign is visible between the headstones and the monument, bearing the names of the seven fallen British servicemen with their unit and age. The painted portrait of Major Roger Chester Nightingale (1909-1944) is flanked by a larger black and white photograph of Littledale. Remarkably, the portrait does not show the lieutenant colonel who was killed at Airaines on 1 September 1944, but the determined face of the second lieutenant in the 2nd Battalion of the King's Royal Rifle Corps in 1923. His uniform, as ever, fitting like a glove, the Sam Browne belt across his chest holding back a man eternally ready for action. Even in 2014, no more recent portrait of Littledale seems to be available save the one from Laufen with his shaved head, or the one of his emaciated features at Stalag XXI-D. There is no dispute about the date of birth, though: 1902.

***

Łódź-Różyca, Poland, 29 September 2016.

The branch office of the national training of the Institute of National Remembrance in Lódz organises a walking tour for schoolchildren from the Lódz region. On the route laid out, youngsters follow in the footsteps of Operation *'Dorsze'*, the codename for the 1941 Resistance operation to help fleeing Allied PoWs from Poland to neutral territory, and whilst doing so, they participate in a historical knowledge competition. This trail is dedicated to one of the main players in this story, Maria Jasińska. It follows two different routes: the route Justynów-Gałkówek-Kaletnik-Różyca and the route Eminów-Będzelin-Różyca. In the end, 300 children will take part in the trail, which includes a walk through the forests around the Koluszki railway junction and a visit to war cemeteries and other memorials in the area. During the walk, the children will stop to gaze at several photographs of Maria, pinned to a tree. The youngsters are told who she was and what happened in these woods. The photos show Maria both as the pharmacy assistant from Lódz and the Gestapo prisoner. After the hike, participants are presented a diploma with her portrait on it as a souvenir.

And Gris? What fate befell him? After the PoWs in Colditz Castle were liberated by the Americans on 16 April 1945, he returned to his home in England. Within a year, he marries Diana Lilias Davidson in Sussex, a veteran of the WRNS (Women's Royal Naval Service) at Bletchley Park. He rises through the ranks and is stationed in Palestine, Malacca, is part of the Rhine Army in Germany, becomes a lieutenant colonel in 1960 and is commander of the 1st Battalion, The Rifle Brigade. Cyprus follows, then Ghana, and finally England. He retires in 1973. In 1991, he publishes his memoirs of his experiences during the Second World War: *In Presence of My Foes: A Memoir of Calais, Colditz and Wartime Escape Adventures*. After his retirement, he becomes president of the King's Royal Rifle Corps' Regimental Association. He dies on 20 November 2006 in Alton.

He is the last of the Posen Three, who escaped that miserable prison camp on 28 May 1941: indeed, he is the only one who survived the war. He takes all his unpublished thoughts and conversations with Ronald Littledale and Mike Sinclair go with him to his grave. Did he really not know what was going on, or was discretion a part of this brave man's valour? Only the walls of Colditz know what was said, if anything was said about that uncomfortable sequence of events in Pirot, Bulgaria. In a letter dated 21 May 2000, he wrote about his friend Mike Sinclair:

> He was determined not to end the war as a prisoner if he could help it. Kenneth Lockwood is quite correct when he told you that Mike never did anything on the spur of the moment. He would plan everything down to the last detail. [...] Mike was a great escaper but an unlucky one. They never worked quite right for him, despite all his efforts.

Would he have thought the same about that last unfortunate attempt by Mike to leave Colditz behind for good, or has the road to Tipperary proved too long for Gris too?

***

March 2022.

The *Instytut Pamięci Narodowej* in Lódz announces the publication of a comic book entitled *Operacja 'Dorsze'*. A short silent video on Facebook features some poignant images. Three soldiers running away in the darkness escaping from captivity... the three being dumped in a rubbish pit along with the day's refuse... a man in civilian clothes jumping out of a moving train... brave Polish citizens, men and women involved in *Operacja Dorsze*... a car on its way to Litzmannstadt... a ferry on the Danube to Belgrade... a horse-drawn cart with silent figures in a forest... a woman in a lighted doorway being arrested by armed Germans... a courtroom with a helmeted soldier on guard... finally, a gleaming hatchet to carry out the sentence.

The question 'Why?' hangs over this story. Why did a major and a lieutenant in the British Army, officers, men of honour, professional soldiers from an elite corps, from a nation with a sense of its own superiority (though it will never admit it), betray those who helped them at the risk of their lives, knowing what the consequences will be? By the time they are arrested in Pirot, they have been on the run for six months after a year of captivity. They are almost in neutral Turkey where lies freedom. No one, including themselves has any idea how long the war will last. The instinct for freedom is strong, but the road to Tipperary long, too long. Sinclair will never explain his behaviour the moment names and routes are written down. He only says to Littledale when they meet, 'We must tell the truth'. Littledale eventually offers some kind of an explanation to MI9. In his debriefing, he notes that he thinks something happened to Sinclair during his interrogation that did not happen to him.

This is not completely unimaginable. In his book *The Colditz Myth*, military historian, Simon MacKenzie, cites examples of PoWs 'being forced to make statements by their German interrogators' threatening their fellow prisoners with death. Lieutenant Kit Silverwood-Cope experiences first-hand what the Germans do to escaped PoWs. For 14 months he remained in hiding with the Polish Resistance. And then the Gestapo catch him, brutally interrogate him and do not hesitate to use torture. They keep him imprisoned for 70 days, trying to find out where he had been, how it is possible that he was able to stay under the radar for so long and, above all, who helped him do so. He gets thrombosis in his leg as a result of severe beatings in Warsaw's Pawiak Prison. But he stays silent. No matter what they throw at him, he does not betray his Polish helpers, but instead ends up classified as *Deutschfeindlich*. Shortly after Littledale's final escape, in November 1942, Silverwood-Cope ends up in Colditz himself. In the summer of 1944, he is examined by the medical committee of the Swiss Red Cross to qualify for repatriation. Despite his poor state of health, the Germans are reluctant to let him go in case his stories about how Jews and PoWs in Warsaw are so badly mistreated reach the outside world. They want him where they can see him, so he must see out the war in Oflag IVC.

It is not definitively known why Sinclair tells Littledale in French to tell the truth. But could any reason be enough justification for the truth, then, to be told, especially when both men were fully aware of the consequences that telling could have? Even worse, on his return to England, Littledale simply admits this in his interrogation with the secret service. This presents a new conundrum: are his religious beliefs so strong that he is obliged to tell the truth?

Torture or threats of torture put to one side, the religious beliefs of both Mike and Ronnie may provide an additional explanation for their unlikely confessions. As noted, Littledale is a devoutly religious person, going so far as to even carry an army edition of the *New Testament* with him, even during escapes, which infuriates Mike. He cannot bear the thought of being arrested in occupied Europe with an English book. According to Gris, Ronnie prays the stars out of heaven when, after jumping off the train with Mike en route to Prague, he hides between some carriages to avoid being discovered by the German police with their dogs. Mike is also deeply religious. Fellow prisoner at Colditz Mike Edwards says of Sinclair that for Mike, 'God was at the top, then the 60th, and that was it'. Never mind the sixth commandment, 'Thou shalt not kill', Mike's hatred for the Germans runs deep. Another Colditz PoW is Lieutenant Pat Ferguson, Royal Tank Regiment, who remarks about Mike: '...his only wish was to get out of the castle and kill as many Germans as possible...'

In occupied northern Holland, deep religious conviction leads Protestant Resistance fighters, when caught by the Germans, to reveal all their group's secrets because their faith forbids them to lie. After all, one of the other commandments (the ninth according to the Anglican Church) reads 'Thou shalt not bear false witness against thy neighbour'. In the *New Testament*, that Littledale carries with him, even if risky to do so, if not in his armoury then in his mind, there are numerous references that consider lying a sin against God. 'Lying is a sin against God: A false witness is not held harmless; and he that blows a lie shall not escape' (Proverbs 19:5). God requires you to speak the truth: 'Lay down therefore the lie, and speak the truth, every one to his neighbour; for we are members one of another' (Ephesians 4:25). Do you find it hard not to lie? Ask the Lord for help! 'Lord, set a guard before my mouth, guard the doors of my lips' (Psalm 141:3). Apparently, a true believer puts the choice not to lie over, above and beyond the sixth commandment to 'not beat to death', because telling the lie contradicts his or her religious beliefs. Telling the truth is more important than preventing someone's death, even if lying would save their life. A further bizarre mental twist justifies all this on the grounds that the speaker of the truth can then at least say that they themselves did not do the actual killing! But is it not a bizarre mental twist but pious religiosity, which considers even resorting to an emergency lie a sin? Seen in this light, it is also understandable that Littledale, on his return to England, again admits to betraying his helpers. After all, this concealment from MI9 would also have been a lie, one of omission. Littledale could have remained silent after his return to England, no one would have found out, though he does not know what would have happened if Sinclair had survived, made it home and then spoke revealingly to MI9, which, of course, never happened. But still, lying is not an option because, as Sinclair says, 'We must tell the truth.'

Awareness of the consequences of their actions permeates the risks they subsequently exhibit, not only in daring escape attempts but also in the way both men are eventually killed. They both knew too well what they were doing, Sinclair in particular. Because for him, on that September day in 1944, there is no rational reason to even think about escaping from Colditz. Unless in the light of what happened that night in Pirot, life had lost an intrinsic part of its meaning: redemption was only to be found in ultimate penance. No price, other than his own demise, was acceptable.

Anyone who tries to tell Sinclair's story will sooner or later come up against the account contained in this book and step away from the truth, a truth that has only revealed itself in the story of Ronald Littledale. Writing the biography of Major Ronald Bolton Littledale solves the riddle of why there has been a lack of a similar biography of Lieutenant Mike Sinclair, the most famous prisoner of Colditz, the most famous escaper of all, who, despite frantic attempts, never managed to escape.

24

A FUNERAL IN BERLIN

It is 13 May 2019, and a special ceremony takes place at the Dorotheenstädtischer Friedhof cemetery in Berlin's Berlin-Mitte district. Located just under a kilometre north of the Reichstag in the heart of the city, the cemetery is Berlin's equivalent to Père-Lachaise in Paris. Since the 19th Century, numerous extraordinary people from the theatre and literary world, composers, film-makers and architects and from 2006, former Federal President Johannes Rau have their final resting place here. On that sunny day in May, an 'interreligious ceremony' is performed in the small chapel on the grounds. The service is led by Pfarrerin Marion Geidel, Rabbiner Andreas Nachama and Catholic Pfarrer Lutz Nehk. The three of them stand behind a small box on a platform. Texts from the Holy Scriptures are recited, a psalm in German and Hebrew and a text from the prophet Ezekiel.

Amongst the attendees sits 81-year-old Saskia von Brockdorff. The day marks 76 years since her mother Erika Gräfin von Brockdorff was beheaded by the Nazis in Berlin-Plötzensee in 1943. Erika von Brockdorff was a German Resistance fighter against the Nazi regime and a member of a Resistance movement called The Red Orchestra. On the evening of 13 May 1943, she and 13 others are put on trial at Plötzensee prison in the Charlottenburg district. She does not have a grave. The Nazi authorities do not want anywhere becoming a place of pilgrimage for opponents of their regime, so therefore, many of their victims are cremated after their death and the ashes are scattered anonymously over various cemeteries in the city. No trace of Gräfin von Brockdorff can be found. Until this moment. For although she too has been cremated, a shocking discovery in 2016 at the former estate of Professor of Anatomy Hermann Stieve, who died of a stroke in 1952, changes everything. Slide preparations of no fewer than 300 victims, mostly women who were executed by the Nazis, are found in

Stieve's collection. The tiny slivers of tissue prepared for further examination under a microscope are a hundredth of a millimetre thick and about one by one centimetre in size. They are set on glass slides measuring two by seven centimetres. Stieve's descendants make the macabre discovery, finding the slides in small boxes, some labelled with the victim's name, others simply being numbered. Stieve's heirs hand over the slides to Berlin's Charité hospital, which immediately commissions an investigation led by Johannes Tuchel, director of the Berlin based Remembrance Centre German Resistance. This investigation reveals, among other things, that Stieve had arranged for a driver to pick up the bodies of executed Resistance fighters from prison. It is said that this driver used a spanner to remove any gold fillings from the victims' teeth. These tiny slivers of tissue are the only traces left of some brave people, who fell victim to Nazi terror. The small coffin in the chapel contains these glass slides. The service marks the beginning of their final burial.

Born in Munich in 1886, Hermann Philipp Rudolf Stieve is one of the most prominent anatomists of his age and sits as chairman of the Anatomical Faculty of the Friedrich-Wilhelm-Universität in Berlin during the Second World War. In addition, he is a doctor and histologist. Although he is not a member of the NSDAP, as a staunch nationalist, he supports Hitler's ideas in the restoration of national pride in reaction to the Weimar Republic, which he found severely wanting. His research into ovaries and the female reproductive system in general, and in particular on the influence of stress on women's fertility is the beginning of a lurid association with the Nazi regime. Between 1907 and 1932, fewer than twenty people a year are executed, most of them male, which means the supply of bodies for scientific research from prisons, as well as from hospitals and psychiatric institutions, is limited. Therefore, a golden opportunity falls into Stieve's lap when Hitler comes to power and the situation changes dramatically. History will show that at least 12,000 to 16,000 civilians are murdered in German prisons between 1933 and 1945. Stieve complains in a letter in 1931 that it is almost impossible to get ovaries from healthy women for his research. A couple of years later, the new regime arrests and executes many of its opponents and thus a significant abundance of research material is provided for Stieve and his fellows.

It is an age of plenty of which every anatomical institute in Germany takes advantage. Each is assigned to a prison that has access to an execution chamber. Stieve is uniquely able to study tissue of reproductive organs from women who are suffering both chronic stress due to the brutal nature of their imprisonment by the Nazis, and acute stress from when they are informed of the time of their execution. NSDAP member or not, Stieve is convinced of the ethical rectitude of his work. Erika Gräfin von Brockdorff is just one of at least 13 female members of Resistance group, The Red Orchestra, who are put on trial in Plötzensee and end up on Hermann Stieve's section table.

Professor Stieve enters into an agreement with the Plötzensee prison whereby all bodies of prisoners shot, hanged or beheaded will be accepted by the institute for examination. Plötzensee will provide many more bodies than Stieve needs for his research, over 3,000 of them. Among them are at least 174 women aged between 18 and 68, and eight men. They are mostly Germans, but also included are Poles, Czechs, French, Belgians, Austrians, a Russian and an American. They are convicted for a variety of crimes: murder, treason or espionage, theft, black market trading, fraud, looting, subversion of the army. There are also three cases of aiding the enemy. Some of the women are pregnant, and according to Ministry of Justice regulations *'Massnahmen aus Anlass von Todesurteilen, Reichsminsiter der Justiz 447-III.a 4 318.39, 19. Februar 1939'* (Measures in connection with death sentences, Reich Minister of Justice 447-III.a 4 318.39, 19 February 1939) it is forbidden to put them to death. Their executions are postponed until after childbirth, and in some cases until the post-breastfeeding period. Among other things, Stieve's research reveals that women can stop menstruating while under chronic physical and psychological pressure, a phenomenon unknown until then. This can also lead the women themselves to think they are pregnant.

Stieve knows exactly who some of the prominent prisoners are, and he makes a point of keeping the urn containing their ashes in order to return them to the families of the dead after the war. When the war ends, he is questioned by the Russian occupation authorities and the university administration and in the process, he gives his interlocutors a list of the names of those he examined. Strangely, he is not prosecuted for his conduct and activities in the Third Reich and is allowed to go free. Until his death in 1952, he remains director of the Anatomical Institute. Today, Hermann Stieve is still a 'posthumous honorary member' of the German Society of Gynaecology.

A researcher called Harold Poelchau now enters the scene. He has a connection to this recent past. He had been a German Resistance fighter and prison chaplain in the war, giving spiritual comfort and counsel to the prisoners at Plötzensee. He knows about Stieve and his list and has much to say. He says that on 30 November 1946 he contacted Stieve and received from him a list of names of people he examined during the war. While he does not have the original wartime documents, which were probably destroyed when the Institute was bombed in the war, the list given to Poelchau seems to have been reconstructed from Stieve's notes.

In a 2013 scientific article in *Clinical Anatomy*, historian and anatomist Sabine Hildebrandt, researcher at University of Ann Arbor in Michigan, describes the list's history. The article's appendix lists 182 people examined by Hermann Stieve, giving not only their names, but also their nationalities, and the dates of their births and deaths. The names of two Polish women stand out:

Number 71-Wiesława Jezierska, aged 30, born on 13 October 1912, died on 9 March 1943.

Number 90-Olga Prokop, aged 20, born on 22 July 1922, died on 9 March 1943.

They are the only two people executed in 1943 for 'aiding the enemy'. At Number 103 is Erika Gräfin von Brockdorff, who is executed a few weeks after Wiesława Jezierska and Olga Prokop on 13 May at the age of 32.

Olga Prokop is Olga Kamińska-Prokopowa; Wiesława Jezierska is her partner at the restaurant in Jagodina, the location used as a secret interchange point on the long escape route from Poland to neutral Turkey. Two of the people passing through the interchange are Mike Sinclair and Ronald Littledale. At the time both KRRC officers are apprehended, Olga is their courier. She is also pregnant.

After Olga gives birth to her son Marek on 25 February 1942, she is taken to *Untersuchungsgefängnis Moabit* (Moabit Remand Centre) in Berlin. Here the long and uncertain wait begins. Time passes slowly in this monotonous place: Olga's thoughts are occupied with memories of her short life. She thinks of her family in Katowice. Of her father, a lawyer. Of her sister Krystyna, a member of the scouting club. Of sports and language studies. Her father's sudden and untimely death in 1939, without being able to properly provide for the family's future, and the carefree existence that was then over for good. Krystyna's daughter will say that in those days, widows of lawyers did not get a pension. Normally, lawyers had enough equity to live on, but Olga and Krystyna's father was only 45 when he died, and he had not been able to save enough to maintain the family's high standard of living. Olga is still in high school in the heart of Katowice when her father died. To support the family, her eldest sister sells off some valuable possessions, and takes a job alongside her studies.

During those long lonely nights in the cell, her thoughts turn to Romek, her great love, killed right at the beginning of the war. At the time, she could find no words of comfort, but from then on, her life's motto and the mission she acted on was '*Slask chcial byc polski*' ('Silesia wants to be Polish').

After fleeing to Hungary in October, she resumed her studies and under the guardianship of an uncle, passed high school. But further studies are now out of the equation. Instead she joins an underground Resistance movement, where she meets another Polish refugee, Jan Prokop. She marries this scoutmaster from Krakow with whom she says she is very happy. But when he flees to England, he leaves Olga behind and alone back in Yugoslavia. That she is pregnant has no bearing on his intentions: he is out of there. They will never see each other again. Then things go badly wrong. While escorting Littledale and Sinclair across the Balkans to Turkey, all three are arrested in Pirot and handed over to the German authorities after interrogation. Did she ever think of the two officers arrested with her? Or they of her? Does she know what they confessed in their statements? Only the thoughts of her son Marek are stronger and keep her going.

During her imprisonment, she is allowed to write letters. One is addressed to her mother, in high school German, which is all she had. But it is enough.

> Dear mother!
> Today marks thirteen months since my arrest. Everything has already been settled. The day before yesterday, on 17 December, my court-martial hearing was held here in Berlin. [...]
> The most important thing is the christening of my son. I would very much like to name him Marek Bronislaw. I really like the name Marek, and besides, he will have an evangelist as a protector in heaven. Bronislaw after my great-grandmother who

loved my son so much [...]

I am very happy that Marek gives you so much pleasure and that you have accepted him with such heart. I was afraid it would give you too much trouble [...] I know you will raise my son well, but remember he is a boy, not a girl, and you must treat him in such a way that he does not grow up awkward. Let him become a full-fledged man and human being, both physically and spiritually. There are many masculine traits in me, maybe he will inherit them; his father is also one hundred per cent masculine. Maybe one day it will come back, show itself to you. I was very happy with him [...] Mom, you raised us both well, I saw it myself.

Kisses, I salute you all, and especially Marek and you, my dearest mother.

Olga

The Nazis are impressed by this young woman. Cynically, they call her 'the Polish queen', not only because of the braid she wears around her head like a crown but also because of her dignified demeanour. In a letter, Olga writes that her trial takes five hours, that she feels good, so good that the judges remark that her behaviour deserves respect. Her trial is held before the *Oberste Kriegsgericht* (Supreme Court Martial) in Berlin-Charlottenburg, where exceptionally dangerous opponents of The Third Reich stand trial. She does not stand a chance. The help she gave Littledale and Sinclair is inexcusable in the eyes of the Nazi judges. The verdict, therefore, can be nothing but death.

She writes letters to her son Marek, even though he is still far too young to be able to read them, or to understand what his mother is saying to him if someone were to read them to him. She urges him to be diligent and study as much as possible. A good education will constitute wealth that no one will be able to take away from him. She would have liked to tell him this herself, but she not allowed.

When Olga and Wiesława are transferred from Berlin Moabit to the women's prison on Barnimstrasse, Olga writes to her mother again on 4 March 1943:

Dearest mother,

As you can see, I am again in another prison, I feel as comfortable here as anywhere else. I can write every six weeks

now, but whether I will ever be able to write again, I doubt very much. Mum, please don't worry. I might be better off there than in this world. I am completely prepared for everything, the only thing that hurts me is having to leave you. I hope one day you will be better, I will be happy about it. I don't know what to write anymore. Everything is over in my soul. I no longer have any plans or thoughts about the future. I have a picture of you and Marek with me. I have great peace. I have never been so calm. Finally, I kiss you all and Marek the hardest.
Olga

In the days before the Nazis execute her for 'aiding the enemy', she has time to write farewell letters, especially to her mother. A prison administration order decrees that these must be in German, presumably so they can be read prior to dispatch. Her soul has calmed. She does not plan or even think about the future now. There is peace within her. Her last letter, written with a steady hand despite knowing that her end is near, begins:

Liebe Mutter,
Diese Brief ist der letzte. Heute Abend werde ich hingerichtet…

(Dear mother, This letter is the last. Tonight I will be executed…)

She continues:

It hurts me, but what can I do. The Führer did not use the reprieve. My belongings I have here will be returned to you. With this letter, I say goodbye to all my family, relatives and friends. Stay with God and think of me sometimes. If there is such a thing as eternal life, I will do everything to make you happy and joyful. I wish you and Marek all the best in this world. And these are my last words to Marek: let him listen to you and let him be like a son to you. Let you replace my love for you. For myself, I only ask for prayer. My sins are not so great that I doubt heaven today. I go to the Father and to the others who are already separated with life. Stay with God. Mum and Krysia, don't forget Marek.

Olga

On 9 March 1943, Olga Kamińska-Prokopowa and Wiesława Jezierska are taken out of their cells, one by one, and taken to the execution chamber, a large room with high windows. The tiles on the floor are scrubbed and gleam in the daylight falling in through the windows. It is the last thing Olga and Wiesława see. Olga is strapped to a wooden bench, her head over the edge at one end. Above her head is a guillotine blade; on the floor underneath is a box for her severed head. Death is sharp and swift. The blade has a two metre drop to end her life, and Wiesława's. On this day, at this time, 200 km to the south, in Oflag IVC, Mike Sinclair is brooding on a new plan to escape from Colditz after the failed attempt in December 1942. 15 days later, a plane from Lisbon taking Ronald Littledale to Whitchurch lands in England.

The German civil service files the lawsuit against Olga under an anonymous Nazi code: *Reichskriegsgericht, Kammer III, Referenz number StPL / RKA / III 423/42.*

Neither her youth nor her beauty saves Olga's life, nor that she has given birth to a child in captivity. The Germans execute men and women younger than her. Just a month earlier, they beheaded Sophie Scholl, 22 at the time, one of the founders of the student Resistance group *'Die Weiße Rose'* from Munich. Unlike Sophie, about whom films are made, for whom monuments are erected and after whom streets are named, Olga vanishes from history. She has no monument, no film, no streets. She does not even have a grave.

Even a last attempt by her mother to save her daughter's life is in vain. Desperately, she sends a letter to Hitler requesting a pardon. Hitler never responds, if he sees the plea at all. She does not know how her daughter dies: although Olga's friends tell her she died a soldier's death after being shot, a lie told out of kindness. The family is never told what happened to Olga's body. They know nothing about Stieve's research at medical college, or how blood was drained from Olga's body, just before her death, for the benefit of soldiers at the front. Was her long, blonde hair cut, which she had always braided into crowns? The only thing Olga's mother gets back are her daughter's personal belongings. Years after the war, Olga's sister goes to West Berlin in search of her grave. She intends to stay overnight at a friend's house, but having visited Moabit prison, she returns home, utterly bereft: she found no resting place at all.

In the spring of 1942, shortly after her arrest and giving birth to her son, Olga is taken to a prison in Vienna, located at Landesgerichtstrasse 11. In June 1942, when Marek is four-months-old, he is removed from his mother's care and placed in the Vienna *Zentralkinderheim* (Central Children's Home). The female prison guards feel sympathetic towards Olga in her desperate plight, and through them, she manages to send word to her family, who have fled from Katowice to Kraków, of what has happened. Her mother Irena and her sister Krystina try everything to get the little boy back, contacting Aleksander Cabaj, a Pole living in Vienna, whom they ask to try and save the child. He replies to Irena as early as 23 July with information about the boy's whereabouts and health. He has more to say. Not only is Marek in good health, he can be handed over any time, as long as it is to a close relative. This, however, requires permission from the *Kinderübernahmestelle des Reichsgaues Wien* (Child Reception Centre of the Reichsgau Vienna).

A child's release can be done in two ways: picking them up yourself or having them brought to you. After the inevitable bureaucratic nightmare involved in obtaining the right papers, an Austrian nurse travels with Marek to Kraków and hands him over to his grandmother and aunt. In August, Irena sends photos of him to Olga in prison. Meanwhile, attempts are being made through the same channels to get Olga's death sentence reduced.

Marek will never know his mother. Nor his father. He completes a polytechnic education and in 1965 joins the *Polska Zjednoczona Partia Robotnicza* (Polish United Workers' Party), Poland's ruling communist party. In the mid-1980s, the Party send him to Moscow for a six-week training course in the finer points of their socialist model. By 1982 and 1983, he is mayor of Siemianowice Śląskie, formerly German Siemianowitz, located north of Katowice. Shortly after the war, the German inhabitants of this place are expelled and deported, and the town becomes Polish. As mayor, Marek Prokop unveils a monument in Katowice on 4 September 1983, dedicated to the Silesian Scouts who gave their lives for their homeland around the world during the Second World War. The monument bears the inscription '*Pomnik Harcerzy Września*' (Monument to the September Scouts) and was created by Zygmunt Brachmanski. It stands about 100 m from the place where, on 4 September 1939, German invaders murdered 104

Poles, including scouts and Silesian insurgents: the yard of the house at 2 Zamkowa Street (today Korfantego Avenue), on the right bank of the Rawa River. This date, 4 September, will be the Feast of Katowice Scouts and the ZHP's informal Feast of the Silesian Flag. 'Everything we will give to Poland...' reads the beginning of the Scout Hymn, reproduced on the monument that recalls those who gave their lives, 'who fell by the bullets, on the gallows, in the camps, at the front.'

Zygmunt Brachmanski speaks of the statue in an interview:

> As of a cracked but defended barricade, metaphysically transforming into the shape of the Scout Cross [...] scout figures emerge. They go out towards life, upwards, towards ideals, towards heaven ... Though they think of those who gave their lives for their homeland.

The monument deserves honour, glory, recognition and eternal remembrance.

Between the four Silesian scout figures on the sculpture is a slender girl. She has the face of Daria, the daughter of artist Brachmanski. It depicts an adjutant of the high school scouts in Katowice, Olga Kamińska-Prokopowa. When Marek has the honour of unveiling the statue, he finally comes into contact with his mother, even if only symbolically. This is as close as he gets. But it is closer than his father ever manages. Jan Prokop remains in England after the war, and starts a new family. He is not interested in his son. However, after many years of silence, Jan sends Marek a package, which his son duly returns to him. Shortly after the unveiling of the monument in which his mother plays such a prominent role, Marek dies suddenly at the age of 45. His wife later explains that his mother's death under the guillotine in Berlin cast a shadow over his entire life.

After the solemn ceremony in the chapel at the Dorotheenstädtischer Friedhof, a procession of Christian clergy, a Rabbi, close relatives, mourners and journalists heads to a small square hole in the cemetery. It is spring, and the sunny day creates a serene atmosphere. A cemetery employee leads the way, holding the coffin carefully. On the grey, concrete edge surrounding the hole are four black ribbons to order the casket to the ground. Two bouquets of white roses lie in the corner. When the coffin has descended into the earth, some of the roses are thrown on the lid. Those at the side of the grave are invited to say the Lord's Prayer and the Rabbi pronounces the Kaddish, the Jewish prayer of mourning. Once those present have thrown a handful of earth into the grave, it is covered with a granite slab. Saskia von Brockdorff emphasises after the burial:

> This is not my mother. But I am glad this place exists. Otherwise, I would have had to go to Plötzensee, that horrible place. Here in this cemetery, it is beautiful. Now she has finally found a place.

It is not inconceivable that Olga's spirit has also found a final resting place.

INDEX

B:

Bader, Douglas Robert Steuart
Famous British Group Captain in the RAF, missing both legs after a crash before the war, prisoner of war in Colditz, involved in escape from Colditz of Littledale, Stephens, Reid en Wardle.

Bergauer, Markéta
Wife of Vladimir Bergauer, involved in Littledale hiding in Prague, murdered by the Nazis on 24 October 1942.

Bergauer, Vladimir
Professor at the University of Prague, involved in Littledale hiding in Prague, murdered by the Nazis on 24 October 1942.

Best, Jack
British lieutenant, escaped from Colditz together with Sinclair in 1944, also appears as a ghost in Colditz.

Black, Graeme
British commando, involved in Operation Musketoon in Norway, via Colditz to Sachsenhausen where he is executed.

Bodenstein
Oberkriminal Assistant, builds, together with Captain Wenz of the Abwehr, a case against Polish Resistance involved in aiding escaped prisoners of war from Fort VIII in Posen.

Bruce, Huge
Lieutenant, Royal Marines, takes part in the Battle of Calais, PoW in Laufen, Posen and Colditz.

Brunclik, Emil
Czech Resistance fighter, involved in Littledale hiding in Prague.

Brunclik, Maria
Wife of Emil Brunclik, involved in Littledale hiding in Prague.

Burn, Michael 'Micky'
British commando, involved in raid on St. Nazaire, operates secret radio in Colditz.

C:
Crawford, John
British officer, escaped from Fort VIII in Posen.

D:
Davies-Scourfield, Edward Grismond Beaumont 'Gris'
Lieutenant, regimental colleague of Littledale and Sinclair, escapes with them from Fort VIII Posen.

Devant, Otto
German guard at Fort VIII in Posen, involved in bribery during escape of Littledale, Sinclair and Davies-Scourfield.

Dolniak, Lech
Brother of Klara Dolniak, cousin of Czesław Wolf, lives in Warsaw.

Dolniak, Klara
A member of the Resistance group around Doctor (Witold Verbno Łaszczyński), Littledale, Sinclair and Davies-Scourfield go into hiding with her uncle Czesław Wolf in Lódz.

Douglas, Peter
British officer, escaped from Fort VIII in Posen.

Drozd, Bernard
Polish Resistance fighter, nicknamed 'The Sailor', involved in Operation *Dorsze* and illegal border crossing of Littledale, Sinclair and Davies-Scourfield, betrays Maria Jasińska.

E:
Eggers, Reinhold
Security officer in Colditz Oflag IVC.

Emsen, Bernard
German guard at Fort VIII in Poznan, involved in bribery during escape of Littledale, Sinclair and Davies-Scourfield.

F:
Fehlau, Johannes
Nickname 'Czekolada', German customs officer at the border with the General Government, bribed with a bottle of vodka.

Fowler, Hedley
British squadron leader, escaped from Colditz in September 1942, travelled with Littledale from Switzerland to Spain, was killed during a test flight in England.

G:
Gabčík, Josef
Slovak paratrooper, trained in Great Britain together with Jan Kubiš and Josef Valčík for an assassination mission against Reinhard Heydrich, Operation Anthropoid.

Geerdts, Oswald
German guard at Fort VIII in Poznan, involved in bribery during escape of Littledale, Sinclair and Davies-Scourfield.

German, Guy
Senior British Officer in Colditz.

Giebelhausen, Albrecht
Kriminal Oberassistent, Abteilung IV der Stapo Litzmannstadt (Lodz), conducts an investigation into the Polish involvement in the escape of English officers from Fort VIII in Posen.

Glaesche, Edgar
Oberst, commandant of Colditz Oflag IVC from 1 August 1942 till 13 February 1943.

Goldman, Sidney 'Solly'
Fuselier, Jew, born in London, worked his way up to chief orderly in the kitchen in Colditz.

Gorczyca, Michalina
Friend of the Klichowski parents, provides a safehouse for escaped officers in Posen.

H:
Hammond, Wally
Mechanic in the engine room of submarine HMS *Shark*, escapes from Colditz to Switzerland by being moved to another camp, together with Tubby Lister.

Hanken, Captain
British officer in Fort VIII in Posen who (presumably) makes contact with German guard Otto Devant in an attempt at bribery for escape attempts.

Harris, Teresa
Wife of Clement St. George Littledale, accompanies him on his expedition to Tibet.

Harvey, Mike
British captain in the Royal Navy, appears as a ghost in Colditz.

Heydrich, Reinhard
Nazi leader and Reich Protector of Protectorate of Bohemia and Moravia during the period of Nazi Germany.

Hindley, George
Gamekeeper at John Bolton Littledale Sr.

Hindley, Samuel
Gamekeeper at John Bolton Littledale Jr., son of George Hindley.

Houghton, Joseph
British commando, involved in Operation Musketoon in Norway, via Colditz to Sachsenhausen where he is executed.

Howe, Dick
British Army captain, succeeds Pat Reid as escape officer in Colditz after his escape.

J:

Jasińska, Maria Eugenia
Pharmacy assistant in Lódz, involved in Operation *Dorsze* and illegal border crossing of Littledale, Sinclair and Davies-Scourfield, murdered by the Nazis on 20 April 1943.

Jezierska, Wiesława
Polish courier in the Balkans, murdered by the Nazis on 9 March 1943 in Berlin Plötzensee.

K:

Kaliszan, Nikodem
Polish Resistance fighter, involved in Operation *Dorsze* and illegal border crossing of Littledale, Sinclair and Davies-Scourfield.

Kaller, Christine
See below, Kallerowa, Krystyna.

Kallerowa, Krystyna
Or Christine Kaller, provides Littledale, Sinclair and Davies-Scourfield with cigarettes, playing cards and magazines in Czesław Wolf's apartment during their time in hiding in Lódz.

Kamińska-Prokopowa, Olga
Polish courier in the Balkans, arrested together with Littledale and Sinclair in Pirot, murdered by the Nazis on 9 March 1943 in Berlin Plötzensee.

Kierczyński, Bolesław
Polish Resistance fighter, nicknamed 'Editor', member of Doctor's cell (Witold Verbno Łaszczyński) in Posen, brother of Miecsysław Kierczyński.

Kierczyński, Miecsysław
Polish Resistance fighter, brother of Bolesław Kierczyński in Lodz, pushed by him to transport British officers across the border.

Klichowska-Gliszczyńska, Maria
Involved in hiding Littledale, Sinclair and Davies-Scourfield in Poznan, murdered by the Nazis.

Klichowski, Zbigniew
Son of Maria Klichowska, assistant to electrician Bronisław Sobkowiak at Fort VIII in Posen, survives the war.

Klichowski, Zygmunt
Son of Maria Klichowska, survives the war.

Kotynia, Tadeusz
Colleague of Maria Jasińska in the pharmacy in Lódz.

Kubiš, Jan
Czech paratrooper, trained in Great Britain together with Jozef Gabčík and Josef Valčík for an assassination mission against Reinhard Heydrich, Operation Anthropoid.

L:
Lange, Johannes
Photographer in Colditz, took many photos in the PoW camp during the war.

Łaszczyński, Witold Verbno
Nickname Doctor, head of a Polish cell in Posen charged with helping Allied prisoners who escaped from German captivity under the name '*Dorsze*' ('Cod').

Lenger, Walter
German logistics supply officer who made a unique colour film in 1939 in Colditz Oflag IVC.

Lister, Don 'Tubby'
Mechanic in the engine room of submarine HMS *Seal*, escapes from Colditz to Switzerland by being moved to another camp, together with Wally Hammond.

Littledale, John Bolton Jr.
Father of Ronald Littledale.

Littledale, John Bolton Sr.
Father of John Bolton Littledale Jr., grandfather of Ronald Littledale, brother of Clement St. George Littledale.

Littledale, Ronald Bolton
British major who successfully escaped from Colditz in October 1942, killed in action in Airaines in 1944.

Littledale, Clement St. George
Son of Thomas Littledale Jr., explorer, big game hunter, travels with his wife Teresa and his cousin William Alfred Littledale Fletcher in 1895 to within 80 km of Lhasa in Tibet.

Littledale, Thomas Jr.
Brother of John Bolton Littledale Sr., Mayor of Liverpool, involved in the rescue of passengers from the *Ocean Monarch*.

Littledale, Thomas Sr.
Father of Thomas Jr. and John Bolton Littledale Sr., great-grandfather of Ronald Littledale, Mayor of Liverpool.

Littledale Fletcher, William Alfred
Cousin of Clement St. George Littledale, travels with him to Tibet.

Luteijn, Abraham Pierre Tonny 'Tony'
Dutch lieutenant, escaped from Colditz together with Airey Neave in January 1942.

M:
Mrs M.
Former British governess, involved in hiding Littledale, Sinclair and Davies-Scourfield in Warsaw.

Markiewiczow, Irena
Provides a safe house for escaped officers in Posen.

Millar, William Anderson 'Dopey'
Canadian lieutenant, imprisoned in Colditz, disappeared after escape, presumably murdered in Mauthausen.

N:
Neave, Airey
First British officer to successfully escape from Colditz in January 1942, involved in the British military intelligence service MI9, I.S.9(d) Room 900 of the War Office, under the name Saturday.

Nielsen-Storackge, A.
Owner of the pharmacy in Lódz where Maria Jasińska works.

Nowak, Henryka
Involved in Operation Dorsze and illegal border crossing of Littledale, Sinclair and Davies-Scourfield.

Nowak, Zofia
Sister of Henryka Nowak.

O:
Ogórek, Stanisław
Brother-in-law of Maria Jasińska, wants to accompany Littledale, Sinclair and Davies-Scourfield to Warsaw.

Ostrowska, Karoline
Former colleague of Maria Jasińska in the health insurance pharmacy, through her contact is made with Maria Zrobek from Gałkówek in the border region.

P:
Pak, Radim
Brother of Zdenka Pakova, after the war he investigates the circumstances under which his sister was murdered.

Pakova, Zdenka
Czech Resistance fighter, involved in Littledale's hiding in Prague, in close contact with the Bergauers.

Pardoe, Philip
Regimental mate of Littledale, Sinclair and Davies-Scourfield, writes memoirs of his captivity in Laufen, Posen and Colditz.

Platt, Ellison
British chaplain in Colditz, keeps a diary

Połczynski, Józef
Pole from Lódz, involved in the transport of four British officers from Lódz to Warsaw.

Prawitt, Gerhard
Oberstleutnant, commandant of Colditz Oflag IVC from 13 February 1943 till 15 April 1945.

Prokop, Jan Stanisław
Husband of Olga Kamińska-Prokopowa, father of Marek.

Prokop, Marek
Son of Olga Kamińska-Prokopowa and Jan Stanisław Prokop, born in 1942 in Belgrade and divorced from mother, after the war as mayor unveils statue depicting his mother.

Puffy
Also known as Mr Olszewski, involved hiding of Littledale, Sinclair and Davies-Scourfield in Warsaw.

R:
Reid, Patrick Robert
British captain, escape officer in Colditz, author of three books about Colditz, escaped with Littledale from Colditz in October 1942.

Rogers, Jim
Mining engineer and officer in The 170th Tunnelling Company of the Royal Engineers, writes memoirs about his captivity in Laufen and Colditz.

Ross, Alec
Medical orderly of Douglas Bader.

Rothenberger, Gustav
Stabsfeldwebel in Colditz, nicknamed 'Franz Josef' because of his distinctive moustache, imitated by Mike Sinclair during his failed escape attempt.

S:
Šašková, Gertruda
Professor of geography and history, involved in Littledale hiding in Prague.

Schaedlich, Georg Martin
German guard in Colditz, keeps a diary.

Schwabe, Maud Thackeray
Niece and one of the heirs of Ronald Littledale.

Silverwood-Cope, Kit
British officer, escaped from Fort VIII in Posen.

Sinclair, Albert Michael 'Mike'
Nickname The Red Fox, British lieutenant and regimental companion of Littledale, escaped and recaptured many times, arrested in Pirot after escaping with Littledale from Fort VIII, involved in betrayal of the Polish Resistance, killed in the last escape attempt from Colditz.

Sinclair, Christopher
Brother of Mike Sinclair.

Sinclair, John
Brother of Mike Sinclair, killed in action in Anzio, Italy in early 1944.

Sobkowiak, Bronisław
Polish electrician at Fort VIII in Poznan, involved in escape of Littledale, Sinclair and Davies-Scourfield from Fort VIII in Posen.

Steele, David Ronald 'Ron'
British sergeant, briefly imprisoned in Colditz, keeps a diary with notes about William 'Billie' Stephens.

Steinberg
Gestapo Lódz, prosecutor in lawsuit against Polish involved in aiding escaped PoWs.

Stephens, William 'Billie'
British Lieutenant Commander, who eventually ended up in Colditz after the raid on St. Nazaire, escaped in October 1942, travels to Switzerland together with Littledale.

Stevenson, Clara Violet
Mother of Ronald Littledale.

Stieve, Hermann
Professor of Anatomy at the Anatomy Faculty of the Friedrich-Wilhelm-Universität in Berlin, involved in autopsies on victims of Nazi rule, including Olga Kamińska-Prokopowa and Wiesława Jezierska.

Sutherland, Kenneth
British officer, escaped from Fort VIII in Posen.

Szczepkowski, Jerzy
Rents a room in the house of Czesław Wolf, acquaintance of Tadeusz Kotynia, establishes contact between the Littledale group and Maria Jasińska, known by the phonetic name 'Teze'.

W:
Wardle, Howard Douglas 'Hank'
Canadian pilot in the RAF, escaped from Colditz to Switzerland with Pat Reid in October 1942.

Wenz
Captain, Abwehr officer Stalag XXID Fort VIII in Posen, builds a case together with Bodenstein against Polish Resistance involved in helping escaped prisoners of war from Fort VIII in Posen.

von Werra, Franz
Luftwaffe captain, the only German to escape from allied captivity, points out the actual circumstances in Fort Henry in Canada to the Germans, after which the situation in Fort VIII changes drastically.

Whitehead, Charles
Pole of British origin, helps several escaped PoWs in Warsaw including Littledale, Davies Scourfield and Silverwood-Cope.

Wieczorok, Bronisław
Polish worker from Lódz, involved in the transport of four British officers from Lódz to Warsaw.

Winton, Peter
British officer, escaped from Fort VIII in Posen, works at the British embassy in Warsaw after the war

Wolf, Czesław
Involved in Littledale, Sinclair and Davies-Scourfield hiding in Lódz.

Wood, Basil Reginald
British lieutenant, prisoner at Fort VIII in Poznan, keeps diary.

Z:
Zrobek, Maria
Lives in Gałkówek in the border region, contact of Maria Jasińska during illegal border crossing of PoWs, friends with border guard nicknamed 'Czekolada'.

BIBLIOGRAPHY

Interviews:

Interview with Gris Davies-Scourfield, Colditz Society Video Archive, Dave Windle.

Private Collection:

Steele, David, *D. R. S. 1940-1945 Lest we forget, The Wartime Memoirs of David Ronald ('Ron') Steele*, London, October 2011-February 2012.

West, Joe, *Colditz Oflag IVC, A story of 3 Distinguished Service Orders*, private document.

National Archives, Kew, UK:

Oflag IVC Colditz, Reference no. WO 208/3288

Major R. B. Littledale, DSO. Service: Army, 2 Bn KRRC [2nd Battalion King's Royal Rifle Corps], Reference no. WO 208/3311

War Diaries 2 King's Royal Rifle Corps 1944 Jan.-Dec. Reference no. WO 171/1327

Account of Escape by Major Ronald Bolton Littledale, D.S.O., 2 Bn. K.R.R.C., 30th Inf. Bde., M.I.9/S/PG(G) 998

Account of Escape of 39457 F/Lt. Hedley Nevile Fowler, 615 Sqn. Fighter Command, R.A.F., M.I.9/S/PG(G) 994

Extract from Interim Report, Interim Account of Escape of Reid, Wardle, Stephens, Littledale, M.I.9/S/P.G.(G) 995, M.I.9/S/P.G.(G) 996, M.I.9/S/P.G.(G) 997, M.I.9/S/PG(G) 998

Instytut Pamięci Narodowej: Komisja Ścigania Zbrodni przeciwko Narodowi Polskiemu; Oddział w Warszawie, Polska:

(Institute of National Remembrance: Commission for the Prosecution of Crimes against the Polish Nation; Branch in Warsaw, Poland):

Nr II C – 90/42 g, Gestapo in Posen to Gestapo Litzmannstadt, letter with two appendices, 19 February 1942

Schlussbericht, gez. Bodenstein, Posen, 30 March 1942

Schlussvermark, Giebelhausen, Litzmannstadt, 8 May 1942

Sd 4 ks 153/42 / I K 109/, Indictment, Posen, 20 July 1942

Statement Maria Jasinska, Litzmannstadt, 11 May 1942

Statement Maria Jasinska, Litzmannstadt, 4 November 1942

Statement Bernhard Drozd, Litzmannstadt, 5 November 1942

Schlussvermark, Giebelhausen, Litzmannstadt, 7 November 1942

8 Sd. Kls. 27/43 – I 97/43, Sondergericht syg.1525, 15 March 1943

Literature:

Bishop, P., *The Man Who Was Saturday: The Extraordinary Life of Airey Neave*, HarperCollins Publishers, 2019.

Booker, Michael, *Collecting Colditz and its Secrets*, Grub Street, 2005.

Brickhill, Paul, *The Great Escape*, Faber, 1951.

Brickhill, Paul, *Reach for the Sky*, W. W. Norton & Company, 1954.

Budziarek, Marek, *Na miarę wielkości, Kronika Miasta Łodzi 1/98,* Lódz 1998

Burgess, Colin, 'Bush' Parker, *An Australian Battle of Britain Pilot in Colditz*, AMHP, 2007.

Burt, Kendal & Leasor, James, *The One That Got Away*, Random House, 1956.

Cartland Institute for Romance Research, *The Colditz Cock*, Imprint unknown, 2012.

Chancellor, Henry, *Colditz–The Untold Story of World War II's Great Escapes*, William Morrow, 2001.

Clinch, Nicholas and Clinch, Elizabeth, *Through a Land of Extremes; The Littledales of Central Asia*, The History Press, 2008.

Cooksey, Jon, *Calais: A Fight to the Finish–May 1940*, Leo Cooper, 2000.

Crisp, Frederick Arthur, *Visitation of England and Wales, Volume 13*, Privately printed, 1905.

Čvančara, J., Janík, V., *Heydrichiáda v ulicích Prahy 2*, 2019.

Davies-Scourfield, Gris, *In Presence of My Foes*, Wilton 65, 1991.

Dozol, Vincent, Annemasse, ville frontière 1940-1944, Université de Lyon, Institut d'Etudes Politiques de Lyon, 2010.

Durand, Arthur A., *Stalag Luft III–The Secret Story*, Louisiana State University Press, 1988.

Ellison, Thomas, *The Cotton Trade of Great Britain*, Effingham Wilson, 1886.

Felton, Mark, *Castle of the Eagles–Escape from Mussolini's Colditz*, 2017.

Forrester, Charles James, *Montgomery and his Legions: A Study of Operational Development, Innovation and Command in 21st Army Group, North-West Europe, 1944-45*, The University of Leeds School of History December, 2010.

Gill, Anton, *The Great Escape*, REVIEW, 2002.

Green, James, *The Colditz Conjurer*, 2022.

Janík, Vlastislav, *Příběh Zdenky Pakovéjim, Protein, časopis YMCA v České republice, ročník XIX*, April 2017.

Kurtz, Glenn, *Three Minutes in Poland, Discovering a Lost World in a 1938 Family Film*, Farrar, Strauss & Giroux, 2014.

Larive, E. H., *The Man Who Came in From Colditz*, Robert Hale, London, 1975.

Mackenzie, S. P., *The Colditz Myth*, Oxford University Press, 2004.

MacKenzie S. P., *Bader's War: 'Have a Go at Everything'*, The History Press, 2008.

McConnell, J. D. R., *Eton: How it Works*, Faber and Faber, First Edition, 1967.

Mills, Giles & Nixon, Roger, *The Annals of the King's Royal Rifle Corps Volume VI: 1921-1943*, Lee Cooper London, 1971.

Mills, Giles, *The Annals of the King's Royal Rifle Corps Volume VII: 1943-1965*, Celer et Audux Club, Winchester, 1979.

Neave, Airey, *Flames of Calais, A Soldier's Battle 1940*, Hodder & Stoughton, 1972.

Niepokonana, Maria, *Maria Jasinska (1906-1943), Marek Budziarek, Lodzianie*, Literatura, Lódz, 2003.

Odorkiewicz, Edmund, *Kryptonim 'Dorsze'*, Śląsk, 1971.

O'Neill, Esther Margaret, *British World War Two Films 1945-65: Catharsis or National Regeneration?*, University of Central Lancashire, 2006.

Pardoe, Philip, *From Calais to Colditz-A Rifleman's Memoir of Captivity and Escape*, Pen and Sword Military, 2016.

Platt, Ellison, *Padre in Colditz*, Edited by Margaret Duggan, Hodder & Stoughton, 1978.

Reid, P. R., *The Colditz Story*, Hodder & Stoughton, 1952.

Reid, P. R., *The Latter Days*, Hodder & Stoughton, 1952.

Reid, P. R., *Colditz: The Full Story*, Macmillan, 1984.

Reid, P. R., *Prisoner of War, The Inside Story of the POW from the Ancient World to Colditz and After*, Chancellor Press, 1984.

Routledge, P., *Public Servant, Secret Agent: The Elusive Life and Violent Death of Airey Neave*, HarperCollins UK, 2002.

Ruft, Reiner, *The Singen Route, The Stories of Nineteen Allied POW Soldiers and Their Escape to Ramsen, Switzerland, Between 1941 and 1943*, GRIN Verlag, 2017.

Rogers, Jim, *Tunnelling into Colditz—A Mining Engineer in Captivity*, Robert Hale, 1986.

Rolf, David, *Prisoners of the Reich—Germany's captives 1939-1945*, Coronet Books, Hodder and Stoughton, 1988.

Shields, John, *Spitfire Pilot Air Commodore Geoffrey Stephenson, The Biography of the Pilot of Duxford's Spitfire MK.I N3200*, Air World, 2024.

Stok, Bob van de, *Oorlogsvlieger van Oranje*, De Haan 1983.

The King's Royal Rifle Corps Association, *Escape to Freedom*, 2004.

Tomaszewski, Irene, *Inside a Gestapo Prison, The Letters of Krystyna Wituska, 1942-1944*, Wayne State University Press, 2006.

Tillotson, M., *Dwin Bramall: The Authorised Biography of Field Marshal The Lord Bramall KG, GCB, OBE, MC*, 1996.

Vance, Jonathan F., *A Gallant Company–The Men of the Great Escape*, Pacifica Military History, 2000.

Walton, M. J. & Eberhardt, M. C., *From Commandant to Captive*, Lulu Publishing Services, 2015.

Williams, Eric. *The Wooden Horse*, Collins, 1949.

Williams, Eric, *The Tunnel*, Collins 1951.

Wood J. E. R, *Detour*, 1946.

Worrell, Gavin J. F., *Lieutenant AM Sinclair DSO, 'The Greatest Escaper of All'*, KRRC Association.

Newspapers, Magazines and Periodicals:

Prisoner of War, Magazine published and distributed by the International Committee of the Red Cross, 1942-1945.

Eton College Chronicle, Year 1850-1944.

Colditz Society Newsletter, 1991-present.

St. George R. Littledale, *A Journey Across Tibet, From North to South, and West to Ladak, The Geographical Journal, Vol VII. No.5*, May 1896.

The Cheshire Observer, 16 September 1944.

The Chronicle, 18 June 1949.

Winged Diplomat, The Swiss Observer: the Journal of the Federation of Swiss Societies in the UK, Band (Jahr) 1962, Heft 1414, 10 August 1962.

Poland (Mr Charles Whitehead, Arrest), UK Parliament, House of Commons, Volume 443: debated on Wednesday 5 November 1947.

The London Gazette 2 February 1923, 3 February 1925, 19 June 1936, 9 October 1936 and 4 January 1938.

Supplement to the London Gazette 2 February 1940 and 4 May 1943.

Łódź Herstories as an Example of Research in the Women, War and Peace Project Supported by Europe for Citizens Programme, Inga B. Kuźma, Edyta Pietrzak, Civitas Hominibus nr 11/2016.

'Dorsze' z Poznania, OKRES HISTORYCZNY, (1939-1945) II wojna światowa, Przystanek historia, Aleksandra Pietrowicz 10 June 2020.

Parish Magazine, Bunbury, 1943-1948.

Sabine Hildebrandt, *The Women on Stieve's List: Victims of National Socialism Whose Bodies Were Used for Anatomical Research, Clinical Anatomy* 26:3–21, 2013.

Stalen van nazislachtoffers begraven in Berlijn, Het Laatste Nieuws, 13 May 2019.

Overblijfselen nazislachtoffers begraven in Berlijn, Metro, 14 April 2019.

Remains of Nazi victims to be buried in Berlin, decades late, RTL Today, 10 May 2019.

Strack, Christoph, Endlich ein Grab: Charité bestattet Gewebeproben von Hitler-Feinden, Deutsche Welle, 13 May 2019.

Winkelmann, Andreas, *Traces of Nazi victims in Hermann Stieve's histological collection, Annals of Anatomy-Anatomischer Anzeiger, Elsevier, Volume 237*, September 2021, 151720.

Other Documents:

Census of England and Wales, 1911.

Poprava 262 spolupracovníků parašutistů v Mauthausenu 24. 10. 1942 - 76 let https://www.fronta.cz/kalendar/poprava-262-spolupracovniku-parasutistu-v-mauthausenu.

Winchester College at War, www.winchestercollegeatwar.com , Online resource Winchester College Rolls of Honour.

Diary of Lieutenant Basil Reginald Wood, Pegasus Archive PoW Stories, https://www.pegasusarchive.org/pow/reg_wood1.htm.

Encyklopedia Konspiracji Wielkopolskiej 1939-1945, Instytut Zachodni, Poznań, 1998.

Kronika Miasta Łodzi, NR 1(88)/2020.

ACKNOWLEDGEMENTS

While writing this book, I have often thought of the glider that British PoWs assembled in the attic of a 16th Century castle, from bed boards and bed sheet covers, without proper tools, without nails, and for nine months under the watchful eyes of a surplus German guard. Did they really think they could fly with this? Did they really think they could make a runway on the roof at the moment supreme, seat two men inside this contrivance, and launch it by pushing down a bathtub full of concrete on a cord, right where Mike Sinclair and Jack Best attempted an escape in January 1944? According to Bill Goldfinch, one of the builders, there was not even a bathtub in the castle, only showers. Did the British even think about flying?

Was it really my idea ever completing this book, or publishing it? Or was it for them, like me, about being intensely engaged in something that had never been done before, without caring about the end result, against all odds? To consider the road to Tipperary more important than the arrival?

For me, the story of Ronald Littledale begins in 2013 when I visit his grave in Airaines and decide, on the spot, to write his story. I owe the discovery of the black page in his life story to Joe West, a member of the Colditz Society. The Society was founded as a successor to the Colditz Association in 1991 with the purpose 'to help preserve historical records and memorabilia, increase awareness and information about Colditz for its members and to perpetuate the spirit and objectives of the former prisoners of Oflag IVC, Colditz.' When I became a member myself and Littledale's story began to intrigue me, Joe responded sympathetically when I asked a question on the Society's Internet platform if anyone could provide me with information about the relatively unknown major, who proved able to escape from Colditz even without a glider. Through the mail, Joe sent me a short essay on whether it was right that Littledale and Sinclair were awarded a DSO for their courageous behaviour, unlike Baron Pierre Fourriere Crevoisiere de Vomecourt, a French aristocrat, who did not receive it. Joe believed that Littledale and Sinclair did not deserve it, unlike Baron de Vomecourt who did. The reason was shocking and lay in the confessions of Littledale and Sinclair after their arrest in Pirot. Joe referred me to the National Archives in Kew for the details where he was by now a familiar face. With great generosity, he gave to me the registration number of the documentation that gave the true background to Littledale's story. Under number WO 208/3311, Littledale's debriefing report was included in the immeasurable amount of information stored in the National Archives. When I later asked Joe if I could get a copy of the debrief from him, he was silent. Sometime later, his wife Sue West answered my email to Joe. Joe was ill, unable to answer, and Sue was greatly uncertain about his future. For a long time, I heard nothing more. Only a few years later did I find out what was going on. And that report, WO 208/3311, turned out to be a painful file, even today.

In March 2019, a dream came true. Together with the Colditz Society, my wife and I returned to Colditz. Apart from visiting the castle for the third time, we also spend the night there, in the former Kommandantur, which today houses a youth hostel, in a bunk bed, perhaps like Littledale 77-years-earlier. Fortunately not under a bag of donkey food. But I also gave a presentation on Ronald Littledale at the request of the Society Secretary. The Treasurer of the Society announces me after some technical assistance by a fellow member of the castle staff, in front of a British audience, with members, some of whom have been to the castle 15 times and are even crazier than I am, or should I say more passionate! I gave a PowerPoint presentation using a laptop I have been dragging around with me. It's about my fascination with Colditz, my book collection and photos and scrapbooks, my model of the castle, sand from the French tunnel, Ronald's family, St. George, Eton, Calais, Laufen, Poznań, Mike and Gris, Prague, Vladimir Bergauer and Zdenka Pakova, Colditz, Switzerland and Airaines. About MI9 I wisely kept quiet. I have requested file WO 208/3311 myself and I know what it contains. I also have a strong suspicion how the company will react were I to bring it up. When I finish my story, I let the applause wash over me.

That I am working on a book drew attention, and potential readers are certainly there. From several members I got a commitment that they will send me information as soon as they return home. One of them is D., a member with '10,000 books' at home on the subject of 'Prisoners of War', down to his bathroom, and during the trip, busy with a folder of photos and drafts and other documents. As early as 1974, when Colditz was still behind the barbed wire of the GDR, he visited the castle, which at the time definitely deserved to be called a ruin. He has been the driving force within the Society for many years at a time when former Colditz prisoners graced the meetings with their stories. On this Society trip, he takes whoever wants to join him on a tour of Colditz after sunset. We go to all those places I know from the stories and the books. The place where three Frenchmen on their way to the dentist ran away in the fog, leaving the guard in despair. The prison, that held commandos captured in a raid called Operation Musketoon in Norway. The blacksmith shop where RAF pilot Douglas Bader had his artificial legs repaired. We pause at the cemetery of the St. Nicolai Kirche. Here, Mike Sinclair was temporarily buried, the only officer shot during an escape attempt. We walk across the bridge over the River Mulde and notice, high up on a building, two stripes where the water level reached during one of the several floods that occurred here in 2002 and 2013. High above us, bathed in light, the great castle floats in the sky. When we reach a spot behind some sheds, where the replica glider landed, we see the gigantic building like a stone balloon high in the sky undulating in the wind. We are back by 10:30 pm, tired but impressed. In the silence on the youth hostel square, I clap my hands. The sound resonates perfectly and keeps buzzing back and forth. How is it possible, I think, that the guards at the time did not hear Littledale as he ran across this square?

D. is a born storyteller. In addition to Colditz, we go to the former camp site of Stalag Luft III, where a mass escape took place in March 1944. At nine in the evening, members of the Colditz Society stand with Harry. It is the name of the tunnel from which the 76 officers escaped. We arrive in the dark at an immense bed of flowers. Behind us is a replica watchtower, and visible among the pine forests is a narrow strip of stone that crosses at right angles the dusty road on which we stand. The stone strip depicts the course of the tunnel, and at the exit, which lies some distance from the edge of the forest, is a large stone against which the sea of flowers gently ripples like water. Of barracks, no trace, nor of barbed wire. Yet it was here, in this place, at this time, 75 years earlier, that in the darkness the courageous escape attempt took place. And here we stand now. D. recounts what happened at that moment. One by one the men crawled out of the tunnel with false papers, suitcases, clothes made out of uniforms and food for a few days, while the guard high on top of the tower looked the other way toward the barracks. Because of an air alert, the lights in the camp were out, and this gave the escapees extra cover. After 76 times, their luck stopped. The men who managed to reach the nearby forest ran north toward the station.

We are silent for a minute and think about the victims. 50 of the 73 men who are eventually tracked down are murdered in cold blood. Using the lights on our mobile phones, we retrace the historic trek to the station. Right now, we can manoeuvre fairly easily through the forest; then there was 15 inches of snow. What must have been going through those heads? We arrive at the back of the Żagań station, walk under the tracks through a tunnel (a tunnel after all!) and enter the hall in the process of being rebuilt. D. points to the ticket counters, and you can see men buying tickets here 75-years-ago. If they were not 'hardarsers', those who decided to walk to freedom on foot. Dutchman Bob van der Stok simply bought a ticket to Alkmaar, visited some family and friends, and was eventually able to get to Spain via France. A group photo is taken in front of the train station. How nice it would have been if the 76 after the war could also have had their picture taken here.

We get talking to D. on the bus and he is willing to send me information about Littledale. Then we ask him if he knows Joe West. He tells us what happened to Joe. He has had a brain haemorrhage and can no longer talk. Salient, not to say relevant detail in his story is that he has taken over Joe's entire archive. The archive that file WO 208/3311 is part of. Which I already have, but I'm keeping quiet about it. After all, the file can also be found on the KRRC Association internet site, except for a single passage that has been omitted 'in the interest of security'. D.'s final response to my request to send file WO 208/3311 is telling. It takes an email reminder to finally receive a debriefing report from Billie Stephens and an Interim Account of the escape of Reid, Wardle, Stephens and Littledale. 'Similar,' as D. calls it, but not the 'real thing' as I call it. D. and the KRRC Association are on the same page regarding the truth about Littledale. But then, I ask, 'Who am I to judge?' Joe is firmer in his judgment and more open minded. About the KRRC Association booklet containing the text of Littledale's interrogation by MI9, he says:

Hi Kees,

I can't remember how much the booklet leaves out and I am surprised that it is still issued because it is total rubbish about 'in the interest of security'. The information is taken from Littledales' debrief by MI9 and I am surprised that he volunteered the information because no one would have known if he kept quiet. Littledale said that he wrote a true statement of the routes and the names of the helpers. Apparently they had been told by the Bulgarians that if they told the truth everyone would be sent to Turkey in a couple of days. Bulgaria had joined the Axis and gave the POW and their confession to the Germans. As a result several Poles were executed and others imprisoned.

Hope that helps
Best wishes
Joe

On Friday 11 February 2022, I read on the Colditz Society's Facebook page, in a casual comment to a post about Colditz traitor Walter Purdy, that Joe West died in January of that year. The spring issue of the Newsletter features his photo and the announcement that he passed away on 1 January.

Society member Dave Windle, who interviewed many former prisoners for the archives, surprised me with some photos of Littledale unknown to me and some passages from the books in which they are included. While researching Littledale, I slowly came to realise how camera shy he was! The photo of Littledale as a young lieutenant for the 1st Battalion in Calcutta in 1932 and the photo taken six years later in Aldershot showing him now promoted to captain and also showing a young Second Lieutenant Sinclair are from *volumes VI and VII of The Annals of The King's Royal Rifle Corps*. Both books unlock the years between the two world wars, the mechanisation of the Corps, the years in the Rhineland, India and Palestine, the battle in Calais and the dramatically ended battles in Airaines.

Every little bit helps. One of the members of the Society sends me a newspaper article from *The Chronicle* following the death of Littledale's mother several years after her son was killed. There is also ample coverage of Ronald himself in the piece.

The Colditz Society membership secretary brought to my attention an essay by Reiner Ruft. Reiner lives in southern Germany and researches the Singen Route about which he has lectured several times to the Society. The Singen Route was a popular route among escaped PoWs to escape from Germany to Switzerland. Supported by original documents, Reiner's booklet, *The Singen Route*, describes in detail the stories of 19 Allied PoWs who managed to reach the town of Ramsen in neutral Switzerland via the route. One of the records included is the first page of a Swiss police interrogation report that briefly notes the story of Littledale, just arrived after his escape from Colditz. When I find out Reiner's email address and ask him if he can provide other pages, he sends me the entire file he was able to trace in Switzerland. Also, my wife and I are invited to walk the route with him and cross the border just as Littledale did. Bikes are waiting for us, and don't worry he says, it is as flat there as it is in Holland. Unfortunately, coronavirus spoils it all, and regularly we reschedule our appointment. When I receive the documents and see the second page of Littledale's interrogation report, I get quiet. A tight, regular handwriting has signed the document. I cannot get any closer to the major.

Through the Cheshire Roll of Honour Facebook page ('Creating a County Memorial Roll to over 30,000 men and women from Cheshire who have given their lives in service of our country since the Boer War (1898) to the present day'), I get in touch with Stephen Benson, who lives just 20 minutes from Bunbury where Littledale lived. According to a post on the page, the Bunbury War Memorial plaques on the gate columns of the church in Bunbury, that include Littledale's name, have been stolen. A short story about Littledale put me in touch with Stephen. Numerous interesting documents including the 1911 Census come to me via the digital highway, and we have a tacit agreement that I will look him up in Bunbury after the pandemic is over.

David Kendrick is Church Historian in Bunbury, and provides numerous interesting facts about Littledale in his hometown. His next announcement almost drives me crazy when I ask him about the signed child portrait of Ronald that hangs under the memorial stone in St Boniface Church:

> This is what I recorded about the sketch of him as a young boy. Not much information but the interesting thing is that when it was taken off the wall in 2019, for cleaning work, I found that if you turned it over, on the back completely out of sight and

unbeknownst to anyone, there is a lot of typewritten information about him. Next time I'm in the church I'll take photos and send to you.

And he delivers as promised. It gets even crazier when he tells us that he is writing this post from Bunbury House where his daughter rents part of the back. Of that house he says 'the house as it is today because the main structure and architecture is completely unchanged from how it would have been when Ronald was growing up there.' David is also Treasurer of the Tarporley Rotary Club, as a charity part of Rotary International. Members of the club meet every two weeks, including at The Hunt Room at the Swan Inn in Tarporley. The Swan Inn has a long history of more than 250 years with the Cheshire Hunt Club. The walls of the dining room display huge lists listing for each year the names of those who have received the honorary title of Master of the Hunt. In 1909, it is J. Bolton Littledale, a prominent member along with his wife, who came here regularly with his hunting friends from the Cheshire Hunt Club. Just in front of his name, applied in ornate letters, is the family crest, a red lion on a white field with three white crosses (a recrossed cross) above it in a row in an azure bar.

The man himself is simpler but mostly more accessible than his job description. François Rouillard (*Premier Adjoint Commune d'Airaines en charge des Finances et des affaires générales* / Vice-Président de la Communauté de Communes du Sud Ouest Amiénois) is very willing when my wife and I walk into Airaines Town Hall to ask if they can tell us anything about the soldiers buried in the cemetery. He can, and shortly afterwards he sends additional documentation. We arrive just in time before the stores close to buy a flower and place it on Littledale's grave.

Whether it is indeed 'a winner of a book' as Elizabeth 'Betsy' Clinch claims is up to the reader to decide. In any case, I am indebted to her and her husband Nicholas for the huge amount of work they have done to provide insight into Ronald Littledale's ancestry and the social class into which he was born, despite finding nothing about my protagonist in her research. Combined with the monk's work of Frederick Arthur Crisp's titled Visitation of England and Wales, I got a fabulous insight into the family of one of the most important side characters of the Colditz saga.

Untold information about the situation in Poland comes from

documents in the possession of Maria Soniewicka of Łódz. She is a niece of Maria Jasińska and possesses translations into Polish of original German documents describing the circumstances following the escape of Ronald, Mike and Gris from Fort VIII in Posen, their journey to Łódz, their transfer across the border with the General Government, and the entire situation surrounding the Polish Resistance fighters who were helpful up to the execution of Maria Jasińska.

Acknowledgements are certainly due to all those anonymous editors who have filled the columns of *The Eton College Chronicle since* 14 May 1863, and occasionally gave me the impression that Ronald Littledale was only playing football, even after his return from captivity and his candid confessions during his interrogation by MI9. Thanks to their accurate reporting, I gained not only insight into Ronald's goings-on during and after his time at Eton, but also a surprising insight into his father John's thought processes. His remark about telling the truth during a session of Pop stands in stark contrast to his son's later conduct, which permeates this biography.

Through em. Prof. Dr. Hans Renner of the University of Groningen, I came into contact with Czech amateur historian, Vlatislav Janik, and historian, Jaroslav Čvančara. Hans Renner himself is from Prague and was in Vienna at the time of the Russian invasion in 1968. Returning was not an option, and with a suitcase containing two shirts, he ended up in the Netherlands. When, while researching the Czech story of Littledale, I came across a wall plaque commemorating Zdenka Pakove in Prague, he asked me if I wanted to do a doctorate on the subject, offered my wife and me his and his wife Justa's apartment in Prague, and got us in touch with Janik. The question about promotion turned out to be the same as whether the British really thought the glider would fly, or whether building it was the real challenge. In 2019, we spent our September vacation at Renner's apartment, a prime location in the heart of Prague. Here, we met Vlatislav Janik and Jaroslav Čvančara, with whom we spoke briefly, a conversation during which Jaroslav concluded that Littledale was indeed not a pilot as he claimed in one of his books. With an 'interpreter,' a cousin of Janik's wife who travels back and forth between the Czech Republic and the Netherlands for his work, we spend several hours with Janik in a restaurant. Janik is an approachable man who is actually a structural engineer working on a large project to commemorate the victims in the aftermath of Heydrich's assassination in 1942. Throughout the city we came across plaques commemorating Operation Anthropoid. This included the address of the Bergauer couple where Littledale spent many days in hiding. Once home, my mailbox overflowed with many documents in a foreign language with numerous photos while I was able to help Janik again with photos of Dutchmen who became victims of Nazi terror in the *Englandspiel* and died in Mauthausen where the Bergauers and Pakova were also murdered.

Museologin Schloss Colditz Regina Thiede immediately sent the photo of the delousing shed in the courtyard of Colditz where Littledale's adventure began for me. I saw the photo at the museum during the Society tour and was pleasantly surprised to finally see the makeshift building after decades of searching.

Then a few words of apology to Rev. Tim Hayward. The clergyman in Bunbury must have considered me very strange, when I asked him information about the Littledales, and after a long time without an answer in my eyes, I asked him if he communicated only with God. My sincere apologies, Tim! Through his mediation, I found out through local amateur historian John Elsworth of Bunbury where Ronald's parents are buried.

Thanks to the efforts of Jolanta de Jong, the *Instytut Pamięci Narodowej*'s comic book on '*Operacja Dorsze*' is on my desk in no time. *Dziękuję*! Bizarre to see the portrayal of the story from the escape from Fort VIII to the jump from the Littledale train. The story is still alive in Poland, that much is clear.

A thorn in the flesh of the writer who thought he was ready with his book is Michael Zwartelé, who, like me, lives in a bookcase, only with the wrong subject. Churchill or Colditz, how hard can it be! His critical thinking and especially his subtle hints 'to kill my darlings' did the book more good than harm. Thanks for that.

A special word of thanks goes to Shelley Di Capri, who helped me enormously with the translation of this book from Dutch into English. Apart from being a natural speaker of the language, she is also very familiar with the story of Colditz. This golden combination has been invaluable in the creation of this book.

The title of the book can be read in several ways. Of course, the betrayal of two of the main characters in the history of Colditz is a central theme in this story, and all its consequences. But in publishing this history, I am committing betrayal of that same history. A history that so far perpetuates the myth of brave, honourable men who ultimately prevail. Only *The Colditz Myth* by military historian, Simon MacKenzie, sheds light on the difference between fact and fiction, between truth and image. *The Betrayal of Colditz* places a bright searchlight on this reality and reveals things some would rather not see. It does not get nicer, but it is more realistic. Perhaps it will cost me my membership in the Colditz Society. So be it. Because in writing this book, following in the footsteps of Anna Sudlitz's Polish radio play *Daleka jest droga do Tipperary*, I hope that after all these big and small steps, the final goal has finally been reached. Although this was not the intention when I started it. The road to the final goal was much more important.

The whole project would have become nothing without the tireless support of my wife, Ingrid Fischer. With her, I visited the castle three times. And it did not stop there. We stood twice at Littledale's grave, once with a wooden cross with a poppy, once with flowers, where I decided to write Ronnie's story. We walked in abandoned forts in Calais, wandered the streets and boulevards of Prague in search of an insignificant alley where Littledale was in hiding with the Berghauers, and we almost lost each other in a kind of a love shack for gay people in the woods surrounding Fort VIII in Poznań. She read my manuscript, commented on it, and made contacts at the moment when I did not seem to finish my study and scoured the internet for information while reality had to be looked for on the street. Together we stood in the small basement under the former Kommandatur in Colditz Castle, looking through the narrow air duct Littledale must have squeezed his body like 'toothpaste from a tube'. Above us through the small trench we saw a blue sky, and I am sure I would have made the deep dive over the river in the glider with her too if it had launched at that moment!

Kees Koenen, Leeuwarden, 2025.

ABOUT THE AUTHOR

Kees Koenen was born in 1964 in 's-Hertogenbosch, The Netherlands. He has two academic degrees in mathematics after studies in Eindhoven, Netherlands, and Oxford. He has been working in the oil and gas industry for more than thirty years, with sub-areas as safety, design, assessment, audits, quality systems, external safety, explosions.

As a child he became interested in the Colditz story when he saw the TV series in the early 1970s. It resulted in a now 50-year study of the castle, the PoW camp, its inhabitants and every other detail related to Colditz. He is a member of The Colditz Society. He collected about 70 books and hundreds of photos related to Colditz.

When in 2013 he visited the grave in France of Lieutenant Colonel Ronald Littledale, one of the few officers who managed to escape from Colditz, along with the much better known Pat Reid, he decided to write a book about him. The story of the almost forgotten Littledale is closely related to Colditz's most famous prisoner: Mike Sinclair. During the study of Littledale and Sinclair, an unknown history emerged.

Printed in Great Britain
by Amazon